Paul Fost

TAROT CARD MEANINGS

VOL I

FUNDAMENTALS

Ishtar Publishing
Vancouver

Tᴀʀᴏᴛ Cᴀʀᴅ Mᴇᴀɴɪɴɢs: Fᴜɴᴅᴀᴍᴇɴᴛᴀʟs
AN ISHTAR PUBLISHING BOOK:
978-1-926667-05-8

PRINTING HISTORY
Ishtar Publishing edition published 2009

1 3 5 7 9 10 8 6 4 2

Ishtar Publishing
141-6200 McKay Ave
Suite 716
Burnaby, BC
Canada V5H4M9

www.ishtarpublishing.com

Printed and bound in the United States.

THANK YOU

ISHTAR PUBLISHING WOULD LIKE TO
THANK YOU FOR YOUR SUPPORT

Look for the 4th word found on page 211 line 10 of this book. Email it to sales@ishtarpublishing.com and receive a $5 coupon redeemable toward your next purchase from Ishtar Publishing.

Look for the 6th word found on page 50 line 4 of Tarot Fundamentals Volume One or Two. Email it to sales@ishtarpublishing.com and receive a $30 coupon redeemable toward your next purchase from Ishtar Publishing.

Paul Foster Case was the founder of Builders of the Adytum, a Mystery School based on the principles of Ageless Wisdom as taught in the Qabalistic-Hermetic tradition. "Adytum" is an ancient Greek word that refers to the innermost part of the Temple, the Holy of Holies, "that which is not made with hands." Builders of the Adytum is an international non-profit teaching and training Order and an outer vehicle of the Inner Spiritual Hierarchy, sometimes called the Inner School, which guides the evolution of Man.

Through Builders of the Adytum's intensely practical curriculum, which includes both lessons and rituals, students are given the opportunity to become more attuned to their innermost Reality, and so become more conscious instruments for the Life Power. They learn to turn to the Interior Teacher, whose wisdom transforms lives.

Paul Foster Case originally wrote the materials in this book as lessons for students of his School of Ageless Wisdom. They were sent out on a weekly basis, which is why you'll find references in them to "this week" or "next week". He meant for his students to spend a week of daily focus on each lesson. There are two lessons devoted to each Tarot Trump. At the end of the first of each of these two lessons, coloring instructions are given for painting the card.

In 1936-37, he gathered these lessons into four books, each of which he typed up a copy and sent to the American Library of Congress for copyright purposes, possibly with the intention of eventually publishing them for non-members. We were fortunate enough to be able to acquire the original copies, typed on Case's typewriter, and have now released all four copies in this compilation.

Although this is a compilation, in order to get the most out of these lessons, **we highly recommend that you undertake them as part of the course created by Paul Foster Case and provided by Builder of the Adytum.**

Interested readers may learn more about this organization through our website at **www.bota.org**, or by calling or writing:

Builders of the Adytum
5105 North Figueroa Street
Los Angeles, CA. 90042
e: 323-255-7141.

CONTENTS   PAGES

CONTENTS PAGES

The Pattern on The Trestleboard

This is Truth About the Self

0. All the power that ever was or will be is here now.

1. I am a center of expression for the primal Will-to-Good which eternally creates and sustains the universe.

2. Through me its unfailing Wisdom takes form in thought and word.

3. Filled with Understanding of its perfect law, I am guided, moment by moment, along the path of liberation.

4. From the exhaustless riches of its Limitless Substance, I draw all things needful, both spiritual and material.

5. I recognize the manifestation of the undeviating Justice in all the circumstances of my life.

6. In all things, great and small, I see the Beauty of the divine expression.

7. Living from that Will, unsupported by its unfailing Wisdom and Understanding, mine is the Victorious Life.

8. I look forward with confidence to the perfect realization of the Eternal Splendor of the Limitless Light.

9. In thought and word and deed, I rest my life, from day to day, upon the sure Foundation of Eternal Being.

10. The Kingdom of Spirit is embodied in my flesh.

THE OBJECT OF TAROT PRACTICE

I f you will stop for a moment to consider the chain of circumstances which led to your reading these words, you will discover one primary motive. That motive is your desire for inner
enlightenment. Even though you approach this study with some
measure of skepticism, so that you wonder how the claims made
as to the effectiveness of Tarot can be substantiated, your inter-
est is founded primarily upon a basic spiritual urge to seek light.

This light–seeking impulse is the first requisite for success in
the use of Tarot. This and a strong determination to persist in
the step–by–step mastery of the details of the work explained in
the course, will enable you to make the most of this study. The
very fact that you are reading this instruction is ample proof that
you are ready for it, because nothing ever happens by accident. A
fundamental principle of Ageless Wisdom is that when the pupil
is ready his instruction will be forthcoming.

This course on Tarot Fundamentals will show you how to use
the Tarot Keys for the purpose of evoking thought, thus bringing to the surface of your consciousness, where you can see and
understand them, those fundamental principles of practical occultism that lie hidden in the hearts of all mankind. All these
principles are based upon a single truth, and knowledge of that
truth is innate in every human being; but not until it has been
found and brought into the light of consciousness is it available
for use. Hence the portals of ancient temples bore the motto,
"Know thyself," and Jesus said, "Seek first the kingdom of God,"
and "The kingdom of God is within you."

Its rich symbolism and ingenious construction make Tarot the
best of all instruments for true occult *education*: that is, for *draw-
ing out* the wisdom hidden within you. Understand, then, at the
very beginning, that the Tarot Keys do not put something into
your consciousness. They call forth something which is already
there. The practical instruction in this course will aid you greatly
in building up an intelligent grasp of the meanings of these Keys.
Clues will be put into your hands that will enable you to use Tar-

1

ot to gain a deep practical understanding of the laws of life. You must follow these clues yourself. Only in this way will Tarot bring out the knowledge which lies within you, and this knowledge is all that can possibly be of any importance to you.

To each prospector in this inexhaustible mine of Ageless Wisdom, persevering study will reveal knowledge that another seeker might never discover. Hence, no matter how high may be his source of information, no interpreter may declare, "This is the full and final explanation of Tarot." There can be no final explanation. No student can exhaust the possibilities of this extraordinary symbolic alphabet, any more than one person can exhaust the possibilities of a language. The most that can be said is that there is a definite manner in which to approach the study of these Keys, just as there are tunnels which lead to the heart of a mine. The function of the earlier part of this instruction is to provide a map or plan of the mine. You who read must enter, and dig out the treasure for yourself.

Your first task must be to master the elements of the esoteric language of symbols in which Tarot is written. Every lesson in this course will enable you to make definite progress in this part of the work. Be sure to pay particular attention to the details of instruction as to procedure, and carry them out to the letter. Nothing will be given you to do that you cannot carry out with a clear conscience and without fear. If you do follow instructions, you will be most agreeably surprised at the change effected in your personality by the time you complete the course. You will find yourself developing ability to concentrate; you will find yourself endowed with keener perceptions and with greater comprehension of yourself and of the meaning of your experience of life.

A mere perusal of these words once a week as they are issued will be perfectly useless to you. You might better far save your time and money. Unless you are willing to devote a certain period each day to this work, so that you can study your Keys, it will be futile to expect results, "Out of nothing, nothing comes." In simple justice to yourself, prepare to enter into the spirit of Tarot practice.

Do these words sound discouraging? They are a deliberate attempt to discourage the idly curious and the superficial. It has been wisely said, "A little knowledge is a dangerous thing." Do not delude yourself into believing that you have no time for this work. It is absurd to say that you have no time for the most important thing in your life, your own spiritual growth. You probably prove this every day of your life by seeking continually for greater enlightenment. You read books; you talk to people about it; you attend meetings and lectures. Yet fifteen minutes a day devoted to Tarot study can promote your growth more than hours of other activities. Your Tarot period is the one part of your day that you cannot possibly afford to miss.

Your first practical exercise will be to commit to memory, if you have not already done so, the eleven statements of *The Pattern on the Trestleboard*, which you received with your Rotascope. These are the words of one of the great leaders of the Inner School, and they are based upon the fundamental teachings of Ageless Wisdom. Commit them to memory in the following manner: Read the entire *Pattern* from beginning to end, instead of trying to learn it piecemeal. Then try to say it over to yourself. Persist in this practice until you have it. Then write it down on paper. This, by the way, is the best and quickest way to memorize any passage. Take care to use it for this work, because it is a correct beginning in learning to organize your conscious processes.

This, remember, is a *pattern* — not a boastful declaration of personal attainment. The truth it speaks is truth about the *Self*, the cosmic Life–power behind all personal manifestations. It is said to be "on the trestleboard" because in the old terminology of the building crafts, a trestleboard is a sort of table on which are laid the plans for the guidance of the workmen.

The *Pattern* should be said every morning upon arising, and every night before you go to sleep. Be sure to do this, even though it seems at present to be a foolish and unnecessary practice. Guard against a mere automatic, parrot–like repetition of the words. Try to think through the meaning of every sentence. Make this effort every time you recite it.

The next lesson will give you greater insight into its meaning. The key to this will be found in the numbering of the statements. Thus in next week's lesson you will really extend your study of the *Pattern*. As a preparation, secure a notebook as soon as you finish reading this lesson. Jot down in it any ideas that may come into your mind as you proceed with this study. The notes need not be extended. Yet it is of greatest importance that they be kept, and *dated*. Observe this last detail with great care.

This notebook is *important*. It is your occult diary, and will contain a record of your progress. It will become of tremendous value to you in your later work. To slight it is to defeat one of the main purposes of this instruction. Use it at every regular study period, and make an entry at that time, even if it is a record of failure to study at the time scheduled. You will need this diary in order to make reports on your progress, and it will have other important bearings upon your development as time goes on. *Keep it in a secure place, and do not show it to anyone.* Heed these instructions to the letter.

Spend your study periods this week as follows:

1. Work at memorizing the *Pattern*. When you have it by heart, begin your study period by reciting it.

2. Read this lesson through slowly, and if possible, read it aloud.

3. Use the rest of the time to look over your Tarot Keys, and endeavor to familiarize yourself with them, so that you can identify each by its number and title. If any Key is especially *attractive* to you, make a note of it in your occult diary. If any Key is particularly *unattractive*, note this also. If any Key suggests to you some idea, however vague, put that into your diary.

With the third of these lessons you will begin to color your Keys, in accordance with instructions you will receive week by week. Colored Keys are imperative for this work, as the symbology connected with the colors is highly important. When you color your own Keys, they take on the character of your personality. They become inseparably linked with you. The attention you must give impresses their designs on the cells of your brain and builds the details of each picture into your consciousness. Making the Tarot Keys part of your very flesh and blood is one of the most important practical secrets of occultism. It is the basis of all the subtler and more potent utilizations of Tarot. Coloring one's own set of Keys is the quickest and best way to achieve this result.

LESSON TWO

THE SYMBOLISM
OF NUMBERS

Number symbols represent truths at once simple and universal, truths immanent in all things and manifest in all phenomena. The science of numbers is at the foundation of every other department of human knowledge. Resolve to master thoroughly the elements of this science as presented in this lesson. In so doing you will be taking an important step toward the understanding of cosmic law, which will eventually put you in harmony with the rhythms of the cosmic life–manifestation, make you ruler of your personality, and free you from restricting limitations in your environment.

Let no fancied ineptitude or dislike for mathematics deter you from entering seriously into this study. You need not be quick at figures, nor do you require a natural bent for abstruse abstractions to undertake this work. You will be able to master the underlying principles in a comparatively short time. Practice will make you proficient in their various applications.

The numerals from 0 to 9 represent successive stages in every cycle of evolution, whether on the grand scale of the cosmos or on the smaller scale of personal unfoldment. The order in the numeral series reflects an order which prevails throughout creation. It is an ancient doctrine that the Master Builder has ordered all things by measure, number and weight. Everywhere in the universe the properties of number are manifested, whether in the revolution of planets round the sun, in the whirling of electrons within an atom, or in the arrangement of parts in a living organism. Not so long since a famous relativist declared that number is one of the few things in the universe which is not relative.

This elementary text will attempt no exhaustive treatment of number symbolism. Such an effort would only bewilder you. For the present what you need is an outline of the fundamental meanings of the ten numeral signs. As you proceed with your studies you can fill in this outline in greater detail.

At first some of the attributions may not be very clear. They may appear to be arbitrary and far–fetched. So do the meanings of all symbols when we first learn them. *Keep your purpose in view.* You are learning number symbols because they are part of the esoteric language which occultists have employed to transmit their knowledge from generation to generation. No satisfactory substitute for this language has ever been devised. By means of it, an advanced occultist can communicate with a fellow adept in spite of the barriers of ordinary speech. With a few lines and figures he can express more meaning than he could pack into pages of words.

When you have fixed in memory the fundamental ideas of this numerical system, you soon learn that none are arbitrary. Then you will begin to see the connection between these ideas, which are printed in capitals at the beginning of each paragraph of attributions, and the other meanings that follow them. The discovery of the links of association that join these key ideas to the others is an important part of your mental training. This discovery you must make for yourself.

Remember, too, that you were told in the preceding lesson that there is a connection between the numbers and the corresponding sentences of *The Pattern on the Trestleboard*. The key words in the *Pattern* are capitalized, and there is a sense in which each key word may be taken as the name of the corresponding number.

MEANINGS OF THE NUMERAL SIGNS

0 — NO–THING; the undifferentiated Power preceding all manifestation; absence of quantity, quality of mass; freedom from every limitation; changelessness; the unknown; immeasurable; fathomless; infinite; eternal Source; the Rootless Root of all creation; the sacred ellipse representing the endless line of eternity; the Cosmic Egg; Superconsciousness.

1 — BEGINNING; the first of the numeral series, because 0 stands for that which precedes all manifestation, and therefore is not properly included in the series; inception; initiative; the Primal Will; selection; unity; singleness; individuality; attention; one–pointedness; concentration; the definite or manifest, as contrasted with the indefinable Source; Self–consciousness.

2 — DUPLICATION; repetition; Wisdom and Science; opposition; polarity; antithesis; succession; sequence; continuation; diffusion; separation; radiation; secondariness; subordination; dependence; Subconsciousness.

3 — MULTIPLICATION; increase; growth; augmentation; expansion; amplification; productiveness; fecundity; generation; the re-

6

sponse of subconsciousness to self–consciousness in the generating of mental images; hence, Understanding.

4 — ORDER; system; regulation; management; supervision; control; authority; command; dominance; the classifying activity of self–consciousness, induced by the multiplication of mental images through the response of subconsciousness to impressions originating in self–consciousness; the Cosmic Order considered as the underlying substance manifested in every form; Reason.

5 — MEDIATION (an idea suggested by the fact that 5 is the middle term of the series of signs from 1 to 9); adaptation; intervention; adjustment; hence, Justice; accommodation; reconciliation; result of the classifying activities symbolized by 4; Subconscious elaboration of these classifications, and the formulation of deductions therefrom. These deductions, projected into the field of self–conscious awareness, are the mental states termed Intuitions.

6 — RECIPROCATION; interchange; correlation; response; coordination; cooperation; correspondence; harmony; concord; equilibration; symmetry; Beauty.

7 — EQUILIBRIUM (the result of equilibration, the concrete application of the laws of symmetry and reciprocation); mastery; poise; rest; conquest; peace; safety; security; art; Victory.

8 — RHYTHM; periodicity; alternation; flux and reflux; pulsation; vibration; involution and evolution; education; culture; the response of subconsciousness to everything symbolized by 7.

9 — CONCLUSION (literally, "closing together", which implies the union of elements that are separate until the conclusion is reached, and has special reference to certain meanings attached to the number 9 through the Tarot Key bearing this number); goal; end; completion; fulfillment; attainment; the final result of the process symbolized by the series of digits; perfection; adeptship; the mystical *three times three* of the Freemasons, and of other societies which preserve some vestiges of the ancient mysteries.

The meaning of a number consisting of two or more digits may be ascertained by combining the ideas indicated by each symbol, beginning always with the digit on the right–hand or units place. Thus the number 10 combines the ideas of 0 and 1, with 1 considered as the agency expressing the power represented by 0. Furthermore, since 10 follows 9, it implies that the finality represented by 9 refers to a single cycle of manifestation only. The completion of a cycle is always a return to the eternal No–thing, 0; but since 0 is essentially changeless in its inherent nature, the eternal Source is eternally a self–manifesting power. Consequently a new cycle begins as soon as the previous cycle ends. Thus the number 10 symbolizes the eternal creativeness of the Life–power; the incessant whirling forth of the self–expression of the Primal Will; the ever–turning Wheel of Manifestation. (See the Tarot Key numbered 10). Thus 10 is the number of embodiment, of the Kingdom, and of the manifested Law. It is also a combination of a characteristic masculine symbol (1) with another recognized the world over as feminine (0).

Memorize the numbers and the key words written in capitals. Set aside ten pages in your occult diary. Head each page with one of the numeral signs and its key word. Then copy each paragraph on the meaning of the numeral signs. *This is important.* To copy anything is to make it more surely yours than if you merely read it.

As the days pass, whenever you get an idea about the meaning of some number, make a note of it in the proper place in your book. If you come upon something in your reading, copy that, too. At this time do not make any special search for additional information concerning numbers. By this, it is meant that you are not to consult other texts on numbers, nor are you to look up articles on numbers in the occult magazines. Simply make notes on ideas that come to you from your own inner consciousness, and copy anything that seems important, whenever you encounter it in the course of your ordinary reading. The main thing to remember is that you are not to go in quest of numerical information.

It will come to you. It will come without special effort on your part. You will be surprised at the amount of material on the significance of numbers that will seem to flow in your direction as if by magic. After a time this part of your notes will seem to you one of the most valuable sections of your occult reference library.

Another good practice is to look up the exact dictionary definitions of every word in the ten paragraphs of explanation given in this lesson. You will gain a great deal of insight from this exercise.

During your study period arrange your Tarot Keys thus:

			0			
1	2	3	4	5	6	7
8	9	10	11	12	13	14
15	16	17	18	19	20	21

Examine this carefully, paying special attention to the numbers of the cards. Try to connect them with the pictures. In the numbers from 10 to 21 try to work out the meanings of the numbers from what you have been told concerning the nine digits and zero. Transcribe your findings into your notebook. Do this, no matter how trivial or vague your first attempts may seem. You must make a beginning. These first endeavors to formulate ideas for yourself are seeds that will bear much good fruit later on.

In the foregoing arrangement of the Tarot Keys you will notice that the zero card is placed above the others, to indicate that No–number, to which it corresponds, is logically superior to, and precedes, the idea of *beginning*, represented by 1. 0 is also separated from the other number symbols because it is not really in the sequence of numbers.

For your information, though you may not be able to use it at first, the Keys in the top row refer to *powers* or *potencies* of consciousness; those in the middle row are symbols of *laws* or *agencies*; those in the bottom row represent *conditions* or *effects*. Thus 1 is the *power* which works through the agency of 8 to modify the *conditions* or *effects* represented by 15; 2 is the *power* which works through 9 to modify the *conditions* represented by 16; and so on through the entire series. Notice also that ten pairs of Keys balance numerically through 11, which is represented by *Justice*, a symbol of equilibrium. Thus 11 is one–half the sum of any two numbers diametrically opposite each other in the tableau, with Key 11 as the mathematical and geometrical center between them, as 1 and 21, 9 and 13, 6 and 16, and so on.

THE FOOL
(THE LIFE—POWER)

The first thing to do before you read this lesson is to take your Tarot Key numbered 0, *The Fool*, and place it before you. Observe every detail closely, so that you can make mental reference to it as you read this lesson. Be orderly about it. Start with the Hebrew letter, which is Aleph, in the lower right–hand corner, then the title and the number. Work progressively from right to left, from the top of the picture to the bottom.

Key 0 represents the manner in which the Absolute presents itself to the minds of the wise. The Absolute is THAT of which nothing may be positively affirmed, of which no definition may be made, because it transcends our finite comprehension. It is the Rootless Root of all being, the Causeless Cause of all that is, yet these names cannot in the least define it. All speculation as to its essential nature is futile. What is important to us is the way in which it manifests itself to our understanding.

Some of the names which have been given to this manifestation are: the Life–power; Limitless Light; L. V. X.; the One Force; the One Thing; the Primal Will. Learn these names. They designate the force you use in every thought, feeling and action, the force you will employ in your Tarot practice. Your advancement will be measured strictly by your growing comprehension of the real meaning of these names.

The first symbol of the Life–power is 0. At this point review what is listed under the numeral sign 0 in the preceding lesson. There you see the key word is NO–THING. The Life–power is limitless. Therefore it is *nothing* we can define, *nothing* we can measure, *nothing* we can fathom, *nothing* that will ever come to an end, *nothing* that ever had a beginning.

0 looks like an egg, and an egg is something which contains potencies of growth and development. As a living form is hatched from an egg, so is everything in the universe brought forth from the Cosmic Egg of the Life–power. The Life–power has within it *all* possibilities. All manifestation, every object, every force in the universe, is an adaptation of the one Life–power. Because its possibilities are truly limitless, it may be specialized in any particular form or manifestation of which the human mind can conceive. It is because of this that so many extraordinary results may be achieved by purely *mental* means.

Because the Life–power is the force behind all manifestation, and consequently behind all growth, it is obviously *the* cultural power. This is vividly suggested by the attribution of the letter Aleph (א) to this Key. Aleph means "Ox." Oxen were the motive power in primitive agriculture. They were used to plow the

11

fields, thresh the grain, and carry the burdens. Agriculture is the basic form of civilization, so the ox represents the power at work in all kinds of human adaptation and modification of natural conditions. In this way the ox symbolizes creative energy, the vital principle of all living creatures. This vital principle comes to us in physical form as the radiant energy of the sun.

Consequently we see that the Life–power is not an abstraction, far removed from our everyday life. We contact it everywhere, in every form. Our senses reveal it to us physically as light and heat from the sun, and scientific research has today confirmed the truth of the ancient intuition that sun energy is the basis of our physical existence.

Just as sunlight is a form of electromagnetic vibration, measurable with physical instruments, so is every other part of the universe, physical or superphysical, composed also of electro–magnetic vibrations. Man's instruments for recording these vibrations have a relatively narrow range, even though they do go far beyond the limits of man's physical senses. But there is an instrument, not made by man, which *can* utilize and adapt the higher vibrations of the radiant mental energy in a manner truly wonderful. That instrument is the human personality, and you possess it. Its function is to give free expression to the Life–power. (Recall statements 0, 1 and 2 of *The Pattern on the Trestleboard*.)

One of the most important forms taken by this energy, and the first you should learn to use, is *air*. You must learn to control actual atmospheric air; in other words, you must learn to breathe properly. We do not recommend here that you indulge in any of the breathing exercises described by some teachers of "occult development." Such practices have no place in your instruction at this time, since they only too often prove dangerous to students who do not fully realize what they are attempting. Just learn to breathe deeply, giving full play to the abdominal muscles during the act of inhalation. Do not make the mistake of trying any forced expansion of the chest. Let the muscles just below your ribs do most of the work. Keep in mind the picture of filling your lungs with air, so as to provide your blood stream with the oxygen it requires. At first many readers of these pages will find that it takes not a little watchfulness to make breathing deep and regular. Consistent practice, however, will soon establish you in good habits, so that automatically you will breathe as you should.

The importance of breath is shown in the symbolism of *The*

Fool. The letter Aleph is the special sign of air in Hebrew eso-teric philosophy. The noun "fool" is derived from the Latin *follis*, meaning "a bag of wind," and to this day we call a noisy, silly person a "windbag." *Follis* also means "bellows", an instrument utilizing air to stir up fire, precisely the office of the lungs in the human body. The yellow tint in the background of Key 0 is also symbolical of air. Add to this the fact that in every civilized lan-guage man uses words which ordinarily mean *air*, *wind* or *breath* to designate *life* or *conscious energy*, and you can readily fathom the significance attached to air by occultists, and realize the im-portance of learning to use it properly.

The Tarot title of the Life–power is highly ingenious. It tells us what we need to know, at the same time throwing the idly curi-ous or the superficial completely off the track. One key to the true significance of *The Fool* is the saying, "The wisdom of God is foolishness with men." Thus it is that those men, found in every generation, who gain unusual knowledge of the Life–power, are often called madmen or fools by their less enlightened breth-ren.

So this title hints at a state of consciousness that has even been termed pathological by some materialistic psychologists, simply because its results were unfamiliar to them and they were in-capable of understanding it. By those who can comprehend its significance, this state of consciousness is termed *superconscious-ness* or *cosmic consciousness*. To attain such a state of conscious-ness is to comprehend the universe in its entirety and to gain complete self–realization. The attainment of superconsciousness may well be given as the ultimate object of your Tarot study. By this you must not understand that some method of practice or instruction outside yourself is going to bring you superconscious-ness in some miraculous manner. Nothing could be farther from the truth. Your study and practice will help you gradually to or-ganize the powers of your personality so that you will be able to express superconsciousness through it.

The only way we can conceive of the Absolute is in terms of our own experience. We always tend to invest it with some hu-man form, from the highest philosophical ideas of a Creative In-telligence down to the grossest types of anthropomorphism. This is what is symbolized by the Fool himself. Behind this personal semblance, however, sages discern something higher — typified in this picture as the white sun — an impersonal Power, manifest-ed as the limitless energy radiated to the planets of innumerable world systems by their suns.

13

In manifestation, this energy, symbolized also by the fair hair of the traveler, is temporarily limited by living organisms. Of these, the vegetable kingdom, represented by the green wreath, is the primary class from which, in the order of evolution, spring animal organisms, typified by the red feather.

The Life–power is forever young, forever in the morning of its might, forever on the verge of the abyss of manifestation. It always faces unknown possibilities of self–expression transcending any height that it may previously have reached. Hence the Fool faces toward the north–west (a direction particularly associated with initiation and the beginning of new enterprises in the rituals of occult schools that dramatize the ancient mysteries). He looks toward a peak above and beyond his present station.

He is THAT which was, is and shall be, and this is indicated by the Hebrew letters IHVH (יהוה) (Yod–Heh–Vau–Heh) dimly shown among the lines of the folds at the collar of his undergarment, for "That which was, is and shall be" is the precise meaning of IHVH.

His inner robe stands for the dazzling white light of perfect wisdom. It is concealed by the black coat of ignorance, lined with the red of passion and physical force. This outer garment is embroidered with a floral decoration, but the unit of design is a solar orb containing eight red spokes and symbolizing the whirling motion that brings the universe into manifestation. The coat is encircled by a girdle consisting of twelve units, of which seven are showing. The girdle symbolizes time, and just as the coat can be removed only if the girdle be first unclasped, so is it impossible to overcome ignorance and passion until man has freed his consciousness from the limitations imposed on him by his belief in the reality of time. No more important single symbol is to be found in Tarot, and what should be noted particularly is that the girdle is artificial, made by man himself, and not a product of nature. In like manner, man's sense of time is an artificial product, a device of man's own creative imagination. It is a most useful invention, when rightly employed, but as most persons abuse it, a prolific source of error.

The mountains in the background represent those abstract mathematical conceptions which are behind all knowledge of reality. As such they are cold and uninteresting to many. Yet the melting snow upon the peaks feeds streams that make fertile the valleys below. So will the principles of Ageless Wisdom feed your consciousness and make fertile your mental imagery, thus transforming your life.

The little dog represents intellect, the reasoning mind functioning at the personal level. In older exoteric versions of Tarot, the dog bites the Fool's leg because, at the period of history when these Keys were first invented, the intellectual consciousness of humanity, distorted by centuries of wrong thinking, was definitely inimical to the spiritual philosophy of Ageless Wisdom. In our version the little dog is friendly, as an intimation that even the lower intellect of mankind has become the companion rather than the adversary of the higher knowledge. Today the intellect is a faithful companion on the great spiritual adventure, but it is at a lower level and must have a master.

During your practice period this week read this lesson once each day. Pay particular attention to anything which may seem obscure to you and endeavor to think *through* it. Give complete attention to everything stated, and set down in your notebook any ideas that may occur to you in connection with this lesson.

This week you begin to color your Keys, using the colors that come with the lessons. You may also use water colors if you know how to apply them. Color only one card each week. If you are pressed for time, take two weeks to complete each Key.

Begin by reading the directions completely. Before applying color to any card, try to visualize exactly what it will look like when it is finished. This is a practical exercise of great value. It not only tends to clarify and make definite your mental imagery, but it also utilizes the suggestive power of the Keys. Be sure to do it before coloring each card.

For the best results you will need two water color brushes, a No. 5 and a No. 1. We recommend Devoe & Reynolds red sable, since they are satisfactory and comparatively inexpensive. A porcelain dish with at least six chambers will also be of help, though not absolutely necessary.

To use the colors, dissolve them in water. Do not use too much water or you will get the colors too thin. A little experimentation will enable you to determine the correct quantity to use. All necessary colors are included in the set. The flesh color, in concentrated solution, is bright orange. The other colors can easily be identified by the color of the paper they are on.

Apply the colors in the order they are given for each card. Long experience has enabled us to determine this order, because of the qualities of the coloring material used. For instance, the reason we recommend you to wait until last to apply the red is that it *runs very readily*. Consequently, if applied too soon it may run into a color you are applying next to it, and thus spoil your

15

work.

A word of caution is necessary with regard to the flesh color. It is very concentrated, and if you are not careful to dilute it properly you will have bright orange instead of flesh tint. Before applying this or any other color, *try it on a sheet of plain white paper*. Thus you will avoid errors on your cards.

To give a lifelike appearance to the cheeks of the human figures, use a diluted red solution. A diluted brown with a trace of orange over the eyes enhances the appearance. But we recommend that you do not try this unless you are sure you can do it skillfully.

Blond hair is yellow, with a little brown added. You can tell the amount by testing on white paper.

The cards can be made more striking if you use white, but this is an opaque color and difficult to use without covering up the black lines. If you feel that you wish to use white, a small tube of water color white or show card white will be satisfactory.

Gold and silver can be used where indicated in coloring directions. This is not by any means necessary, and gold and silver are difficult to apply. Wherever gold is called for use yellow, or yellow with a trace of orange added to make a golden yellow. For silver use white, or leave blank. If you wish to use gold and silver, you can procure them for about ten cents a cake.

If your colors do not appear bright enough it is because you have applied them too diluted. This can be remedied by going over them again until the desired shade is secured. When this is necessary, be sure that the first coat is thoroughly dry before you apply another. Otherwise you will get a spotty, muddy appearance. But if you try out your solutions before applying them, you will have no difficulty. Begin with a very small quantity of water, and gradually dilute the solution until you arrive at the shade desired.

By following these directions carefully you should be well pleased with the results. Again let us suggest that you read the directions for *each* card carefully before applying any color. In this way you will avoid coloring portions that should be left blank for another color. Experience has taught us that this precaution is *very necessary*.

If you spoil a card, place it face down in a basin of water over night. By morning most of the color will have come off, so that you can try it again after it is dry.

0. THE FOOL

Yellow: Background, circles on garment (but not flame in top circle), shoes.

Green: Trefoils surrounding circles on outer garment, and other tendril–like figures. (Not belt). Leaves on rose, wreath round his head.

Violet: Mountains. (Use somewhat diluted solution, since they are distant mountains. The peaks are snow–capped, so do not paint where snow is to be.)

Brown: Eagle on wallet, precipice in foreground whereon the Fool stands.

White: Sun, inner garment, dog, rose, eye on flap of wallet, mountain peaks.

Flesh: Hands and face. (Since it is obvious where flesh color should be used we shall not indicate it hereafter. There are two places where it should not be used — the hands and face of the angel on Key 6, and the human figures on Key 20.)

Blonde: The Fool's hair.

Citrine: The Fool's hose. (Citrine is an olive green, secured by a mixture of orange and green. This is the only place where it is used.)

Gold: Star on shoulder, girdle, knob on staff.

Silver: Moon on shoulder.

Red: Feather, lining of outer garment where it shows at the sleeves, spokes of wheels, flame in top circle on coat, wallet (except eagle and eye).

Keep the symbolic interpretation of each detail in mind as you color it. When your set of cards is completed, *do not allow others to see or handle them.* The one exception to this rule is that you may show your work to another student if by so doing you can really help him. But even then your Keys should not be handled by anyone but yourself. They are part of your equipment, and should be used by you alone — not for any selfish reason, but in order that no magnetism but yours be impressed upon them.

LESSON FOUR

THE FOOL
(Cont.)

Now that you have colored the first of the Tarot Keys, you are in a better position to understand the details of the symbolism, of which only the main outlines were given in the preceding lesson.

The white sun behind the Fool is placed in the upper right–hand corner of the design. Look at Keys 10 and 21, and you will see that in those pictures this place in the design is occupied by the head of an eagle, symbol of the zodiacal sign Scorpio. Astrologers take this sign as the ruler of the reproductive mechanism of the human body. Hence the sun indicates the idea that the ONE FORCE typified by the Fool is actually related to the reproductive power of living organisms. On its practical side our work has to do with the control and adaptation of the force which is ordinarily expressed in reproduction.

The color of the sun is a reference to the Primal Will. On an ancient occult diagram called the Tree of Life, the first manifestation of the Life–power, corresponding to the statement numbered "1" in *The Pattern on the Trestleboard*, is called the *Crown*, and is represented by a white circle. From this white circle proceeds a path corresponding to the letter Aleph and to the Fool.

Here is a suggestion that the cultural power represented by the letter Aleph and by this Key is identical with the Primal Will, and in a sense proceeds from that Will when a cycle of manifestation begins. Furthermore, the position of the sun in the picture, because it relates to reproduction, intimates that manifestation is the reproduction and extension of the power of the Primal Will. In the Hermetic Wisdom symbolized by Tarot, one of the fundamental principles is that the manifested universe is not something made by the Life–power out of some kind of material other than itself. Rather is the manifestation to be considered as the projection of the Life–power into the relative conditions of time and space as we know them. It is therefore understood in this ancient doctrine that the universe is of the same essential nature as the Life–power. It is the expression of the creative

Word, or Logos, and even the exoteric Christian creed speaks of the Logos as "begotten, not made."

The green wreath encircling the Fool's hair symbolizes the fact that the green leaves of plants actually do bind sunlight, just as the wreath binds the Fool's yellow hair. Capturing sunbeams and binding them into organic form is the principal work of the chlorophyll which is the green coloring matter of plants. This is what makes green vegetables so valuable as food. They constitute one of the most important forms in which the Life–power is available for your use. See that you eat enough of them.

The feather rising from the wreath is a wing–feather of an eagle. It represents animal life, a step higher in the scale of organism than the vegetable kingdom. It is red, the color of desire and action. The only true aspiration is the desire to be *something*, the desire to express some particular form of the Life–power *in action*. What do you aspire to be and do?

The wand over the Fool's shoulder, like a yardstick, represents the idea of measurement. It shows us the necessity for measuring the possibilities of the Life–power. We cannot measure the No–Thing itself, but we can and must measure what we intend to accomplish by means of it.

The most important thing to measure is our own place in the universe. According to the Bible the full measure of man is this: "You have made him but little lower than God, and crown him with glory and honor. You made him to have dominion over the works of your hands; you have put all things under his feet."

The wand is black because it represents occult powers. There is a secret force in human personality which is brought into manifestation whenever we take our own measure truly, and correctly measure the conditions of our environment. Thus the black wand stands for the hidden forces called into play by our exercise of the mental power of measurement.

The wallet suspended from the wand represents the powers of subconsciousness, which depend from or upon the self–conscious power of measurement. Memory is the basic power of subconsciousness and memory is essentially reproductive. Hence the wallet is blazoned with the device of a flying eagle, which refers both to aspiration, as having its roots in subconscious desires, and to the reproductive forces associated with the eagle as one of the emblems of the zodiacal sign Scorpio. The eagle is also the bird of Zeus or Jupiter. As king of birds it suggests dominance over the element of air. Here it may also be noted that the sacrifices to Jupiter generally consisted of bulls and cows, so here is another correspondence to the meaning of the letter Aleph.

On the flap of the wallet is an open eye. This is the All–seeing Eye of Freemasonry, the Egyptian Eye of Horus, the eye placed in a delta or triangle on the reverse side of the Great Seal of the United States. The particular aspect of Horus here indicated is Hoor–pa–Kraat, the Egyptian god of silence, depicted as a child seated on a lotus, holding his forefinger to his lips.

The symbol of the Eye of Horus has many occult meanings, some of which will be touched upon in later lessons. Here it is placed on the flap of the wallet in the position usually occupied by a lock, and it means: SIGHT is that which both locks and un-locks subconscious powers. It is the way we *look* at ourselves and at life that determines whether we are mere puppets of subcon-sciousness or masters of its hidden powers.

There are ten dots, representing stitches, on the flap of the wallet. They symbolize the ten basic aspects of the Life–power, and thus they correspond to the statements numbered from 1 to 10 in *The Pattern on The Trestleboard*. They are analogous to the wheels on the Fool's coat.

The rose represents desire. Its thorns symbolize pain and its bloom typifies beauty and joy. It is white, like the sun, to inti-mate that through right cultivation of the desire nature we may bring it into unison with the Primal Will, so that our desires may become conscious expressions of the actual underlying tenden-cies of the cosmic order. To control desire, to cultivate it aright, to use it in such a way that we enjoy the beauty it can bring us without suffering the pains that result from misuse — this is one of the great practical secrets. Hence this rose is a cultivated flower, and the youth carries it gaily, without pricking himself.

The eight–pointed star and the crescent on the left shoulder of the Fool's black garment are symbols of the sun and moon, of the positive and negative modes of light. They have many profound meanings in occult science, but all these meanings are develop-ments of the fundamental doctrine that all things are manifes-tations of the action and reaction between the solar or electric and the lunar or magnetic currents of the Great Magical Agent, or L. V. X.

The yellow circle enclosing a triple flame, shown on the Fool's breast, represents the doctrine that the One Force is essentially that which is manifest to us as light and fire. This particular sym-bol refers to the formless state of the One Force, prior to the beginning of a cycle of manifestation.

The ten wheels were touched on in the preceding lesson. Here we may add that in Hermetic Wisdom they represent Spirit. Each is surrounded by seven trefoils which represent the seven basic modes of activity which we shall hereafter learn to associate with the seven alchemical metals and with the seven interior stars of the Yoga philosophy. The trefoils are green, the color of immortality, to show that they typify eternal phases of the Life–power's activity. One of the Wheels contains a Hebrew letter Shin (ש), (the letter on the 20th Tarot Key). It is a symbol of the fiery Life–Breath and of the spiritual energy which brings all things into manifestation.

The abyss which yawns at the Fool's feet is in contrast to the height on which he stands. It symbolizes "that which is below." It is nature, the relative, the phenomenon or effect, in contrast to Spirit, the Absolute, the noumenon or cause. At the bottom of the abyss is the valley, the scene of labor, of constructive activity, of struggle and competition, in contrast to the ideas of perfection, superiority and supremacy which are suggested by the Fool's position on the mountain–top. The valley is what the Chinese philosopher calls the Mother–Deep, what the Hindus term *Prakriti*, the mysterious power of the Supreme Spirit. Because the valley is the field of experience, it also corresponds to ideas that Hebrew Wisdom relates to the noun *Chokmah*, Wisdom; and on the Tree of Life before mentioned, the path of the letter Aleph terminates at the point on the diagram to which *Chokmah* is referred.

In practical psychology the abyss represents what we are accustomed to call subconsciousness. The natural metaphor for this plane of consciousness is "depths." Thus in an article by Dr. Putnam on the work of Freud, the pioneer in psychoanalysis, we read: "In the course of these investigations Freud and Jung and their followers have dived more deeply than anyone before into the mysteries of the unconscious life."

The traveler is on the verge of descending. Thus the picture shows the Supreme Spirit, or super conscious aspect of the Life–power, as we think of it prior to the beginning of a cycle of self–expression. The wayfarer is unafraid because he knows he cannot be injured by his descent into the depths, and because he is aware that he will certainly raise himself to the greater height toward which he is directing his eager gaze.

22

This picture is a representation of that limitless Force which is the central reality in every human life. It stands for what you really mean when you say "I AM." It is an image of the *Something* in you that sees far beyond the seeming limitations of your present environment and circumstances. *That Something has brought you thus far on your journey toward supreme attainment. That Something is what makes you want to succeed, what makes you want to enjoy better health, what makes you want better circumstances.*

Because it knows itself perfectly, knows how limitless are its possibilities, how resistless its powers, how boundless its opportunities, that *Something* in you will not let you alone. Though you may seem to be at the end of your resources, it urges you to press on. Though you may be past what men call middle life, it knows that it is forever young, and knocks importunately at the inner door of your mind, trying to let you know that in the very core of your being is a power which knows nothing of age or defeat or ill–health — a power which over and over again has worked its miracles of healing and rejuvenation, has transformed disaster into victory, lack into abundance, sorrow into joy.

In short, the Fool is a picture of the limitless power of your own inner, spiritual, super conscious life. In order to get more and more of that power into expression every day from now on, you must begin by thoroughly impressing your subconsciousness with this image of that One Force.

The method is simplicity itself. Just *look* at this picture five minutes every morning during the next week, and five minutes every evening. Remember that *Sight* is the power which locks and unlocks the wallet of subconscious forces. When you do this, look at the details of the design, one after another. Simple as it is, this exercise will transfer the picture from the printed Key to the cells of your brain. Thus the Key will become an integral part of your personality, will be made an element of your flesh and blood.

This is one great secret in the practical use of Tarot. Until you have built the Tarot Keys into yourself they do not exert their maximum power. When you have done so they will evoke powers from within you which will change your whole life.

Continue to use *The Pattern on the Trestleboard*, and keep up your regular practice period as in preceding weeks. Pay particular attention to your notebook. Even if the entry be only a word or two, keep a record of the ideas that come to you as you use the Tarot Keys. This practice period should include one of the two five–minute examinations of the Fool.

LESSON FIVE

THE MAGICIAN
(SELF — CONSCIOUSNESS)

B egin this lesson by carefully examining, as a whole and in detail, Key 1, *The Magician*. In this connection review the meaning of the number 1, given in Lesson Two.

All that is represented in the symbolism of the Key is a development of ideas associated with this number. The Magician typifies the beginning or inception of the process whereby the limitless possibilities of the Life–power are brought into expression as manifested actualities. The Key represents the *initiation* of the creative process on all planes of nature. In human personality the creative process is begun by the phase of consciousness that we term *self–consciousness* or *objective mind*. Self–consciousness is the distinctly human aspect of mental activity. Objective mind is the waking mind that you are using to read these pages.

Self–consciousness initiates the creative process by formulating premises or seed–ideas. Subconsciousness accepts these as *suggestions*, which it elaborates by the process of deduction, and carries out in modifications of psychological and physiological function and structure. These two sentences outline a most important process. You use it continually, whether or not you know that you do, because it is the basis of your intellectual knowledge and the determinant of the state of your physical health. All of your physical and mental states are the results of your mental imagery. You have the clue to success in occult practice when you thoroughly understand what is implied by the statement that *any mental image tends to materialize itself as an actual condition or event.*

Geometrically the number 1 is a point, particularly a central point. In *The Pattern on the Trestleboard* the statement attributed to the number 1 is, "I am *a center of expression* for the Primal Will–to–good which eternally creates and sustains the universe." The beginning of the creative process is the collection of the Life–power at a center, and its expression through that center. The sun of our solar system is such a center. It transmits the Life–power in a form in which it can be utilized.

The idea is shown in two ways by the letter Beth (ב), printed on Key 1. Ancient forms of this character represented an arrow–head, and the name for this implement in Greek was *kentron*, from which come the English words, *center* and *concentration*. The letter–name means "house", which is a definite location used as an abode. In the sense used here it refers to whatever form may be termed a dwelling–place for Spirit, and the form particularly referred to in this lesson is *human personality*. The personality is a center through which the Spirit or real Self of man expresses itself. Do not be abstract about this. Think of *your* personality as a center of expression for your own inner Self. Try to realize what Jesus meant when he said, "The Father who dwells within me, He does the works."

The title of this Key, *The Magician*, definitely identifies the picture with Hermes or Mercury, who presided over magic. You will remember that Mercury was the messenger of the gods and in this capacity, served to *transmit* or *express* their wisdom. This correspondence to Hermes is also connected with another meaning of the number 1, which as representing singleness and therefore isolation, stands also for privacy and concealment, and thus for occult or hidden knowledge. Magic is the art of *transformation* and it is closely related to *the* Hermetic Art, alchemy. In human personality, self–consciousness is the transformer. It and it only, is able to set in motion the forces which bring about change, variation, and so forth. The fundamental magical practice is *concentration*, or one–pointed attention to some selected area of one's environment.

The practice of concentration enables one to perceive the inner nature of the object of his attention, thus leading to the discovery of natural principles, which when applied, enable us to change our conditions. Hence concentration helps us solve our problems, and thus we may understand why the old alchemists wrote: "Our Mercury enables us to prepare the universal solvent." The higher phases of the art that begins with concentration are those which have to do with the underlying principles of human existence. Thus, one reason you are using the Tarot Keys as objects for concentration is that they represent the basic modes of human consciousness.

Learn the following definition:

Concentration is the collection, at a center or focus, of units of force. These units are always units of the Life–power, because every unit in the universe, regardless of the form it takes, is made of that One Force. You will understand that you do not concentrate attention. Attention is the *means* that enables you to concentrate units of *mental energy*. The result is that you intensify this energy so that you can direct it usefully. When you intensify the rays of the sun through a convex lens, they will burn your hand if you direct them upon it, but if you place your hand in the sunlight passing through a pane of window glass, the result is merely a slight sensation of warmth. Never forget that when you practice concentration you are directing a *real force*.

Note the posture of the Magician in Key 1. With his right hand he draws down power from above. With his left he makes a gesture of concentration. He is directing power drawn from higher levels to planes below that of his own self–conscious existence. He does this for a specific reason. This picture shows clearly the magical process involved in an understanding of the correct practice of concentration. The plane below the Magician is shown as a garden, which is a symbol of subconsciousness. When you concentrate you seek always to impress some definite image on subconsciousness, thus accomplishing some particular modification of the subconscious field of activity.

One important point to observe is that the Magician himself is not active. He is acting as a channel for a power that comes from above his level and, after passing through him, this power sets up a reaction at a level lower than his. As in the illustration of the convex lens, the lens, though it is the agency which intensifies the rays of the sun, does nothing itself. In this connection it is interesting to note that the old Hebrew name for the mode of consciousness represented by the Magician is *Intelligence of Transparency*, clearly intimating the idea that self–consciousness effects transformations because something works *through* it.

Again, the digit 1, as the beginning of the numeral series, is the sign of a thing standing in relation to other things. What stands in relation to other things is connected with them by various links or bonds. Magic is really the science of the hidden relationships between things. The practice of magic is based on the law of correspondence expressed in the Hermetic axiom: *That which is above is as that which is below, and that which is below is as that which is above.*

The bond between things is fundamentally their co–existence as manifestations of the one Life–power. All things are of one substance. All things are governed by one great law. All things are masks of a single Reality. Hence all things are parts of a great whole from which nothing can be detached. Anything done to the part affects the whole. In human relationships this is unalterably true, and therefore was it said: "Inasmuch as ye have done it unto the least of these my brethren, ye have done it unto me."

Magic is the art which produces effects by a mastery of the secret forces of nature. It is the science of Zoroaster and Hermes — *the* science of which all others are branches — the science that sent its representatives to pay homage to the Child of Bethlehem. It is the science of initiation. A true initiator is one who has mastered this hidden science of causes, and knows how to direct the universal creative force so as to bring about, by methods that

27

seem miraculous to those who do not know the secret, the full realization and physical embodiment of the aims and purposes expressed by his mental imagery.

A perfected magician uses his objective mind, or self–consciousness, in the manner depicted in this Tarot Key. Endeavor therefore, as you work with the coloring of the design, to impress all its details on your memory. In the next lesson you will find their significance explained; but for the coming week you should concern yourself with nothing but the coloring, and with getting the design, as a whole and in detail, into your mind.

DIRECTIONS FOR COLORING

Yellow: Background, spearhead on table, lily stamens.

Green: Foliage.

Blue–green: The serpent girdle.

Brown: Table.

White: Inner garment, head band, spear shaft, uplifted wand, lily flowers.

Gold: Pentacle or coin on table, sword hilt, circle at end of spear shaft.

Silver: Cup.

Steel: Sword blade. (Mix a little blue with gray.)

Red: Outer garment, roses.

Read this lesson once daily during your practice period. Be sure to look at the Key for five minutes in beginning the period. In this lesson there is enough material for a great deal of careful study. Do not slight it because you think you understand it after one or two readings.

THE MAGICIAN
(Cont.)

As has been said in the preceding lesson, the earliest form of the letter Beth was a crude picture of an arrow–head, which because of its uses suggests acuteness and the power of penetration. It is a symbol, therefore, of those powers of mind which are expressed in nice perception, in keen discrimination of differences, in accurate estimation of values. The fundamental *mood* represented by this form of the letter, connected as it is with hunting and warfare, is that of alert intentness; and for right use of the powers of consciousness pictured in Tarot by the Magician, this mood of alert, watchful attention to the succession of events constituting our waking experience is of primary importance. Nobody becomes a true magician, a wielder of the subtle forces of nature, who permits himself to be preoccupied with subjective personal states of mind to such an extent as to blur the sharpness of his objective awareness of events and things in his environment.

Note, too, that an arrow–head has no energy of its own. The force whereby it cleaves the mark is a derived force, and the arrow is merely the agency whereby that power is transmitted. An arrow–head is an instrument which transforms the propulsive force of the bow into penetrative force. It specializes bow–force into arrow–force.

The sound of the letter, the same as English "B", is a concentrated projection of the breath. Hold the palm of your hand near your lips as you say "B", and you will feel the air strike your hand like an arrow shot from a bow. Contrast this with the unmodified free breathing represented by the sound of the letter Aleph, an almost soundless vibration of air, made with lips open and relaxed, whereas the sound of Beth is a centralized expulsion of breath through lips almost closed. This illustrates the principle of contrast determining the arrangement of the letters of the Hebrew alphabet and the sequence of the Tarot Keys assigned to them.

Without going any farther, therefore, we have found that the

29

earliest forms of Beth agree with its sound. They are definite representations of a force intensified by concentration and projected toward a specific mark. By transference to things of the mind, these meanings of the letter are related, in a way neither arbitrary nor fanciful, to keen perceptions, discriminative power, alert awareness of events in one's environment, and consequent ability to see through superficial appearances into the inner realities of which those appearances are veils.

As the Tarot Key to which this letter is assigned is numbered 1, there is here a clear intimation that it represents the first step in your practical work. You have already taken that step by determining what, more than anything else, you want to be and do. You have set the mark at which you are aiming the entire energy of your life. Realize that the energy so aimed is derived from the super conscious level of the universal Life–power that is pictured in Tarot as the Fool, and you will have placed yourself symbolically in the position shown by this picture of the Magician. Observe that he lifts his *right* hand toward the sky. The right is the stronger hand, and what is meant here is that the act of establishing contact with super–conscious levels of energy is the highest and most potent use of self–consciousness.

By inductive reasoning, based on accurate observation of our lives and circumstances, it becomes evident that the succession of events of which our personal experiences are a part is under the direction of a supervising Intelligence, higher than the objective mind of the ordinary man. Just what this supervising Intelligence may be in itself we find it of little use to ask. The main thing to recognize is that it *is*, and that it is a *real presence* at every point in space, always.

The white wand held in the Magician's hand is a phallic symbol. It represents the concentrated and purified physical nerve force which the ignorant waste in uncontrolled gratification of sex desire. Such want of control is due largely to ignorance of methods for transmuting this powerful drive of what psychoanalysts term the *libido*. Methods for such control vary according to the temperament of the person who employs them. What for one would be rigid and irksome asceticism is relatively easy for another. Extremes of asceticism are never necessary for students who have learned the fundamental principle of control, which is this: *The practice of mental creation and constructive thinking automatically transmutes the urge of the libido from physical to mental fields of expression.*

Over the head of the Magician is an arbor of roses. An arbor is the simplest kind of shelter or house; hence this bit of symbolism is in agreement with the meaning of the letter Beth. Red roses are emblems of desire, and here they mean that all creative and constructive work of self–consciousness is a response to the motivation of desire for some specific practical result.

The horizontal figure 8 over the Magician's head reminds us that 8 is the particular number associated with Hermes or Mercury. It also represents education and culture, under the patronage of Hermes, and is likewise a numeral sign of dominion, strength, and control of the forces of nature through the agency of the law of rhythmic vibration — the basis of all practical magic. The horizontal 8 is also the mathematical symbol of infinity, hence of the limitless Life–power. Finally, it represents the law that *opposite effects are produced by identical causes.*

For instance, the same law which makes iron sink is what ship–builders apply in order to float iron vessels; the law that makes a kite fall to the ground is utilized to keep an airplane aloft; and the laws which result in disease, misery and failure are the same laws which intelligent adaptation employs in order to manifest health, happiness and success. *By changing the methods whereby you exercise your subconscious forces, you may produce effects just opposite to those which you have experienced in the past.*

You do not have to acquire new powers. You change your life–expression by applying power that is already yours. You simply learn to use your forces in a *different way.*

The Magician's left hand points to the ground. The gesture is one of concentration. It is made with the left or secondary hand, because success in concentration depends on conscious recognition of the fact that the force we concentrate by our acts of attention comes down to us from super conscious levels. Furthermore, the left hand is a symbol of the habit–mind, and thus the pointing finger of this hand represents habitual concentration, the result of long and persistent practice.

The black hair of the Magician is a contrast to the Fool's yellow locks. Black is a symbol of ignorance, darkness, and inertia. The band surrounding this black hair is white, typifying purity, light and wisdom. This detail of the picture therefore represents the limitation of ignorance by enlightenment.

The red outer robe typifies action and desire. Its color is associated with the planet Mars, said by astrologers to govern reproduction and to be the force expressed in all muscular activity. Note that this robe is unconfined by a girdle. It may be removed at will. This detail means that self–consciousness may or may not be involved in physical action, as we may determine in any given instance. Yet observe that the Magician is not fully clothed without his red robe. The perfection of self–consciousness is in its control over the various physical and bodily manifestations of the Life–power. But it can cease from conscious action and devote itself at any time to the contemplation of the inner mental states symbolized by the white undergarment. The color of this garment is a reference to truth or wisdom. The blue–green serpent girdle symbolizes eternity, because it swallows its tail. Its color will be more fully explained in Lessons 29 and 30.

The table before the Magician is the field of attention. It is made of wood grown in the garden. Its columnar legs are surmounted by Ionic capitals, in reference to architecture. Architecture is presided over by Hermes or Mercury and is also directly connected with the meaning of the letter–name Beth. The Ionic Order is shown because it was used in the Ephesian temple of Diana, a moon goddess. In Tarot the moon is associated with subconsciousness. The intimation here is that the materials utilized by self–consciousness are derived from subconsciousness, even as the power self–consciousness applies to the control and arrangement of these materials is derived from superconsciousness.

The implements on the table are those employed in ceremonial magic. The wand with a spear–like head is a symbol of *Will* and of the element of fire. The cup made of silver, metal of the moon, is a symbol of *imagination* and of the element of water. The sword of steel is related to Mars, but it also stands for *action* and for the element of air. The coin or pentacle is related to Saturn, and it also represents *form* and the element of earth. All magical transformations result from the power of self–consciousness to produce varying manifestations of will, imagination, action and physical embodiment.

These four implements represent also what is known in Hermetic Wisdom as the *Power of the Word*. According to the occult doctrine, language has a force not generally recognized. Furthermore, there are certain words, special combinations of *sound* and *ideas*, whereby extraordinary results may be produced when such words are correctly pronounced or intoned. Because the Tarot pictures have been influenced by Hebrew esoteric ideas, the particular word symbolized by the four magical implements is the four–lettered name, or *Tetragrammaton*, ordinarily written "Jehovah." It really has no pronunciation, but should be read letter by letter, Yod–Heh–Vav–Heh. The corresponding English letters are IHVH. Yod (I) is the wand, Heh (H) the cup, Vav (V) the sword,

32

and final Heh (H) the coin or pentacle. This is the name dimly embroidered in the folds of the Fool's white garment, at the neck. Its meaning is: *That which was, is, and will be.* In connection with the Key you are now studying, it means that self–consciousness utilizes the four aspects *of a single reality* in all its adaptations of the forms and conditions of human experience.

The garden in which the Magician stands represents the field that is cultivated by the objective consciousness. This field is subconsciousness, and here is a hint that the whole series of events and all the forms of circumstance of which we become aware through sensory channels are really events and forms resulting from the activity of subconsciousness.

All that surrounds us is the manifestation of subconscious forces; and because the objective mind can control subconscious force directly, and modify and adapt the rhythms of its vibration, a trained magician is able to exert by mental means a degree of control over his environment which amazes those of his contemporaries who do not share his knowledge and skill.

Two principal forms of subconscious activity are symbolized by the roses and lilies in the garden. They represent desire and knowledge.

The roses are red, to represent active desire. Five are shown because every desire is rooted in some one of the five senses. Every rose also represents the number 5, because all roses have five or some multiple of five petals. 5 is the number of adaptation and adjustment and self–consciousness, the special *human* expression of the Life–power, acts by adaptation. Thus 5 is the number of man, embodying the personal factor which carries the development of natural forces beyond the mere averages attained without the introduction of this human factor.

The lilies are white, to represent abstract perceptions of truth, or knowledge of principles and laws, apart from considerations of desire. They also represent the number 6, because they have six petals. In its symbolic meaning, 6 represents universal energies like light, heat, electricity, chemical forces, and so on. Through concentration we perceive the true nature and laws of such energies. There are four lilies because all pure science is knowledge of those powers the ancients termed fire, water, air and earth. In modern parlance these are radiant energy, fluids, gases and solids. They are the forms taken by the *Word* typified by the Magician's four implements.

Summing up the meaning of this Key, we say that self–consciousness is the primary human expression of the Life–power.

It constitutes your awareness of your environment, and this is really awareness of mental impressions received through bodily sensation from the world around you. The activities of that surrounding environment are activities of the powers of subconsciousness.

Self–consciousness is consciousness of being *one*, standing in relation to *others*. "I am, and that is not–I." At a still higher level of unfoldment, what is usually called "*myself*," that is, the physical body, is included among the things that are not "I". Beyond this is a stage in which the personal consciousness is recognized as being, like the physical body, merely an instrument for expressing the power of the real Self.

In partly developed persons, the objective mind creates the illusion that the Self is peculiar to a particular personality — that the personal self is a unique entity separate from all others. Concentration and meditation lead to freedom from this illusion, by enabling us to see that it *is* an illusion. When you have come to this recognition, you no longer think and act as if you were a separate being. You know that your personality is an instrument through which the *One Force* typified by the Fool finds expression.

Remember, the Life–power works *through* your self–consciousness. Your will, in so far as it really is will and not a delusive shadow, is a specialization of the universal will. To know this is to be certain that your true will is irresistible. This establishes confidence in the happy outcome of all your undertakings. It is the only knowledge that will make you truly Self–reliant, free from any trace of worry or anxiety, and therefore able to give undivided attention to the experience of the present moment. This consciousness enables you to live in the NOW, and because in reality it is always NOW, this consciousness permits you to live in eternity, instead of being time–bound, instead of relating yourself either to the past or to the future.

All the practical training of this course aims at the unfoldment of this consciousness. Until you receive the next lesson, review this one carefully until you are sure you understand every detail of the symbolism of *The Magician*. This Key was originally designed to awaken the power of attention. Attention is the great secret. When the etheric vibrations of external objects are concentrated on a brain–center by acts of attention, these vibrations have a tendency to organize that center in accordance with the intrinsic nature of the particular thing attended to. Thus the brain–center becomes attuned to the idea which is the inmost reality of the form observed. Then comes conscious perception of that inner reality and one sees *through* the form of the thing into its essential nature.

Be alert, then, to the life round you. Use all your instruments of sensation to gather accurate information. Resolve to see into life instead of merely looking at it, and you will find the world transforming itself before your very eyes. This is the great, the essential, secret of magic. Use this Tarot Key daily to sharpen your powers of observation and attention. Be sure to record your impressions *daily* in your occult diary.

LESSON SEVEN

THE HIGH PRIESTESS
(SUBCONSCIOUSNESS)

B efore you read this lesson, study carefully the symbolism of Key 2, *The High Priestess*. Remember that Tarot uses the universal language of pictorial symbolism, and that the deeper part of your mind is perfectly familiar with that language. One purpose of the Tarot Keys is to evoke thought, and if you look at a Key before you begin to read our explanations, you bring these hidden meanings nearer to the surface of your mind, so that it is easier for you to grasp the significance of what is written in these pages. Devote at least five minutes to this preparation, and longer if you have time.

Among the meanings of the number 2, as given in the earlier lesson, is *Subordination*. This word gives you a clue to the relationship existing between subconsciousness, represented by Key 2, and objective mind or self–consciousness, represented by *The Magician*. The figure in Key 1 is engaged in controlling the powers of subconsciousness, and these powers are always amenable to his suggestive influence. It is because of this fact that you are able to use these Keys to bring into vigorous manifestation the latent forces of your inner life. The principle involved here has been fully explained in Lesson 3 of *Seven Steps in Practical Occultism*. Review that lesson and Lesson 2 of the same course in connection with your present study.

The psychological law there stated, that subconsciousness is perfectly amenable to control by suggestion, makes it obvious that the important thing to be careful about is what kind of suggestions you formulate in your self–conscious mind, the main source of the suggestions received by subconsciousness.

Subconsciousness, you will recall, is represented by the garden in Key 1. The fertile soil of this garden will grow *any seed* planted in it by the Magician. If you plant careless observations and incorrect reasoning, the tares and weeds of conscious thought, subconsciousness will develop these seeds of error a thousand fold, with all sorts of uncomfortable consequences. On the other hand, if you learn to concentrate, to make your mental imagery clear and definite, if you make accurate observations from which you draw correct inferences, the seeds planted in your subconscious garden will bear fruit in the renewal, revivification and regeneration of your whole personality.

37

The ability of subconsciousness to develop seed ideas in this manner may be formulated thus: *Subconsciousness is possessed of perfect powers of deductive reasoning*. If you are uncertain as to the difference between inductive and deductive reasoning, consult a good dictionary before proceeding farther. Always, when you study, have a dictionary at hand, for you will need it frequently in the course of this instruction. You will find that this practice of making sure of the precise meaning and use of words will be of immeasurable benefit to you in the orderly organization of your mental processes.

Geometrically the number 2 is the *line*, the extension of the *point* (No.1). This is related to the subconscious power just mentioned, by which the consequences of conscious thought and observation are developed. You will not fail to note that the extension of the central point of a circle into a diameter (an extension in two directions) divides the circle into *two* parts, each the exact *duplicate* of the other. In this power of duplication may be perceived the basic function of subconsciousness, *memory*. This brings us to a third psychological principle: *Subconsciousness keeps a perfect record of all experience, and therefore has perfect memory.* Not only does it retain all the experiences of a single personality, but it holds also a summary of the race experience, and this is the source of the greater part of our intuitions and scientific discoveries.

When Hebrew letters were scratched rudely on stone, the character for Gimel (ג), the letter printed on Key 2, was a crude picture of a bow. This is one reason that it comes after Beth in the alphabet. The original character for Beth was an arrow–head, and in the development of weapons, bows follow arrows. Primitive races began by throwing their darts by hand. The invention of the bow came later. The bow carries the arrow to its mark, yet it is secondary, considered as an implement suggested by the dart or arrow. A bow, moreover, *extends* the range of the arrow. Similarly the subconsciousness represented by the letter Gimel is what carries your conscious determinations to a successful conclusion, what makes your decisions "hit the mark". Yet the activities of subconsciousness are derived from, and secondary to, the operations of self–consciousness pictured by Key 1.

Subconsciousness is the propulsive, driving force in human personality. Keep this idea of *propulsion* in mind. Link it up with the noun "propeller", that which drives a boat or an airplane. Self–consciousness aims and steers. Subconsciousness provides the motive force.

As a symbol the bow is feminine, and the characteristics of subconsciousness are those which are naturally associated with the feminine sex. It is the protective, maternal, nutritive, reproductive aspect of consciousness, always represented in esoteric literature under the guise of feminine symbols. Among these, in addition to the bow, are the ark, the crescent moon, the cup, the ship, the sistrum of Isis, almonds, ovals, lozenges (diamond–shaped figures), and many others, including some that we shall find in Tarot.

The letter–name, Gimel, means "camel". Perhaps the early forms of the letter suggested the name, because the head and neck of a camel somewhat resemble a bent bow. Again, the Hebrew verb *gaumal*, spelt with the same three letters (גמל) (G M L) as the noun Gimel, means (1) to carry a load; (2) to ripen (as fruits), and both these ideas are representative of the action of subconsciousness.

One familiar action of subconsciousness is "mind–wandering." This enables us, when we fall into a state of reverie, to pass from thought to thought until we have traversed a vast field of ideas. Until we learn to control this power of associating image with image, it interferes with concentration and with all other directed use of our mental powers. It is like a camel running wild. When we learn to drive it, this same power of association will take us quickly to any chosen goal.

As the seat of memory, subconsciousness "carries the load" of our personal experience. It also carries a greater load than this, for subconsciousness is a universal phase of the Life–power's activity, and "personal" subconsciousness is merely a particular manifestation, through a single organism, of this universal subconsciousness. Hence, when we have learned how, we may gain access to the records of *all* experience through tapping the cosmic or universal subconscious memory.

Other implications of the letter–name Gimel are: *transportation*; *motion from place to place*; *movement to and fro, as of the regular journeys of caravans over trade routes*; *hence, commerce, exchange, interchange, reciprocation, alternation, correlation, correspondence*; *communication, dissemination of information, and consequently, education and science*. Study all these words carefully with a dictionary. They are descriptions of your subconscious powers.

In the esoteric doctrines of Israel, the letter Gimel is said to correspond to the Moon, which is a "ship of the skies", just as the camel is "ship of the desert". In the human brain, the Moon center is the pituitary body, which, besides the functions generally known to physiologists, is understood by occultists to be a transmitting station, through which the mental states of self–consciousness are relayed to centers below it in the body.

Among the ideas suggested by the Moon are: *reflection*; *pe-*

riodicity *(from its waxing and waning)*; association, accompaniment, correlation *(because the Moon is a satellite, consort, or follower of the earth, and in like manner subconsciousness follows the lead of self–consciousness.)*

As a crescent the Moon suggests a bow, the original form of the letter Gimel. Thus it is connected with the goddess named Diana by the Romans and Artemis by the Greeks. Diana is a *huntress*, and to hunt is to follow, to inquire, to pursue. Subconsciousness follows up the suggestions and observations of self–consciousness. Even while we sleep, it is reviewing all our experiences, ruminating (like a camel chewing its cud) over what we have sensed, felt and reasoned. During sleep this nocturnal mental luminary carries out the mental processes which lead to the consequences of what we have thought, observed and consciously reasoned out during the day.

Diana or Artemis is a virgin goddess, and because she presides over childbirth, she is closely related to Hekate, who for the ancient Greeks combined the characteristics of moon goddess, earth goddess, and queen of the underworld of shades, the abode of the dead. Hekate had a share in the rulership of earth and sea; gave aid in war, in athletic contests, and in hunting; protected herds and children; but she was particularly the goddess of magic, mystery and occult powers generally. She also presided over the meeting–place at which roads cross. Indeed, it is principally from the attributes of Hekate that the symbolism of the second Tarot Key is derived. *All the powers attributed to these moon goddesses are actual powers of your subconsciousness.*

Note that one key word for this picture, based on its connection with Gimel and the Moon, is *association.* Not only ordinary association of ideas within the limits of your own mind. A wide kind of association, symbolized by the fact that a camel's journeys connect distant places. *Subconsciousness has perfect connection with all points in space.* This law is the basis of the phenomenon of telepathy. It is also the law that will put you in touch with your true Teacher, when you have developed to a point where you are ready for higher instruction. This same law has many other applications in practical occultism.

40

During your practice period this week, color Key 2, in accordance with the following directions:

Yellow: left foreground, small space at right foreground.

Green: Palms on curtain behind High Priestess (not centers).

Blue: Background, from yellow foreground up. Her robe. The robe should have white in it also where it shimmers down in front and out of the picture. It represents flowing water.

Gray: Throne, veil background (veil need not be painted unless desired.)

White: Inner garment, cross on breast, head drapery, right pillar, centers of palms. Hebrew letter on left pillar.

Silver: Crown.

Brown: Scroll (diluted to look like parchment).

Red: Pomegranates on curtain behind High Priestess (seeds a deeper tint than skins).

Read this lesson every day. Contemplate Key 2 five minutes each day before reading the lesson. When you have studied the lesson, place Keys 1 and 2 side by side. See how many contrasts you can find between the two pictures and between the ideas they represent. Write these in your notebook. This practice is valuable, both to improve your powers of observation, and to establish in your consciousness the reciprocal relationship that exists between these two Keys.

Use Key 2 to stimulate your memory. Before trying to recall anything, look at this picture or bring it before your mind's eye. Take the hint it gives. The High Priestess sits at ease. There is no strain about her. When you wish to recall anything relax your body and let your mind be passive. The current of associations will then flow freely, and after a little it will bring the desired information to the surface of your mind.

THE HIGH PRIESTESS
(Cont.)

The title of this Key means literally, "the chief feminine elder". It applies perfectly to Hekate and the other moon goddesses of the ancients, including the Egyptian Isis and the Hindu Maya or Prakriti. Under the figures of these goddesses, the priesthoods of old time concealed their knowledge of the powers of subconsciousness.

Remember that the subconscious powers are universal as well as personal. In the teaching received by us it is held that this subconscious activity is the real substance of all the things we call "physical objects". What appears to us as wood or stone, as various metals, as the "matter" of the forms round us, is held to be actually the subconscious level of the activity of the *One Force* pictured in Tarot as the Fool.

A few years ago this idea would have been scoffed at by scientists. Today several prominent physicists do not hesitate to say that the real substance out of which atoms are built is "probably" *mind–stuff*. This "probability" of modern scientific speculation is an established certainty for the Inner School to which we owe the invention of the Tarot Keys. *The actual substance of the physical plane, from which all forms perceptible by the human senses are built, is mental energy, working at the subconscious level.* Hence the Tarot Key which represents this primary "material" is rightly named "the chief feminine elder", for it symbolizes the original receptive, reproductive and form–building power in the universe. This it is to which you have access through your personal subconsciousness, which is like a bay opening into the ocean of universal subconscious mental energy. The Inner School, working experimentally upon this hypothesis, long ago demonstrated its accuracy by works of power involving extraordinary control of physical forces and conditions by *mental* means.

The predominant color of Key 2 is blue, which is that attributed in one occult color scale to the Moon and to the letter Gimel. This color is also associated in occultism with the element of water and with subconsciousness.

Much of the symbolism of the High Priestess is directly connected with memory. Her scroll contains the complete record of experience, but two things are requisite if you are to read it. First you must practice concentration. By careful observation and vivid awareness of what goes on round you, you focus your mental camera, and the resulting images are sharp and clear. Secondly, you must understand and apply the laws of recall, as set forth in the symbols of this Key.

The pillars represent two of these laws by their form and color, and another law by their position. You can easily recall ideas or things which are *like* each other; ideas or things in sharp *contrast* to each other; ideas or things *near* each other in space or time. Here are three rules in practical mnemonics. If you use these identification tags consciously when you file your experiences, you can make a mental index that will give you the ability to recall any phase of your experience at will. Link what you wish to recollect with something like it. Contrast it with something entirely different. Notice what things are near it in time or space.

Now examine the symbols on the veil behind the High Priestess. The members of the pattern are repetitions of the two symbols used (pomegranates and palms, which symbolize opposite forces, and so refer to the law of contrast). The fourth law of recall is *frequency*. In the first lesson of this instruction you had an opportunity to put this law into practice when you learned *The Pattern on the Trestleboard*. Along with frequency goes *recency*, since we tend to recall recent experiences more readily than others.

All these laws of memory are various processes of *association*, dealt with in connection with the meaning of the letter Gimel, as covered in the preceding lesson. There we spoke of universal association and intercommunication. The law which makes this possible is closely bound up with all the meanings of the number 2, and is graphically symbolized by the robe of the High Priestess.

This robe represents the element of water, which is in turn a symbol of *root matter*, or Prakriti, as Hindus call it. The wavy lines of the robe represent *vibration*. This is one of the most important words in all occultism (and one of the most abused by ignorant dabblers). We live in a vibratory universe, and it is vibratory activity in the *root matter* that brings us into touch with other points of the universe. Those points are themselves centers of the conscious energy of the universal Life–power. The same law of vibration at work on the physical plane brings to us the radiant energy of the sun, and the various rays of influence converging upon this planet from every point in space.

The *root matter* is identical with subconsciousness, of which water is also a symbol. Water was the first mirror, and because mirroring is duplication or reflection, the symbolism of water is closely related to the meanings of the number 2. It is the conscious energy of the One Force, acting upon itself in its subconscious aspect of *root matter*, which brings into being all physical structures, *including the cells of your body*.

The function of every cell is the result of the Life–power flowing *through* that cell. This is the truth behind the statements developed in Lesson Four of *Seven Steps*, and that lesson should be reviewed in connection with this one.

Watch your daily experience closely and you will soon be able to detect the operation of subconsciousness in your own life. As you become increasingly familiar with these principles and the way they work, you will put then more and more into conscious operation, with the result that you will gain greater control over the forces of your personality. Persistent practice in directing your personal forces leads eventually to the attainment of extraordinary control over physical conditions, and this control is exerted by purely mental means.

The veil behind the throne of the High Priestess is a symbol of virginity. The design upon it refers to the associative powers of subconsciousness. The units of the design are palm leaves and pomegranates, which are respectively masculine and feminine symbols. Note, however, that the pomegranates are red, the color of the masculine planet Mars, while the palms are green, representing the feminine Venus vibration. This is only one of many places in Key 2 that represents graphically the *union of opposite forces*. The veil itself, because it joins the two pillars, is a symbol of that union.

The pillars, which are alike in form but opposite in color, symbolize all pairs of opposites, such as light and darkness, attraction and repulsion, affirmation and negation, active and passive, manifest and unmanifest. In each of the foregoing pairs the first is represented by the white pillar and the other by the black one. The letter on the white pillar is Yod (`), the initial letter of the Hebrew word *Jachin*. That on the black pillar is Beth (‌), the initial of *Boaz*. Thus these pillars are related to those of the porch of Solomon's temple. (See 1 Kings 7:13–22, for the Biblical basis of the Masonic pillar symbolism.)

The lotus buds at the top of the pillars refer to the subconscious activity that is the cause of all growth and development in organic life. They are buds because this Key represents the potencies or possibilities of subconsciousness, apart from their actual manifestation in response to self–consciousness.

The cubic stone upon which the High Priestess sits is important in symbolism, but its meanings are too extended for full treatment here. The cube is a symbol of salt, which crystallizes in cubes, and thus it is a symbol of earth and the physical plane. But the cube is also a symbol of truth and order, because all its faces are equal and all its boundary lines are equal. This cube is of *stone*, a word which has esoteric meanings signifying union, life and wisdom. Briefly, the cubic stone in this Key means that all operations of subconsciousness are founded on immutable principles of truth and order operative throughout the physical plane as well as in higher fields of manifestation.

The robe of the High Priestess, besides representing the *root matter*, is a symbol of flowing and fluidity, and typifies the ever–changing forms of life–expression. Observe that it seems to flow out of the picture. It is the source of all the streams and pools shown in subsequent Keys.

The crown is of silver, the metal attributed to the Moon. By its form the crown shows the waxing and waning lunar crescents with the full moon between them. They suggest periodicity and alternation, as well as the reflecting and reproductive power of subconsciousness. The Moon actually polarizes sunlight, so here is another reference to the polarity symbolized by the number 2.

The cross on the High Priestess' breast is white to represent light. It is also the primitive form of the letter Tav, the last letter of the Hebrew alphabet, corresponding to the 21st Key. It has many meanings, some of which will be touched upon in later lessons. At this point its four equal arms may serve to remind you of the four implements on the Magician's table, and of their combined activity.

The scroll represents memory, the record of experience and the basis of history. The word TORA signifies *law*, and is a rearrangement of the letters of ROTA, the Latin for "wheel". This is a reference to the Law of Cycles or Rotation, which will be more extensively dealt with later on. This Law of Cycles is closely connected with the Law of Spiral Activity represented by the form of the rolled–up scroll. Both these laws are aspects of the great Law of Rhythm.

The right hand of the High Priestess is hidden, because the

more powerful aspects of subconsciousness elude all our attempts to analyze them. The left hand, therefore, is the only one that is visible, to intimate that we perceive, so to say, only the end results, or relatively superficial manifestations, of the activity of subconsciousness.

Finally, this Key symbolizes seven great Hermetic Laws or Principles. These laws have been discussed by many writers on Ageless Wisdom. They are:

1. *The Law of Mentalism*, the law that the totality of the universe is essentially mental. This is indicated by those details of the symbolism which suggest that subconsciousness is actually the "matter"' or substance of all things.

2. *The Law of Correspondence*, indicated by the meanings of the letter Gimel.

3. *The Law of Vibration*, represented by the meanings of the number 2, and by the wavy folds of the blue robe.

4. *The Law of Polarity*, typified by the pillars.

5. *The Law of Rhythm*, symbolized by the crown, since the basis of rhythm is periodic action like the waxing and waning of the Moon. Note that this is the *crowning* symbol, intimating that rhythm is the dominant law in subconscious activities.

6. *The Law of Cause and Effect* is symbolized by the scroll and the word TORA, for the Law of Cause and Effect is the clue to the meaning of the whole record of existence.

7. *The Law of Gender*, represented by the palms and pomegranates on the veil, and by the contrast between the pillars and the veil behind them.

We shall have occasion to refer to these seven Hermetic Laws again and again in this course. Some years ago an excellent little elementary treatise on these Laws, entitled *The Kybalion*, was published in Chicago. The text was written down by the late William Walker Atkinson, but the material itself is from very ancient sources. We shall embody some of its more important teachings in this and other courses, together with other Hermetic doctrines received by us from the same Inner School to which Mr. Atkinson was indebted for his knowledge of the *Kybalion*.

46

The main lesson you should now learn from Key 2 is that your personal field of subconsciousness is *materially connected* with even the most distant of the stars. "Your" subconsciousness is a temporarily restricted portion of universal matter in its potential mode. Mind–stuff is the original material from which everything is made. Through various processes, all essentially mental, this mind–stuff undergoes changes in form which make it *appear* as physical objects. The original material is mind–stuff, and a great secret of practical occultism is that this mind–stuff may be shaped by conscious control of mental imagery. Through your personal subconsciousness you have access to the inexhaustible universal supply of original material, and *you may make it what you will*.

Use Key 2 in this week's practice, and be sure you make full use of your occult diary.

LESSON NINE

THE EMPRESS
(CREATIVE IMAGINATION)

This week look at Key 3, *The Empress*, for five minutes before reading the lesson. Remember that every Key of Tarot is a symbolic picture of some aspect of your consciousness. These Keys are all portraits of yourself. As Eliphas Levi tells us, the Tarot speaks by evoking thought, and not thought in the narrow intellectual sense, but all the various forms of mind–power of which personal life and consciousness are but the outward forms of expression. Looking at the Keys is the fundamental method for bringing the deeper potencies of your life closer to the surface. Have at hand always, whenever you study one of these lessons, the Key to which it relates, and look often at the picture as you read.

Multiplication is a key word attributed to the number 3 in Lesson Two. To multiply is to cause to increase in number, to make more by natural generation. Multiplication is the act or operation of increasing by multiplying.

Creative Imagination is the way the principle of multiplication manifests itself in your mental life. The secret of the process is given in that part of the definition of the number 3 which speaks of "the response of subconsciousness to self–consciousness in the generation of mental images." Just as 3 is produced by the combination of 1 and 2, so also is the Empress a symbolic combination of ideas represented by the Magician and the High Priestess. In Key 3 is shown the activity which results from their harmonious union.

The number 3, as the sum of 1 and 2, is the union of the ideas of individuality (1) and repetition (2). The repetition of the unit through the agency of the duad is reproduction, and reproduction is manifested as renewal, generation, development, growth, fertility, fecundity. Hence the number 3 is the number of production, formation, organization, propagation, elaboration. As a number representing organization it suggests arrangement, and the right adaptation parts to the whole. This implies anticipation, expectation, purpose, plan, contrivance, invention. All the meanings of the number 3 are developed in the symbolism of the Empress, because this Key represents that working of your subconsciousness which results in the activities indicated by the words corresponding to the number.

49

The Hebrew letter printed on this picture is Daleth (ד), which means "door". Originally it represented the flap of a tent, and then any sort of door — the leaf, not the opening. Hence it suggests power to admit or bar, to retain or to let out. The door has been always a feminine symbol representing birth, reproduction.

Some authorities, indeed, say that Daleth represents the womb, which is the door of personal life, opening to receive the seed, closing to retain the germ of life during the period of gestation, and opening again to send the newborn creature into the world. Similar activities on planes above the physical are indicated by the same symbol.

Subconsciousness receives the seed impulse of observations made in periods of concentrated attention. Then follows a cycle of development within the field of subconsciousness. When this cycle is completed a new idea, or an invention, or some new plan comes forth through the door of subconsciousness into the field of self–conscious awareness. The form of this completed result of creative imagination may be altogether different from the form taken by the original seed thought; but the life in that form is continuous with the life in the seed thought, just as the life in a human body is continuous with the life in the spermatozoon and ovum from which that body has been developed.

Note that in this operation of subconsciousness there is an apparent accretion of materials round a vital center. This is as true in purely mental as it is in physical creation. In this connection remember that the Greek noun *Delta*, directly derived from Hebrew Daleth, represents both the feminine organ of generation and the accretion of alluvial soil at the mouth of a river, as when we speak of the Delta of the Nile or the Delta of the Mississippi.

It is thought by some that the original hieroglyphic for Daleth represented the radiance of sunrise, the entrance of light into the world through the gateway of the East. This probably accounts for the attribution of the direction East to Daleth, and for this letter's being the sign of what Qabalists call the Luminous Intelligence.

Radiance is vibration produced by solar force. The sunshine is not the sun. The brightness and splendor are effects produced by the action of the luminary. His rays make the sun visible. They are his power. Hence, because the sun is one of the principal emblems of the Supreme Spirit, sunshine represents the mysterious power of spirit, the manifesting agency which Hindus call Prakriti, and of which the *Bhagavad–Gita* says: "My great Prakriti is the womb into which I cast the seed; from thence is the birth of all creatures."

Radiation of solar energy being the basis of all vegetable and animal life is what brings about gradual unfoldment of consciousness. It is also the cause of those physiological changes whereby a human personality manifests higher orders of consciousness. This radiant energy is also the actual physical force that assumes definite forms in our acts of creative imagination. Keep this in mind in order to intensify your feeling that you are using *real powers* in your occult work. In their essence, to be sure, these powers are purely spiritual. Those teachers are perfectly correct who say there is really no such thing as a separate entity called "matter".

On the other hand, those relative states and conditions of the manifestation of spiritual energy that constitute the field of investigation for physical science are also perfectly *real*. Whatever of illusion there is about them is the erroneous human notion that the physical manifestations of the Life–power are separate from the finer and subtler manifestations which are termed psychic, astral, and so on. According to the Ageless Wisdom symbolized in Tarot, all forms of manifestation are expressions of a single energy that enjoys an unbroken and unbreakable continuity. That energy is real, and its reality extends "downward" into the physical plane just as truly as it extends "upward" into realms of finer and more intense vibration. "That which is above is as that which is below, and that which is below is as that which is above."

Mental images are patterns or matrices for physical conditions. Mental objects, in their plane, have just as definite reality and validity as physical objects. Creative imagination, represented by the Empress, is the process of internal development and arrangement which precedes the external manifestation of physical conditions corresponding to mental patterns. Under ordinary conditions, the mental images are gradually precipitated into physical expression through a series of subtle transformations so complex that we cannot trace the links in the series. Those extraordinary personalities, the adepts and Masters, are able to speed up this series of transformations so that their mental images are almost simultaneously manifested as physical actualities. This is the secret of instantaneous healing, of such works of power as the change of water into wine, or the miracle of the loaves and fishes.

Yet it must be remembered that these extraordinary manifestations are no exceptions to the general rule. For the merest tyro, as well as for the adept, mental imagery is the basis of bodily and environmental conditions. The states of body and environment that you are experiencing now are the fruition of your mental images. If you want different external conditions you must change the images. This is the secret of dominion.

Thus it is valuable to utilize every legitimate device to make us realize that our mental imagery is a manifestation of real power, of power that has definite physical potencies as well as meta-physical reality. The chaotic conditions of our present political and economic systems are a direct result of chaotic, disorderly mental images held in the minds of millions of human beings. To change the conditions the images must be changed, and to attain this desirable result (which requires that each person shall undertake the cultivation of his own mental garden), it is first of all necessary to help people to understand that outer circum-stances are physical embodiments of mental patterns.

The Empress, among the Tarot Keys, is the symbolic statement of the harmonious and constructive direction of mental imagery. This will be more apparent next week, after you have considered the meaning of the various details of the symbolism. This week, as usual, we are concerned with impressing these details upon your mind as you color the Key. As heretofore, plan your work so as to complete the coloring on the last day of your week's study. Thus all week long you will be educating yourself through pictorial symbolism, the natural language of subconsciousness, in what the great Inner School of adepts and wise men knows about the operation of creative imagination. Such visual educa-tion is more valuable than any verbal interpretation, because it calls into actual operation the very powers which the symbols represent.

DIRECTIONS FOR COLORING

Yellow: Background, shoes, staff of scepter.

Green: Foliage, grass, wreath. Robe (except cuffs, girdle, collar edging and panel). Ball on scepter.

Blue: Stream and waterfall.

Brown: Tree trunks beside waterfall.

Gray: Stone bench.

Gold: Stars, collar edging, girdle, cross and bar on scepter.

Silver: Crescent.

Copper: Shield (except dove). Mix red and brown to secure cop-per color.

Blonde: Hair, wheat ears.

White: pearls, panel in dress, cuffs of dress, dove, highlights in waterfall.

Red: Roses, triangle on breast.

In your study period ponder this: *The point where the working power of subconsciousness may be controlled is the point where thoughts take form as definite mental images.*

A statement like "All is Good" is not a definite mental image. Statements of truth do no work unless they are linked to specific images of the operation of the principles stated. These images must be concrete. They must prepare mind and body for action. This is in no sense a denial of the importance and value of abstract statements of principle *as helps to right understanding*. The point is that intellectual statements of truth must be supplemented by concrete imagery before the mighty forces of the inner life can be made to emerge as actual forms and conditions of the physical plane.

THE EMPRESS
(Cont.)

The noun "empress" comes from a Latin root meaning "to set in order, to arrange". This, you will see, is in agreement with some of the meanings of the number 5, given in the preceding lesson. In Tarot, The *Empress* represents the inner side of the process that establishes order, and the Key following it in the series has to do with the outer side of the same process.

By contrast with the High Priestess, who is a cold, virgin figure corresponding to the Moon, the Empress is warm and maternal. She is the Great Mother, pregnant with the world of form. In this figure all the mother goddesses of the ancient world are synthesized, but she is particularly Aphrodite or Venus.

Venus is also the astrological attribution of the letter Daleth, according to the school of Qabalism represented in these pages. Here two points of occult teaching may be noted in passing. According to H.P. Blavatsky's *Secret Doctrine*, the human race owes much to an earlier development of consciousness connected with the planet Venus. Again, in the Rosicrucian *Fama Fraternitatis*, the entrance, to the mysterious Vault comes to light when one of the Brothers happens to move a tablet of brass, a metal associated with Venus; and in certain rituals based on this tradition, the side of the Vault which forms the door is attributed to Venus, just as in the Qabalah Venus is assigned to a letter named Daleth or "door". Furthermore, the Vault itself has seven sides, and this heptagonal construction is found in many alchemical diagrams typifying the perfection of the Great Work. Such perfection is, of course, a victory over all obstacles, and this idea of Victory, linked with the number 7, is also associated with Venus because Qabalists call 7 the Sphere of Venus. Put very simply, one meaning of all these mysterious hints is that the mental activities personified by the various mother deities, of whom Venus is a great type, are those which lead to the discovery of the Great Secret and to the completion of the Great Work. Hence we find the idea of Wisdom associated with the letter Daleth in the Qabalistic *Book of Formation.*

But the same book also attributes Folly to this letter. For the very same activities that, rightly understood and applied, can lead to the discovery of the Great Secret and enable us to succeed in the Great Work are those that drive the greater number of human beings into all sorts of foolish thought and action.

Tarot shows us the positive, constructive phases of the activity represented by the Empress. There is no representation of the negative, destructive activities. If all the Furies were represented in one horrifying figure, the picture would fall short of the dreadful menace of perverted and distorted mental imagery. Always remember that subconsciousness accepts as true, and proceeds to develop by deduction, whatever suggestions are impressed on it by the habitual mental attitudes of self–consciousness. Subconsciousness is particularly susceptible to the power of words, *especially the words we use as predicates after the initial statement, "I AM".*

Hence the really practical occultist watches all that he says, to the end that he may give utterance to no statement which he is unwilling to see realized in his external circumstances. Not even in jest will he say anything that belittles the "I AM". He learns early in his instruction that the "I AM" is, in very truth, a magic "Word of Power". This is the "Lost Word of which so much has been said and written — lost because the profane world has forgotten its significance and its actual power, but found generation after generation, by those who have ripened into understanding.

The Empress then, is Mother Nature, personified as Venus. She clothes herself in the web of manifestation that entangles the minds of fools; but the wise see through appearances, and to them Nature unveils herself. The veil that conceals truth is the veil of human ignorance, and it may be removed by proper selection of mental imagery. The creative force is always at work in Nature, but the application of that force is left to the individual man, since subconsciousness has no power of discrimination.

The color associated with the letter Daleth is green, and this color predominates in Key 3, as it does in nature. Note that green is produced by the mixture of blue and yellow, which are the colors attributed to the High Priestess and the Magician, respectively.

55

The Empress is a matronly figure, and traditional interpretations tell us that she is pregnant. This is in harmony with the fact that creative imagination is the result of the impregnation of subconsciousness by impressions originating in self–consciousness.

Her hair is yellow, like that of the Fool, symbolizing radiant energy. It is bound by a wreath of myrtle, a plant sacred to Venus. Myrtle is an evergreen shrub, and thus, like the acacia, is a symbol of immortality.

On her head is a crown of twelve golden six–pointed stars. This connects her with the woman in *Revelation*, clothed with the sun and crowned with twelve stars, with the moon under her feet. Older symbolic representations identify her with the Queen of Heaven. Six–pointed stars represent universal forces, hence the symbolism of the crown refers to the twelve modes of cosmic activity associated with the twelve signs of the zodiac. One idea conveyed here is that subconsciousness is affected not only by the objective mind, but also by an influx of power descending directly from the superconscious, or celestial, level of the Life–power's activity.

Her green robe is bound by a golden girdle, above which there is shown a red triangle. By its shape, the triangle is a Greek letter Delta, corresponding to Daleth. It is red to show the influence of the universal fiery energy in the activities of subconsciousness.

The Empress' scepter is surmounted by a globe bearing a cross. This is a symbol of dominion. Older symbolism is that the globe and cross form a union of feminine (globe) and masculine (cross), or positive and negative, modes of the activity of the Life–power on all planes of manifestation.

The shield is of copper, the metal sacred to Venus. The dove on its face, also sacred to Venus, is the Christian symbol of the Holy Spirit. This also connects with the number *three*. Thus, P.F.G. Lacuria, in *The Harmonies of Being*, writes:

"The number three reveals to us the harmony of the Holy Spirit. The number three is the return to unity, which seems to be broken by the number two. It is in uniting the Father and the Son that the Holy Spirit realizes itself; on this account it may be considered as the efflorescence of the unity."

(The reader should be careful not to let the theological terminology of this passage blind him to its profound occult meaning.)

Beneath the feet of the Empress is a crescent moon. Besides further emphasizing her correspondence to the woman in *Revelation*, it represents the fact that all activities of subconsciousness that have to do with growth, development, reproduction and imagination are activities based on rhythm.

The stone seat is richly ornamented, in contrast to the severe simplicity of the cube on which the High Priestess sits. This shows the result of the operation of self–consciousness upon subconsciousness, which results in modifications and adaptations of nature — in the arts, fine and useful. Here is another symbolic hint that the Empress is Venus, goddess of art and beauty.

The ripened wheat in the foreground represents the completion of a cycle of growth. It carries with it the same idea of multiplication that is indicated by the number 3. Note that the *seed forms* are multiplied. Every act of creative imagination elaborates the conditions spontaneously provided by nature into new forms which themselves become points of departure for further growth.

The stream and pool in the background represent the stream of consciousness that has its source in the robe of the High Priestess. The symbol of water falling into a pool is also an intimation of the Law of Gender, of the reciprocal relationship between the male and female modes of conscious energy. This stream is a symbol of that which in analytical psychology has come to be known as *libido*, the driving energy of conscious life. The stream is modified and directed by the self–conscious activities symbolized by the Magician, and the pool represents the accumulation of those influences at the subconscious level. The stream waters the garden and makes it fertile.

The cypress trees in the background are ten in number, corresponding to the ten circles on the dress of the Fool. The cypress is also a tree sacred to Venus. Attributed to the same goddess are red roses, of which there are five, representing the five senses, and having the same meaning as the five roses in the Magician's garden. Yet another Venusian symbol is the necklace of pearls. There are seven pearls showing, representing the seven planets known to ancient astronomers, and the seven interior stars (or chakras) in the human body. These seven are of like meaning to the seven ornaments showing on the belt of the Fool. Note that when these beads are strung in a necklace they are related together and put in order. Furthermore, a necklace like this one touches the throat at the level of the Venus center which is located at this point. The intimation is that the Venus center is the one through which the seven centers are to be brought into orderly correlation, so that the forces playing through them may be controlled. This correlation may be called the secret of entrance into adeptship, and thus the Venus center may be thought of as the *door* to mastery. All this ties up with what has been said about

Daleth and Venus at the beginning of this lesson.

You will find that regular use of the Empress will enrich your faculty of creative imagination and stimulate your inventiveness. It will give you power to make new combinations of ideas, and ability to develop old ideas into something better. There is no picture in the entire series which is more needed in these days. We live in an age when cheap printing and motion pictures, combined with the cut–and–dried life of our cities, are endangering our imaginative power. We take too much of our imagination at secondhand from the screen and the printed page. In direct consequence of this, consulting psychologists and other advisers are continually called on to help in the solution of personal problems which have arisen simply because people do not realize, let alone utilize, the tremendous power of imagination. Our prisons are packed to overflowing simply because men and women are unable to imagine the consequences of their own acts. People fail in business and in other undertakings for the same reason.

This Key will help you to use imagination positively and constructively. Through your eyes it tells your subconsciousness what powers it has and how they should be exercised. Possibly you may not grasp the inner meanings of the symbols at first. *But your subconsciousness will*, for this picture, like the other Tarot Keys, *is written in your subconscious mind's own language*. Pictorial symbolism is the language of dream, of reverie, of fantasy and imagination. *It is not an intellectual affair, although intellect may analyze it*. It goes far deeper. Use Key 3 whenever you find yourself apparently sterile of ideas, and it will help to start an abundant flow of mental imagery.

LESSON ELEVEN

THE EMPEROR
(REASON)

4 | THE EMPEROR

T his week use Key 4, *The Emperor*, as the basis for your five–minute meditation before taking up the lesson. As you look at it, remember that the Emperor, as his name shows, is the consort and complement of the Empress. Compare the two Keys, and discover for yourself as many points of contrast between them as you can. Make a list of these contrasts *before reading this lesson*.

The key word of the number 4 is ORDER. Closely allied meanings are system, regulation, management, supervision. Thus the number 4 clearly relates to the classifying activity of self–consciousness, induced by the response of subconsciousness to impressions originating in self–consciousness. This classifying activity is REASON.

Mental imagery is useful to us chiefly after it has been systematized or put in order. It then becomes valuable in our daily lives in the regulation, supervision and management of our affairs. When mental imagery is not so systematized, we are creatures of our emotions and desires; impractical dreamers, unable to meet adequately the problems life presents to us. Note that verb "presents". Life's problems are not evils. They are *gifts*. For there is no problem that does not conceal a principle that, when understood, may be applied to the production of manifold useful and beautiful results. Reason helps us to discover the principles hidden in problems. It is what enables us to face life's experiences squarely.

The Emperor is an executive. The noun *emperor* means "he who sets in order", and setting things in order is the chief function of an administrative officer. Thus the title is closely bound up with the various meanings of the number 4.

That which the Emperor administers is the progeny of the Empress. She is his consort, subject to her husband, and her motherhood depends on him. On the other hand, the exercise of his sovereignty depends on her motherhood. Unless the universal subconscious activities bring forth the universe, the cosmic self–consciousness has nothing to govern. It is because she brings forth that he has something to rule.

This is true also in man, who is called in occult terminology the Microcosm, or "the universe in little". The activity of imagination is subconscious response to impulses originating in acts of attention and observation carried out by self–consciousness (the Magician). But the Magician, who appears now as the Emperor, would have nothing to control or transform if subconsciousness did not send up from its depths a stream of images to be classified and arranged by the exercise of reason. Thus in Key 4 we find the Emperor seated on a height *overlooking* a stream in his domain. This is the same stream that waters the Empress' garden, and has its source in the shimmering robe of the High Priestess.

Geometrically, the number 4 corresponds to the square, an old symbol of the physical plane and of things concrete. Specific mental images, in definite, logical order — "precept on precept, line upon line" — are the basis of reason and good sense. The number 4 is also closely connected with the idea of measurement, and it is only by reason that we are able to take the measure of our experience so as to interpret it correctly. Without such right measurement of experience, we continue to mistake the illusory for the real, and thus manifest all sorts of conditions which bring misery, poverty and disease.

The Hebrew letter Heh (ה) means "window". A window admits light, symbol of knowledge, and air (the Life–breath, Spirit) into the house (Beth) of personality. A window also permits outlook, survey, supervision, and so on. Hence Qabalists attribute the function of Sight to the letter Heh. Windows, so to say, are the eyes of a house. Sight is also closely allied to reason. When our reasoning results in understanding of the truth about some problem we say, "I see". We are strikingly reminded of the importance of sight in this connection by the 29th chapter of *Proverbs*, which says: "Where there is no vision, the people perish."

In the Hebrew language the letter Heh is used exactly as is the English definite article "the". Reason is a defining activity. This shows us, first of all, that reason is a phase of self–consciousness, because to define anything is to *name* it, and self–consciousness is associated in occultism with Adam, the namer. There is a curious colloquial expression one often hears that is commonly used thoughtlessly in connection with something unknown or queer. The expression is, "Name it, and it's yours." Whatever the origin of the statement, it is an actual truth when we understand the real significance of naming anything. It will pay you to meditate on this idea.

Definition limits, sets boundaries, specializes, particularizes, and enters into details. The qualities thus indicated are precisely those that enter into the making of a constitution for any social organization, from an entire nation on down. Its constitution is the *supreme authority* for any such organization. Laws are definitions, and it should be borne in mind that what we call "laws of nature" are simply definitions and descriptions of the sequence of events in some particular field of *human observa-*

tion. Thus it is highly important for an occultist to understand clearly that our personal definitions (or naming) of the meanings of our experience and existence constitute suggestions that are accepted without reservation by subconsciousness. In one sense every man makes his own law, writes the constitution of his own private world. His life–experience is the manifestation of that constitution through the activity of subconsciousness. Take this statement literally, but remember that right understanding of its truth requires that you shall comprehend man as something more than a personality who is born, lives a few short years upon this sphere, dies, and vanishes forever.

Aries, the first of the twelve zodiacal signs, is assigned to the 4th Key. As the first sign it symbolizes the outgoing, ordered, cyclic motion emanating from the Primal Will — the beginning of cosmic manifestation. This sign rules the head and face, especially the eyes, and dominates the higher functions of the brain.

Aries is ruled by the planet Mars, the planet of war and conflict, but also the protector of fields against enemies. In occultism, the Mars force is not only that which rules the brain's higher functions. It is also the fiery activity which gives energy to the entire muscular system. Thus it is the instrumentality of execution and realization. Through Mars man deals with the world round him, and sets that world in order.

The Sun is exalted (that is, finds its highest expression) in Aries. We may understand from this that the highest manifestation of solar energy in our world is that which is expressed in those functions and powers of man that are governed by Aries and symbolized by Key 4. For all these functions and powers are actually dependent for manifestation upon transformations of solar energy in the human brain. Of all mechanisms or organisms on the face of the earth, the human brain is the most wonderful and most powerful. The brain is run by solar force, as is every other bodily organ.

Strictly speaking, the brain does not transform solar energy into thoughts. What it does do is to transform this energy into rates of vibration which enable the personal consciousness to receive ideas already inherent in the Universal Mind, and continually being broadcast throughout all space. The principle is similar to that used in radio, where an electric current in the receiving set establishes vibrations that may be attuned to the broadcasting station. The receiving set does not make the music. Neither does the brain make thought. The brain simply provides the necessary conditions, as does a receiving set, whereby thought can find expression.

The Emperor, then, represents the Sovereign Reason. In nature every law reflects reason. Reason is the source of all the operations of the Life–power in the world of manifestation. The Emperor is the Establisher, the Founder of all things, and the Framer of the Universal Constitution. In the field of human personality, the universal constituting power is specialized in man's ability to see through outer appearances into the real nature of his environment. Actually, this power of vision is something that embraces the whole complex machinery, mental and physical, by which the spirit within becomes aware of the manifested universe.

As you color the Key this week, compare its symbolism with that of the Empress, with a view to making note, not only of contrasts between the two pictures, but also of details which bring out the idea that the power of the Emperor is *complementary* to that represented by the Empress. The directions for coloring are:

Yellow: T–cross and circle in right hand.

Green: Foreground.

Blue: Stream at base of cliffs.

Gray: Stone cube, except ram's head.

Violet: Belt, flaps on tunic (not borders or medallion on left shoulder).

White: Borders of tunic flaps, belt, medallion, ram's head, beard and hair, border of inverted T on globe in left hand, sleeves.

Gold: Inverted T and cross on globe, framework and points on helmet.

Brown: Slopes from height in foreground to stream's edge.

Orange: Background, above mountains.

Steel: Leg armor and breastplate.

Red: Globe in left hand (not inverted T or cross), helmet (except borders and points), mountains and cliffs.

Note also that numerically the Emperor is the union or sum of the Magician and the Empress. This is one reason for identifying the Emperor with the Magician. Another is that the sum of the numbers from 0 to 4 is 10, and the digits of 10 reduce to 1 by addition. Thus the Emperor is *essentially* 1, or the Magician, but *the extension of his power* is 10, or the Wheel of Fortune.

But 4 is also the sum of 2 and 2, and the multiplication of 2 by 2. Here is a hint that the Emperor, though he seems to be other than the Magician, is really an expression of the mysterious power of 2, the *root matter* symbolized in Tarot by the High Priestess. It will also appear, upon reflection, that Reason is really an expression of memory. Under all the forms of reasoning is the fundamental activity of *retention* and *recollection* symbolized by the High Priestess. Develop these number hints in your notebook.

LESSON TWELVE

THE EMPEROR
(Cont.)

In the preceding lesson, the general meaning of Key 4 is given as *Reason*. This has two aspects, as do the attributions of all the Tarot Keys. The universal aspect is that rational quality of the Cosmic Mind which sets in order all the manifestations of the Life–power. The personal aspect is the reflection or particularization of this universal rational quality in the field of man's action and experience. Thus Key 4 represents the Life–power as the Sovereign Reason, the Great Lord ruling all manifestation, and at the same time pictures that in yourself which enables you to control the conditions of your external environment.

Note, first of all, that the seat of the Emperor is just like the seat of the High Priestess — a cube. Since the days of Pythagoras, this one of the five regular solids has been taken as representing the physical plane. It is also a symbol of order, regularity and truth, because it is composed of equal faces, has lines of equal length, and also because every face is a square, corresponding geometrically to the number 4.

A cube, moreover, is bounded by *twelve* lines, *eight* points and *six* faces, and since the sum of 12, 8 and 6 is 26, the numeral value of the divine name, I H V H (Jehovah), which signifies "That which was, that which is, and that which will be," the cube is not only a symbol of *manifested Reality*, but it also implies that this Reality, even on the physical plane, is none other in truth than the real presence of the Limitless Life–power that is the Sovereign Ruling Principle of the universe. Hence, in the Tabernacle of Moses and in the Temple of Solomon, the Holy of Holies, where dwelt the *Shekinah*, was a cubical room. Similarly, in the *Book of Revelation*, the heavenly city which represents the completion and perfection of the divine order is in the form of a cube, for its length, breadth and height are said to be equal.

The white hair and beard of the Emperor identify him as the Ancient of Days, or Great Lord, designated by the Hebrew noun I H V H. For the same reason he is shown in profile, so that only

one eye is showing. This is an ancient piece of symbolism, intimating that even our highest vision of Reality is necessarily one–
sided and imperfect.

The ram's head on the side of the cube, the same design in
the medallion on the Emperor's shoulder, and the astrological
symbol of Aries at the top of his helmet, refer primarily to the
attribution of the zodiacal sign, Aries, the Ram, to this Key and
to the letter Heh. This ram symbol is very ancient. In India it denotes Agni, the god of fire. Used as a common noun, the Sanskrit
word Agni is an alternative name for the element of fire, usually
termed Tejas. In works on Hindu occultism, the Agni Tattva is said
to be the subtle principle of sight. This agrees with the attribution of sight to the letter Heh and to Key 4.

The white lambskin apron that is the distinctive badge of a
Freemason has a direct connection with the ideas we are now
considering. First of all, it is a square with a triangular flap. This
combination of square and triangle is shown in Key 4, where the
head, chest and arms of the Emperor are enclosed in a triangle,
while his legs form a rough cross, suggesting the same idea as
the square.

Furthermore, the lambskin refers directly to the sign Aries. That
sign is the first in the series of twelve composing the astrological
year. Thus it represents the first stage of a time cycle, before the
various events of that cycle have come to pass. Hence in Freemasonry the apron is subtly termed "the emblem of innocence,"
because the strict meaning of "innocence" is "absence of knowledge", and even omniscience cannot possibly include knowledge
of a particular event, as a *completely realized actuality*, until that
event has really come to pass.

Again, the lambskin apron is conferred upon the candidate
as he stands in the North–East corner of the lodge. Similarly, we
find that to the letter Heh, representing sight and the sign of the
Ram, the direction North–East is attributed. This direction is the
combination of East, attributed to the Empress, symbol of Venus,
and North, attributed to the letter Peh and Key 16, which stands
for Mars, ruler of Aries. This is another hint that in Key 4 we have
represented a combination of the powers of Mars and Venus. We
touched on this in the preceding lesson, when it was pointed out
that the Emperor, consort of the Empress, would have no sub-
jects to govern unless his mate had borne him children.

The combination of the number 3, suggested by the triangle
in which are the Emperor's head and arms, with the number 4,
suggested by the cross formed by his legs, is another intimation

of the same combination of masculine and feminine powers. This idea is emphasized by the shape of the Emperor's scepter, which is a modified form of the astrological symbol for the planet Venus. This means that the Emperor's active power of regulation has to do with control of mental imagery. A similar hint is given in the old Greek myth of a clandestine relationship between Mars and Venus.

The helmet, surmounted by the symbol of Aries, is also ornamented with twelve triangular points, of which six are visible. These are analogous to the stars on the Empress' crown and to the jewels on the Fool's girdle. The space between the bars of the helmet is red, so that the colors of the Emperor's headdress, gold and red, are those of the Sun and Mars, both active in Aries.

The globe and cross in the Emperor's left hand are symbols of dominion. They are similar in form to the ornament at the top of the Empress' scepter, but her globe is green and the Emperor's globe is red. These are complementary colors, the green corresponding to Daleth and Venus, the red to Heh and Mars. The little cross at the top of the globe is composed of five equal squares, referring to 5, the number of the letter Heh (ה).

The inverted T on the globe represents Tav (ת), the final letter of the Hebrew alphabet. To the letter Tav, or T, Qabalists attribute the planet Saturn. Saturn is the astrological symbol of restriction, hence the inverted Tav on the globe of dominion intimates that the Emperor's rulership and authority are expressed in his ability to reverse Saturn, that is, to reverse the action of that aspect of the Life–power's self–expression which seems to limit our freedom. Such reversal of apparently restrictive conditions is precisely what you may accomplish by right use of the Constituting Intelligence represented by Key 4.

This right use consists in a higher vision of reality. A higher vision firmly based on accurate observation of the actual situation on the physical plane. For in true occult science there is no attempt whatever to deny the reality or importance of the physical world. What is denied is the opinion held by materialists concerning the physical world. True occultism combats the error of materialism, but in order to do so it has no need to resort to silly denial of the physical world, neither does it attempt to explain away by any kind of high–sounding verbal trickery, the actualities of time and space.

The higher vision includes insight into the powers of man as well as accurate observation of the physical conditions surrounding him. Such insight makes it evident that when we have

67

watched a train of events as it occurs in nature, apart from the introduction of the human personal factor, our watchfulness is always rewarded by a rational perception of the law or principle at work in the train of events we have observed. This law or principle is seen with reason, the eye of the mind, and sooner or later the vision of principle stirs up the inventive power of subconsciousness. Then, through the combination of invention (creative imagination) and reason, the human personal factor enters into the situation.

New trains of events are set in motion, new forms are produced, new conditions are made manifest. By the very same law that makes iron sink, man floats great ships of steel. In obedience to the law that makes a stone thrown in the air fall to the ground, airplanes have already developed far beyond anything the Wrights could possibly have foreseen. *By seeing things as they really are, instead of as they superficially look, the Sovereign Reason, manifested through the human brain, reverses one by one all semblances of bondage which afflict mankind. For the Spirit of the universe is a Spirit of freedom; yet this freedom is the perfect liberty of a rational order, operative on all planes.*

Reason and insight are always contrary to mass–opinion; hence they invariably stir up conflict. Hence Jesus, foreseeing the more immediate relative consequences of his ministry, declared that he came to bring a sword, rather than peace. The peace comes with fulfillment, not in the initial stages of the work. Thus the Emperor is shown as a man of war, in contrast to the peaceful scene shown in the preceding Key. Every step forward in man's dominion over the conditions of his environment has been bitterly contested by those who prefer to adhere to the "good old ways". The mass mind resents innovation, prefers its comfortable errors, and scoffs at the great seers. But the Sovereign Reason is protected by the armor of truth, which is here represented as being made of steel, a metal attributed to Mars. For the final test of any vision is to carry it into action, and since Mars is ruler of action, what is symbolized here is that even the mass mind surrenders its follies when confronted with the beneficent results of true vision expressed in action. Many a person who crosses the continent by airplane today would have laughed scornfully at the idea of such a flight, had someone suggested such a thing fifty years ago.

The skirt of the armor and the flaps that cover the Emperor's arms are violet. In the color scale on which these attributions are based, violet is primarily the color of the planet Jupiter, represented in Tarot by Key 10. It is also the color attributed to the sign Aquarius, represented by Key 17. The planet Jupiter is understood astrologically as the representative of expansion (which is, observe, the opposite or reversal of contraction or restriction.) It is also the planet symbolizing law, scientific research, and so on, as well as the planet dominating religion.

Now, though this anticipates a little, Key 10 represents the scientific vision of the mechanism of the universe, as it is seen by great seers. Hence the violet flaps of the Emperor's dress mean: *Reason clothes itself in the vision of reality.* And since this vision is a revelation of the truth about man as well as of truth about the universe, the color violet also links up with Key 17, which is obviously a symbol of precisely that revelation. In Key 17 it is associated with the sign Aquarius, because the Inner School has long foreseen a great unveiling of truth during the Aquarian Age that even now is just beginning.

The mountains in the background are of igneous rock, which is colored red to emphasize the fiery quality of the sign Aries. These barren rocks are in sharp contrast to the fertility and productiveness of the Empress' garden. They represent vividly the sterility of mere intellection — use of reason for its own sake without any practical application to life. They also represent the fruitlessness of mere regulation and arrangement unless there is something warm and vital to set in order.

This fourth Tarot Key is intended to impress upon you a clear pattern of the ruling power of consciousness. Whenever you exercise true reason, whenever you interpret an experience correctly, whenever you frame a satisfactory definition, you are actually using the power that defined the universe in the beginning. That power, at work through you, is the maker and framer of worlds, and the maker and framer of your personal world. *It rules everything now. At this moment, and always, it has absolute command over every circumstance, and condition.*

Read, with Key 4 before you, these last stanzas of Angela Morgan's poem, *The Cosmic Fire.*

> DUST! Why, the Future laughs at our dull sight;
> Laughs at the Judgment linking man to sod —
> Damning him ever with decay and blight
> When at his center burns the blaze of God!
> The Force that flung the far suns into space
> Pushes and throbs through an eternal plan;
> The Mind that chains the singing stars in place

Implores fulfillment in the soul of man.

O GOD, give us the whirlwind vision! Let us see
Clear-eyed, that flame creation we call earth,
And Man, the shining image, like to Thee.
Let the new age come swiftly to the birth,
When this — *Thy* world — shall know itself divine;
And mortals, waking from their dream of sense,
Shall ask no proof, no message, and no sign —
Man's larger *sight* the unanswerable evidence.

THE HIEROPHANT
(INTUITION)

By this time you will have become used to a definite method of studying these lessons that you will use throughout the entire series. There are two lessons for every Key. In the first, the meanings of the number, title and letter are dealt with, the emphasis being placed on the general meaning of the whole Key.

During the week that you study this lesson you also color the Key, so as to fix its details in memory, and prepare you for the more detailed analysis of the symbolism that is given in the second of the group of two lessons. Every day you begin your study period by meditating on the Tarot Key for five minutes. Then study the lesson, reflect on it as you read, and write in your diary any observations that may occur to you.

Your Key this week is number 5, *The Hierophant*. After you have looked at it for five minutes, review the meanings of the number 5 given back in lesson two. Note that this symbolizes the results of the classifying activities of Key 4. A subconscious elaboration of these classifications, and the formulation of deductions therefrom that are projected back into the self–conscious level, results in the mental states termed intuitions. Even the form of the figure 5 suggests this, for the top is a right angle composed of straight lines, and its bottom is a swelling curve. The straight lines are masculine, and so related to self–consciousness; the curve is feminine, representing subconsciousness.

Note the cyclic action of the mental process that gives rise to intuitions. Every idea thus projected into self–consciousness is another suggestion to subconsciousness and becomes the beginning of yet another series of deductions.

The working out of this process may be instantaneous. This is what happens when we "think rapidly", as most persons express it. On the other hand, it may be a matter of days, or longer. A common example of this, and one that you have probably experienced many times, is when one reads a difficult passage in a book. At first reading it may be very obscure, but the next time one sees it, it is perfectly simple and clear, even though one may have given it no conscious attention during the interval.

Intuition means literally, interior teaching. As here treated, intuition is understood as being direct perception of the eternal principles that may be applied to the solution of human problems and to the establishment of human control over nature. This direct perception is the result of *union* of the personal consciousness with the superconscious I AM, the Central Self, termed "the blaze of God" in the poem quoted in the last lesson. Such perception makes a human being *immediately* aware of those eternal principles, but it does not stop there. Included in this awareness is also a perception of the way the principles may be put into practice for the solution of some particular problem.

There is a distinct difference between intuitions of this sort and those whose roots go no deeper than the "upper layer" of subconsciousness that is merely a record of personal experience. The deeper levels of subconsciousness contain the record of the race experience; they correspond to what Carl Jung calls the "collective unconscious". Intuitions coming from the upper, personal level of subconsciousness are what we commonly call "hunches". Intuitions that have their origin in superconsciousness clothe themselves in the symbolic imagery of the race experience stored in the collective subconsciousness. These may be correctly termed *spiritual intuitions*.

The word *union* is the key to the reception of spiritual intuitions. Unless there is a real union between the personality and the Central Self, there never can be an expression of superconsciousness, and one does not touch the high plane where eternal principles are perceived. This idea of union is symbolized in many ways by Key 5.

The Hebrew letter Vav (ו) means "nail" or "hook". Both meanings represent union, since nails are used to join the various parts of a house, and a hook joins the object fastened to it to the support to which the hook is attached.

Notice that the idea of *sustenance* is also connected with the nail or hook, since it is by nails that the house is sustained and a hook is that from which something depends. When the Central Self is linked consciously with the personality, one gains first–hand knowledge that all things are sustained by and depend upon that ONE SELF.

The idea of union is still further carried out by the primitive form of the letter Vav, which was a crude picture of a yoke, such as is used to harness oxen. Remember that the letter Aleph means "ox" and you will see that here is a hint as to the means of "harnessing" the limitless energy of the Life–power. Think over this hint, and record the results of your thinking in your occult diary.

The root of our English noun *yoke* is the Sanskrit *yoga*, the exact translation of which is "union". As commonly taught, yoga is a system of practices designed to bring about the union of the higher and lower natures of man. A similar idea is suggested by the noun *religion*, which means literally "to bind together again". The religious doctrine of atonement (at–one–ment) is another expression of the same idea. It is evident that anything so deeply rooted in all of the world's religions must have some profound philosophical and practical basis.

The practical application of the idea of union is to be found in the function of hearing, which is attributed to the letter Vav, and thus to Key 5. It is not simply physical hearing that is referred to here, but what is known as "anterior hearing". Knowledge of the higher aspects of reality comes to us through the "soundless sound" of an Inner Voice, which often speaks as distinctly as any voice heard by the physical ear. The reason is that the hearing centers in the brain, when developed to a certain extent, are stimulated by higher rates of vibration that serve as a means of communication with the Central Self. The same receptivity of the hearing centers also puts us into communication with those advanced human beings who compose the Inner School.

Here a word of warning is necessary. The awakening of the greater receptivity of the hearing centers may put us in communication with intelligences by no means wise or good. Do not be frightened at this. There is a sure way to distinguish between the "voices" and the VOICE. The "voices" often flatter. They promise great things – wealth, knowledge, prominence, power, and so on. Sometimes they appeal to spiritual pride, by announcing that the person who hears them is destined to save humanity from some dire catastrophe. Always they demand implicit obedience and, if they give what purports to be occult instruction, they require its recipients to follow it without criticism, and they often require the abandonment of any other kind of instruction. The counsel they offer in practical matters is often silly, and at best is usually merely expedient.

The true VOICE *never* flatters. Often it gently, but firmly, points out our shortcomings. It seldom promises anything. It never coerces. What it always does do is to point out some universal, and therefore eternal, principle that applies to an actual problem confronting one. It does not say, "Do thus and so," but instructs us concerning the law of nature involved in our problem, so that we can see for ourselves what ought to be done.

Hence the mode of consciousness associated with the letter Vav and Key 5 is called the *Triumphant and Eternal Intelligence*, because the Inner Voice invariably indicates the principle that will work out as a successful course of action, and in so doing reveals a law of nature that applies not only to our personal problem, but also to many others of like characteristics.

Wise men throughout the ages have taught and practiced union with the Central Self. Everywhere and always they have agreed that release from every limitation comes to those who awaken to recognition of this power that is always present in human life, a power that sets men free when they know it and act in obedience to its law. That power is understood clearly by those who have learned to distinguish the Great Voice from the lesser, and often dangerously misleading, *voices*.

Geometrically, the number 5 corresponds to the pentagon, or figure of five equal sides, and the pentagram, the five–pointed star developed from the pentagon. The pentagram is one of the most important symbols in occultism. Each of its five lines is divided in exact extreme and mean proportion (the famous Golden Section or Divine Proportion). With a single point uppermost, it suggests the head and four extremities of the human body, and is thus understood as a symbol of man, the microcosm. Just as the number 5 is the number of mediation (being the middle term between 1 and 10), so is man the mediator between God and nature. Remember this last sentence. It is a key to many mysteries of Tarot and of practical occultism.

The zodiacal sign Taurus, the Bull, is attributed to Vav and to Key 5. Taurus is an earthy sign, yet the symbol of the bull is closely related to that of the ox represented by the letter Aleph. That letter, you have learned, is a symbol of the Life–Breath, Spirit, and superconsciousness. Yet here is a symbol that is practically the same, attributed to the element of earth, which stands for the physical plane. Here is a clear intimation that the spiritual and the "material" are, for the wise, essentially identical. The Divine Force that is health to the soul, medicine to the body, and the source of all true wealth, is *omnipresent*. In the thinking of the average person, that Divine Force, if recognized at all, is thought of as being far off, and a sharp distinction is made between Spirit and matter. For the wise man who has achieved union with the One Self, no such separation is possible. To such a knower of Reality, the substance of anything whatever is the actual presence of the One Spirit.

Taurus is ruled by Venus and is the sign of the Moon's exaltation. Reflect a little upon this, and you will see that Intuition comes as the progeny of the Empress (Venus), who is the High Priestess (Moon), in her highest expression of active creation. This is one way of saying that the only way to contact superconsciousness is through the agency of subconsciousness.

The older exoteric Tarot named Key 5, *The Pope*. This is a direct reference to the attribution of the function of hearing to this Key. For tradition has it that the first pope was the Apostle Simon, nicknamed "Peter", the "Rock". Simon, or Simeon as the Hebrew has it, means *hearing*. If you will read the passage in Matthew 16:13 to 19, on which the papal tradition is based, you will see there a clear intimation that Simon's answer, for which Jesus commended him, was the result of interior hearing.

Hierophant, the esoteric title of this Key, means literally "revealer of mysteries or he who shows that which is sacred". In the ancient Greek mysteries, the hierophant was the teacher who explained the meanings of the sacred symbols. Thus the Inner Voice represented by Key 5 will reveal to you the deeper mysteries of Tarot, and the inner or sacred meanings of its symbols. When this occurs you will have not only a true understanding of the meaning of life and its expression, but you will have also a practical working knowledge of it. Again, note that explanation is a linking process, uniting the knower with what is known.

Finally, this Key follows the Emperor, who represents Reason, in order to show: (1) that he who would be instructed by the Inner Voice must first have trained his mental vision, so as to see his situation clearly, even though that situation presents a problem; (2) that though Intuition goes beyond Reason, it is not a substitute for reasoning, as some lazy–minded persons suppose when they confuse their personal "hunches" and the messages of "the voices" with the clear instruction of the Inner Teacher.

Read this lesson carefully, with your occult diary at hand. Remember that this Key, besides being a symbolic presentation of esoteric doctrine, has power to arouse your intuitive ability, because the symbols act as forceful suggestions to your subconsciousness, which is the channel of Intuition. The force of these suggestions will be intensified as every detail of the symbolism is impressed on your subconsciousness while you carry out the following directions for coloring the Key.

Yellow: Crown (not trefoils, crossbars or circle at top), yoke behind ears (except fringe), staff in left hand, orphreys (Ys) on priests' vestments.

Green: Garments of figures in foreground (except collars, sleeve edges, flowers and orphreys).

Violet: Fringe of yoke.

Gray: Background (light), pillars, and throne (darker shade for throne).

Gold: Crown ornaments, key with handle pointing to priest whose garment is embroidered with roses (except dots in circle).

Silver: Crescent at throat, key with handle pointing to priest whose garment is embroidered with lilies (except dots in circle).

Blue: Undergarment showing at bottom. The scarf or border of the outer robe should   be blue–green.

White: Undergarment at throat, navel and sleeves. Shoes, collar and sleeve edgings of chasubles, dots in key circles. Lilies on chasuble at right.

Red–orange: Outer garment (not scarf or border), dais. (Mix equal parts red and   orange).

Red: Roses on chasuble at left.

THE HIEROPHANT
(Cont.)

In the preceding lesson you learned that in some versions of Tarot Key 5 is called *The Pope*, in reference to the attribution of hearing to the letter Vav. In the Bible passage to which you were referred, note that the traditional first pope is called not only Simon Peter (Hearing, the Rock), but also Simon Bar–jona, or Simeon, son of Jonah (Hearing, son of the Dove). In this connection, remember that the dove pictured on the Empress' shield is not only the Christian symbol of the Holy Spirit, but also a bird sacred to Venus, ruler of the sign Taurus, represented by Key 5.

In Key 5 the principle of antithesis that runs throughout the Tarot is shown particularly by the contrast between the shaped stone that is a prominent detail of the design and the rough rock in the background of Key 4. The Hierophant sits between two carved stone pillars, upon a stone throne, in a stone temple. The Emperor is out–of–doors, for the mental activity he represents is concerned more particularly with the ordering and arrangement of external conditions. The Hierophant, like the High Priestess, sits within, for the mental activity he symbolizes has chiefly to do with the revelation of the inner significance of the conditions the Emperor rules.

Actually, the Hierophant and the Emperor are not two, but one. This is shown by the older title, *The Pope*, which means literally, *the Father*, and thus refers to the conditions of primitive society, in which the head of the family was also the chief authority on religious matters. When the Magician has brought into existence a family over which he rules as father and king, he assumes the responsibility of transmitting his wisdom to his children. Thus he becomes the Revealer or Hierophant.

Furthermore, "Father" is a technical term used by Hebrew sages to designate the second aspect of the Life–power, named Wisdom, and associated with the second statement in *The Pattern on the Trestleboard*. That Key 5 represents the communication of wisdom from the Parent Source is obvious.

The Emperor wears armor, but the Hierophant wears the vestments of the peaceful priestly office. These vestments are adaptations of feminine garments, to indicate that Intuition is the

78

extension and development of reason, effected when the special and particular conditions of a given external situation are linked up with the inner, subconscious memory of universal principles, first pictured in Tarot as the scroll of the High Priestess. The insignia of the Emperor are those of earthly rulership, while those of the Hierophant represent spiritual dominion.

The outer robe is red–orange, the color assigned to Taurus. It is trimmed with blue–green edging, which is the color complementary to red–orange, and refers to the sign Scorpio. The undergarment is blue like the robe of the High Priestess, and has a similar significance. Over this is the white robe that symbolizes enlightenment. The outer robe is fastened at the throat (which is a part of the body under the rulership of Taurus) by a silver crescent, suggesting the exaltation of the Moon in Taurus.

The crown is similar to the triple papal crown. It is egg–shaped, denoting that the One Force (that is, the reality represented by the symbol of the Cosmic Egg) bestows spiritual sovereignty on man, whose life includes all *the potencies of the universe*.

The ornament hanging from the crown, behind the ears of the Hierophant, is a form of yoke, referring to the primitive meaning of the letter Vav. It falls behind his ears to call attention to these organs of hearing. (Note that as only one eye of the Emperor is shown, so in Key 5 only one ear of the Hierophant is visible. These two details refer to singleness of vision, in Key 4, and to the hearing of the One Voice, in Key 5.)

The golden staff represents the dominion of the Life–power through the planes of nature, represented by the knob and three bars. These bars are analogous in meaning to the three crowns, and the knob at the top of the staff corresponds to the circular ornament that surmounts the crown. The lowest bar and the lowest crown represent the element earth and the physical plane, symbolized by the Magician's coin or pentacle. The next bar and crown, counting upward, represent the element air and the formative world or astral plane, symbolized also by the Magician's sword. The upper bar and crown stand for the element water, the creative world or mental plane, and thus correspond to the Magician's cup. The knobs at the top of the staff and crown represent the element fire, and the spiritual plane or archetypal world, represented also by the wand on the Magician's table.

The keys crossed at the Hierophant's feet represent the Sun and Moon, for one is golden and the other is silver. They suggest that an understanding of the power of light (gold) and its reflection (silver) unlocks the mysteries of life. The wards of the keys show a bell–and–clapper design denoting the importance of sound vibration and of the function of hearing in the discovery of these secrets.

The priests who kneel before the Hierophant wear robes upon which are embroidered replicas of the flowers growing in the Magician's garden, making the two figures stand for desire and knowledge. The orphreys or Ys on their garments are variants of the yoke symbol, colored yellow, the tint associated with Mercury and the Magician, to show that both desire and knowledge are under the direction of self–consciousness.

The throne, which is ornamented, and therefore a product of human adaptation, is of stone. The Hebrew noun for "stone" is *Ehben*, spelled אֶבֶן, in English transliteration, A B N. Esoterically this word is itself a symbol of union because its first two letters spell אַב, (AB), Ab, the Hebrew noun meaning "father", while the last two spell בֵן, (BN), Ben, the noun meaning "son". (Hebrew is read from right to left.)

Thus אֶבֶן, *Ehben*, signifies esoterically the union of the Father (God) and the Son (humanity), together with many other variations of meaning. You may also learn something by putting the Keys bearing these three letters in a row, so that the pictures spell *Ehben*.

In harmony with what has just been said, older versions of Tarot call Key 5 *The Pope*, or Father, but attribute this Key to the letter Vav, which Hebrew sages attribute to an aspect of the Life–power known as the Lesser Countenance, and also as the Son.

As you read previously, the word Father has special reference to the aspect of the Life–power named Wisdom, and the Paternal Wisdom is said to be the seat of the universal Life–force. In the same system of occult philosophy, the name Son is applied to the sixth aspect of Reality, corresponding to the sixth statement in *The Pattern on the Trestleboard*. This sixth aspect is understood as being the particular manifestation of the universal Life–force as the human Ego. Thus, whenever stone is used in Tarot symbolism, you may know that it refers to some phase of the union of the human ego with the divine Life–force.

The pillars, like those of the High Priestess, represent the Law of Polarity. On each capital you will notice that part of the design resembles the letter U, one English equivalent for Vav. The rest of the ornamentation on the pillars represents the union of feminine and masculine potencies, and thus relates to the Law of Gender.

The background is gray, a color associated with that same

Paternal Wisdom that the Hierophant symbolizes. Gray is a balanced mixture of white and black, another suggestion of the union of the unknown and the known, or the blending of spirit and matter. Gray is also the result of the mixture of any pair of complementary colors, so that it is a symbol of the blending of the influence of all pairs of opposites. Of similar import is the checkered border of the carpet covering the dais, intimating by the alternation of light and dark squares the alternation of day and night and thus the Law of Rhythm, or periodic alternation.

Ten crosses of equal arms appear on this Key – one on each hand and foot of the Hierophant, four (enclosed in circles) on the carpet, and two in the handles of the keys. They represent the ten great aspects of the Life–power that are also symbolized by the ornaments on the Fool's robe and by the ten cypresses behind the Empress. They also represent the mystical number 4,000, because each cross is a letter Tav, as written in ancient Hebrew, and the value of this letter is 400. The number 4,000 is one of several numbers used to represent *perfection*. It is a symbol of the ALL.

This Key shows the One Life–power as being the Teacher of humanity. By its correspondences and associations it instructs us that our personal contact with that Inner Teacher is through mental hearing.

This teacher is the Guru so often mentioned in Hindu books, which abound in counsels that may be summed up in the admonition: "Reverence the Guru." In order to receive instruction from that Teacher, you must first of all recognize his presence in your life. This lesson and the Key it explains are intended to help you to that recognition, and to the understanding and discrimination that will enable you to distinguish the Inner Voice of Intuition from telepathic invasions from other personalities, incarnate or discarnate, human or non–human.

If you wish to avail yourself of guidance and instruction from the One Teacher, study this lesson carefully. The steps to be taken are:

1. Acknowledgement of the actual presence of the Teacher;

2. Daily acts of attentive *listening* for his instruction;

3. Careful study of the content of all messages received through interior hearing. True intuition unfolds principles,

81

not merely expedients. It is always concise, clear, and the meaning is unmistakable. True intuition never flatters. More likely it will reprove. It never misleads, and can stand the most severe spiritual, moral and intellectual tests. As Lao–tze says, "Its counsel is always in season."

4. Obedience to the instruction. When you distinguish a true intuition, carry it out in action.

THE LOVERS
(DISCRIMINATION)

Contrary to our procedure in the previous lessons of this course, we shall consider the meanings of the Hebrew letter Zain (ז) before we go into those of the number 6. We do this for the reason that the meanings of the number grow out from, and are dependent upon, certain other meanings of the symbology of Key 6, as you will perceive presently.

In Hebrew the letter Zain means "sword". Among other things, a sword is an instrument of *cleavage*, something that is capable of making sharp divisions. This refers to a human faculty that the Hindus call *Buddhi*. It is the *determinative* or *discriminative* faculty, the power to perceive *differences*. This power is at the root of self–consciousness, since it is only with the self–conscious mind that things are perceived as many apparently unrelated parts rather than as single *unity*.

Note carefully that the *Many* are only *apparently* unrelated. Buddhi is the power that makes things and conditions *seem to be real in and by themselves*. Yet these seeming realities are but reflections of the *One Reality* in the universal subconsciousness. The occult teaching is that all such reflections, that is, everything that changes and is impermanent, are phases of illusion, and therefore in the absolute sense unreal. Since it is the attention of self–consciousness to particular ideas that acts upon subconsciousness to bring these ideas into active expression, this power of being able to perceive differences, that is, to *create illusions*, is a fundamental necessity in order that individual self–consciousness may be manifested. Otherwise all would be undiffused substance, unperceived by any one, and hence, in effect, without existence, having subsistence only.

You will avoid confusion as to how self–conscious perception makes self–consciousness possible if you will remember that manifestation is simply the way the ONE IDENTITY appears to *itself*, and the instrument of its self–perception is that which the faculty of self–consciousness in man. As *The Book of Tokens* puts it: "For the sake of creation the One Life that I am seemeth to divide itself, becoming Two." The two units resulting from this semblance of division are termed, respectively, the *superior* nature and the *inferior* nature. Though distinguished as superior and inferior, the one is really as important as the other, for the superior nature is that which we are considering in this lesson as Buddhi, represented in Tarot by the Magician, while the inferior nature is the universal subconscious matrix that reacts to the direction of the superior nature. This is symbolized primarily by the High Priestess.

84

Discrimination becomes most valuable to man when he uses it to perceive the difference between the real and the unreal. As long as he is a slave to appearances, he perceives unreality; but when he begins to awaken from the dream of sense to the inner knowledge of his true nature, he begins to understand reality. Tarot pictures reality in terms that subconsciousness understands. It tells man the truth about appearances. Hence intelligent study and contemplation of its symbols constitutes a phase of right discrimination. It is a practical method whereby you turn from the unreal to the real.

The number 6 means *reciprocation*. Reciprocation is the act of giving and receiving mutually. You now see why a discussion of discrimination precedes that of reciprocation. Reciprocation is a relationship between distinct and separate entities, or between parts of an organism or mechanism. As it is to be understood here, reciprocation is the relationship existing between the self–conscious and subconscious phases of mental activity, for the self–conscious mind *gives* suggestions that the subconsciousness *receives*, works out, and *gives back* to self–consciousness. Furthermore, in connection with Key 6, as will be more definitely established in the next lesson, reciprocation is also the relationship between superconsciousness and the human personality, when the latter is considered to be the combination of the two poles of personal mentality, self–consciousness and subconsciousness.

Self–consciousness, remember, is not the Self. The true Self is One, and identical with superconsciousness. Self–consciousness is simply that phase of the Life–power's activity that constitutes consciousness of the Self, but the Self that is the subject of self–consciousness is itself superconscious. Subconsciousness designates the totality of the Life–power's activity below the level of self–consciousness.

Reciprocity between opposites, when it is harmonious, is always of the same nature as that which we call *Love*. An inharmonious relationship is akin to *Hate*, which is the inversion of Love. Both love and hate are human emotions, but an eminent Master of occult wisdom once made a statement that they are *spiritual* emotions. This means that they are really root emotions, and that all other emotions and desires take on the character of either one or the other of them. The Bible says that God is Love; hence we perceive that we approach God through emotions and desires that have the attractive, beautiful quality of the primal Love impulse, rather than the selfish and separative motivation of hatred.

85

A little thought will make clear why this is so. If both Love and Hate are spiritual, they must alike be eternal and immortal. When cosmic manifestation takes place, the process of involution becomes operative. This process is the separation of the ONE THING into the appearance of many parts. The force of Hatred is involutionary, and properly belongs to that phase of manifestation. Hence the German seer, Jacob Boehme, speaks of God's wrath as the involutionary power, and in the same connection speaks of the fiery anguish of the turning wheel whereby all things come into separate manifestation. But we, as human beings, are upon the path of return, or in process of evolution. In other words, we are headed back toward Unity. Consequently the force we must employ is the synthesizing, attractive force of Love, and our desires and emotions must be colored by that force. It is always a uniting force of great power. We utilize the separative faculty of discrimination, which we have already developed, to enable us to understand the illusive nature of separativeness, and to help us to determine the true color of our emotional life. Key 6 tells us that the Way to Freedom is the Way of Love.

The title, *The Lovers*, brings out the idea that pairs of opposites are not antagonists but complements. The lovers are not simply the man and woman in this Key – these symbols in the picture stand for all opposites, as well as for the special opposition of self–consciousness and subconsciousness. Thus the main lesson to be drawn from the title is that right understanding of the universe shows it to be, in all its details, an expression of the power of love, as the right and balanced relationship existing between the various pairs of opposites of which the universe is apparently made up.

The astrological attribution to Key 6 is the zodiacal sign Gemini, the Twins. Here again you see the same symbolism of discrimination and separateness. This is accentuated by the astrological symbol for this sign, which is II. This symbol also brings out the fact that opposites are really different aspects of the one thing, just as heat and cold are different aspects of something that we call temperature, past and future of that which we call time, and so on. As *The Kybalion* puts it:

Everything is dual; everything has poles; everything has its pair of opposites; like and unlike are the same; opposites are identical in nature, but different in degree; extremes meet; all truths are but half–truths; all paradoxes may be reconciled.

The planet Mercury rules Gemini. This planet is represented in Tarot by the Magician. Here again you see that self–consciousness is the phase of mental activity that utilizes and controls the faculty of discrimination for the acquisition of knowledge and understanding of the true meaning of our conditions and environment. No planet is exalted in Gemini, because right discrimination balances the activity of all planetary forces without exalting any one above the others.

The Mercury power, or self–consciousness, is the maker of interpretations, and has rulership over subconsciousness through the law of suggestion. When we make unskillful use of this power we interpret experience incorrectly. The result is confusion in the mind, which confusion is reflected into our external lives as misery of various kinds. As we become better trained, our interpretation becomes more accurate, and order takes the place of chaos in our mental life and our outer circumstances.

Discrimination begins by accurate classification of differences, by learning what the pairs of opposites are. It passes from this knowledge to a yet higher perception, in which it finds that each pair of opposites is really a dual manifestation of a single activity. Then it goes on to discover that these reconciling unities are themselves under the law of polarity. In other words, when we succeed in discovering the unity that is the reconciler between two known opposites, we have found also something that is either the positive or negative pole of another pair of opposites.

This, however, does not go on indefinitely. The process of right discrimination leads at last to mental recognition of a UNITY that transcends *all* pairs of opposites, a UNITY we cannot define or even speak about, a UNITY for which SILENCE and DARKNESS are symbols. This UNITY is no mere intellectual abstraction. It may be directly known, immediately perceived, even though no words or forms can be found to express it. Such direct cognition is the outcome of true discrimination, the result of our learning to unify the pairs of opposites, and so rise above their influence.

Hence the mode of consciousness associated with Zain in the Hebrew Wisdom is "Disposing intelligence". To dispose is to arrange, to classify, and to set in order. Primarily, however, it means "to pose apart", or to separate. Thus we may expect the symbolism of Key 6, to be considered in the next lesson, to indicate an activity characterized by duality, contrast, and a tendency to divide things and conditions into separate classes, sharply distinguished from each other.

The function assigned to the letter Zain and to Key 6 is that of the sense of Smell. An ancient occult treatise says: "Properties are discerned by the nose." Smell is always associated in language with discrimination. Our English word "scent" is from a French verb meaning "to discern by the senses". Odors are known to be among the most powerful, and at the same time most subtle, means of stimulating the mental associative function. Hence, in Egypt the god Thoth, corresponding to Hermes or Mercury, was sometimes represented as having the head of a jackal, on account of that animal's keen sense of smell.

This week, as you are studying Key 6, and coloring it, be on the lookout for examples of the seven laws mentioned in Lesson Eight. Note, too, the various points of contrast between this Key and the one that precedes it. Write your observations in your occult diary.

You must not think that this diary is supposed to be a record of extraordinary events or discoveries. It may become just that as time goes on. But its use now is of great importance. Now is the time to review all practical instruction from Lesson One on, so that you are sure you have attended to all the details, such as setting aside a few pages for the development of the meanings of numbers, and so on and so forth. Careful attention to these little points will facilitate your progress.

The color instructions for Key 6 are:

Yellow: In every case, except the sun, the yellow in this card is beside red, or red and green. The five fruits on the tree behind the woman are yellow with red cheeks. The flames behind the man are yellow with red at the base, after the manner of the blue and yellow in a flame from an old–fashioned gas jet. The angel's hair is yellow, red and green. The angel's flesh is yellow, but diluted somewhat, so as to give the appearance of flesh.

Blue: Background, but not above angel's head.

Green: Foreground and foliage, serpent round the tree, angel's hair, with yellow and red.

Violet: Angel's garment, mountain (diluted)

Gold: Sun and background above angel (make yellow, if not gold).

88

White: Clouds.

Blonde: Woman's hair.

Brown: Tree trunk behind woman.

Red: Angel's wings. See also note under *Yellow*.

This week keep close watch upon your desires and impulses. Check up on your tendency to obey impulses without first submitting them to the light of reason. Make an effort to discriminate between helpful actions and unimportant ones, between those that are purely selfish and those that reflect the influence of the unifying force of love.

Be careful to discriminate intelligently. There is altogether too much of the idea that in order for an impulse to be good it must be unconcerned with personal happiness or pleasure. No bigger mistake can be made, for love expresses itself in happiness, joy and well–being. Poor discrimination may make some persons believe that happiness and well–being are concerned with selfishness, but anyone who has developed a sense of "other–consciousness", or awareness of the relation between one's own mental and physical states and these of other people, is under no such delusion.

Keep this practice up from now on. Unselfishness and consideration for others are marks of the master of true occultism.

THE LOVERS
(Cont.)

The sun in Key 6 is golden. Thus it is a symbol of that which is the goal of all practical occult work, namely, enlightenment or illumination. It also represents the *One Force* that is differentiated into the various pairs of opposites.

The angel is Raphael, archangel of air, and angel of the planet Mercury, which rules Gemini. His hair, by its form, suggests flames. The yellow represents the influence of Mercury. The red stands for Mars, and for action and passion. The green is the color of Venus, and is a symbol of the power of imagination. Thus in the colors of the angel's hair are blended the colors of the planets that rule Aries, Taurus and Gemini. The suggestion is that in discrimination we must make use of reason (red, corresponding to Aries and the Emperor), and imagination and intuition (green, corresponding to Taurus and the Hierophant), in order to make right classifications (yellow, corresponding to Gemini and Key 6).

The yellow color of the angel's skin is a reference to the element of air, or the Life–breath. This is because Gemini is an airy sign, and also because yellow is associated with Mercury.

His wings are red to show that right discrimination includes right desire, and finds expression in right action.

His robe is violet, the blending of the red of action with the blue of mental substance. Violet is also the color of royalty and dominion, showing that right discrimination leads to right control of conditions. See also what is said of this color in Lesson Twelve.

The angel represents superconsciousness, and is therefore shown resting on clouds, to indicate that the powers and activities of superconsciousness are partly hidden from us because we have not yet developed, as we shall in due season, the organism in our brains through which superconsciousness is realized.

Note that the angel's name, Raphael, means "God is the healer". This agrees with the Egyptian doctrine that Thoth (or Mercury) is the god of medicine. It also refers to the idea that right discrimination leads to the recognition of that Unity that is the ALL. The true healing is the attainment of inner and outer *wholeness*.

The mountain in the background is a symbol of attainment and realization. It is the height whereon stands the Fool, and on which the Hermit is shown in Key 9. Here it is in the background, to indicate the truth that we are able to discriminate correctly because there is that in us that has already reached the loftiest pinnacles of understanding.

The man represents the Magician, the Emperor and the minister whose chasuble is ornamented with lilies in Key 5. He is also the Adam of the Bible allegory of Genesis. In Tarot, he represents self–consciousness. Behind him is a tree whose leaves or fruit are flames, and each is triple. They represent the twelve signs of the zodiac, which astrologers subdivide into three divisions, or decanates, for each sign. Hence they represent the twelve basic types and the thirty six sub–types of human self–consciousness or personality.

The woman corresponds to the High Priestess and the Empress, and to the minister wearing roses in Key 5. She is also Eve, the mother of all. Thus she is a symbol of subconsciousness. The tree behind her is the tree of knowledge of good and evil, in contrast to the tree of life behind the man. It bears five fruits that represent the senses, and also those five subtle principles of sensation that occultists know also as the five elements: ether, fire, water, air and earth.

The serpent coiled round the tree represents Kundalini, the serpent–power of Hindu Philosophy. It is also the serpent of temptation, *Nachash*, (נחש), N Ch Sh, whose name bears the same numeral value, 358, as the name *Messiah*, (משיח), M Sh I Ch. What is meant here is that the serpent–power of vibration is the force that at first leads us into delusion, but in the end, when it is rightly understood and applied, rescues us from all the miserable consequences of the earlier error.

The man looks at the woman, but the woman looks at the angel. All that self–consciousness observes directly is the activity of subconsciousness. Yet under the influence of right discrimination subconsciousness can be made to reflect the activity of superconsciousness.

This, however, is brought about by right exercise of the powers of self–consciousness. All our miseries and limitations result from subconscious developments of the erroneous interpretations of experience made by self–consciousness. Subconsciousness has no power of independent inductive reasoning, and its production of mental imagery is determined by the premises, or mental seeds, planted by self–conscious thinking.

The first step in taking advantage of this law is to learn it, as you have just done. Then it follows that if we plant correct premises, subconsciousness will work out the corresponding consequences. Since subconsciousness is the bodybuilder, and ruler of the complex chemical, electrical and other phenomena of the organism, if we interpret our place in the universe correctly, an inevitable consequence will be that, through the work of sub-consciousness, our organisms will be so adjusted that they will adequately express this true interpretation.

In this Key the man and woman are shown nude, because in right discrimination self–consciousness conceals nothing of its own nature from itself, and the true working of subconscious-ness is also perceived by it. No disguise is assumed by either member of the mental pair. They have nothing to be ashamed of, nothing to conceal. Their relation is that of lovers, not that of opponents, and thus we know that this Key is a symbol of mental health and of the right adjustment of the relationship between self–consciousness and subconsciousness. Here is no confusion. The two stand apart, each in the right place.

Because subconsciousness is amenable to suggestion, you can remind it that it is the Uniting Intelligence, reflecting into your field of personality the absolute knowledge of the supercon-scious plane, and communicating to you the inexhaustible power of that higher level of being. In making this suggestion you are simply recognizing the truth that the highest function of sub-consciousness is to act as such a reflecting agency. The sugges-tion releases subconsciousness from the dominion of your former misunderstandings, and should be formulated somewhat as fol-lows:

Speak directly to subconsciousness, as if to another person, and say: *Henceforth you are free from the influence of any misinter-pretations of appearances that may result from the inaccurate operation of my conscious thinking. You will refuse to accept any such misinterpretations, and you will be guided by the influx of superconscious life and wisdom. Under this influence you will set my body in perfect order, through this wisdom you will guide me aright in all my affairs, and by the reflection of this boundless power into my personality you will give me ability and strength to accomplish all that I have to do.*

This is a positively magical formula. Use it as given here, elabo-

92

rating it, if you feel the need for some specific development of the general idea. It will work marvels of transmutation in your life.

Read this lesson once daily, and look at Key 6 five minutes every day, before reading the lesson.

At least once daily pause long enough to call up the mental images of the Keys you have studied, from Key 0 to Key 6. Remember that these are portraits of certain aspects of your own real selfhood. Try to realize, as you complete this brief mental review, that what the Keys picture is actually operative from moment to moment throughout your life. Hence it is always true that what you are just about to do, whether it be work or play, is in some sense an expression of the powers pictured by these Keys. If you think of this, you will transfer Tarot from the printed designs into your brain, and thence into your daily experience.

LESSON SEVENTEEN

THE CHARIOT
(WILL)

Review the meanings of the number 7, in Lesson Two, before reading this lesson. In the Hebrew language, which has had so much influence upon the philosophy of Tarot, the word for "seven" is spelled with the same letters as a verb signifying "to be full, filled, satisfied", as a noun meaning "abundance, plenty", as an adjective that is translated "satiated, satisfied, full", and as a verb meaning "to swear", that is, to vow, to confirm by a solemn oath, to express solemn intention of purpose.

Note that among the meanings of 7 are mastery, conquest, peace, safety, security. These are all related to the root–meaning of the verb signifying "to be filled, satisfied". Peace and safety are associated with abundance and plenty. Conquest, another meaning of 7, is the outcome of carrying definite purpose into action. Peace is what follows conquest, and conquest is the establishment of equilibrium between contending forces. As an ancient occult ritual puts it: "Two contending forces, and one reconciler between them." Hence we may expect to find in connection with the number 7 and the Tarot Key bearing that number indications of a power that can establish harmony, can bring order out of chaos, a power of adaptation and adjustment.

That power is *Will*; but the occult conception of Will is different from the ordinary notions, because occultists look upon Will as being in no sense a personal faculty. Will is not something that strong–minded people possess, and timid people are devoid of. Instead, it is the living, motivating power behind the entire universe, and every person and thing in the universe has an equal share in it. Remember the words of *The Pattern on the Trestleboard*: "All the power that ever was or will be is HERE, NOW." The difference between persons is not in degree of Will power, as a possession. We all have access to a limitless supply. That wherein we differ is the degree of our ability to express this power through our personalities.

Will power is a universal, cosmic energy, not a personal force, So long as men suffer from the delusion that they have any Will power *of their own*, just so long will they be held in bondage. It is absurd to think of Will power as one's personal property, as a personal attribute. One night as well claim ownership of the air one breathes!

There is only *one* Will power in the universe, and that power is expressed through all the various laws of life. Through want of right discrimination a man may suppose himself to have something he calls "will" that he can oppose to the laws of life. Thus the Tarot Key that has to do with Will follows the one that represents discrimination. If one sees, as Key 6 shows, that the power source behind and above self–consciousness and subconsciousness (the two aspects of personal life) is a superconscious reality, superior to every personal limitation, then it is a logical consequence to see that the mighty energy of Will power is really super–personal.

So much for reasoning. If we turn to the report of those men whom history designates as masters of life, what do we find? Invariably those whose achievements express the superlative degree of mastery are persons who solemnly declare that they have *no will* of their own. Moses was one such. So was Buddha. So was Jesus, who said, "*I have no will* save to do the will of Him that sent me." And the counsel of these masters of life to those who seek to follow in their footsteps is always: "Above all else, rid yourself of the delusion of self–will, and learn to be receptive to the inner guidance of the only Will power there really is, which is the Will of the one Life–power."

The meaning of the letter Cheth, (ח), printed on Key 7, is *field* or *fence*. Both meanings imply *enclosure*. Primarily this field is the universe, which includes all manifested objects and energies. In man the field is the personality, and the master, or cultivator, of this field of personality is the true I AM, or Inner Self.

The idea of a field brings out the fact that personality is something that can be cultivated. That is to say, the potencies of Will power can be brought into active manifestation through the functions of a personal vehicle that has been properly prepared. Will power may be likened to the seed from which all possibilities are developed. It is also the fruition of these possibilities when they have been brought from latency into active manifestation. A little thought upon this idea will shed a flood of light on the true function and purpose of personality, and its value to man as the instrument of his spiritual progress. But it must be always an instrument, never mistaken for the workman; always the field, never the cultivator. You are not your body, your emotions, nor your intellect. If you were, you could not apply the possessive case to them, for you do not possess what you are.

Hence to the letter Cheth is assigned the mode of consciousness named "The Intelligence of the House of Influence." The word translated "Influence" means also "wealth, abundance." What is meant here is that the master consciousness, the state of mind that permits the greatest possible expression of Will power, the highest degree of control of the field of circumstance, is that which grasps the truth that human personality is the abode or dwelling–place of a power that flows into the self–conscious and subconscious levels of personality from above those levels. This is the true Will power, free from every restriction whatsoever, the only *free* Will there is.

A field is a definite, limited area. A word is a definite idea, limited to a form that makes it intelligible. A word endows an idea with a specific, concrete meaning. Thus the function of speech is related to the letter Cheth and to Key 7. This refers not only to the spoken word, but also to the unspoken language of thought.

Our habits of speech are the indices of our Will development. The words we use continually, every day, and the meanings they have for us, are the patterns of our life–expression. This does not mean that persons who use large and unusual words are express-ing life more completely than those whose speech is simple and homely. Quite the contrary. But accuracy in the use of words, care in the selection of words so that they convey true meanings, choice of positive, strong, courageous words – these are among the most important requirements for the unfoldment of Will power. Such words result in correspondingly positive mental, emotional and physical states. Their opposites result in confused thinking, chaotic emotions, and physical disease.

In occultism there are certain special words that have specific vibratory power when they are spoken or sung. Such words are the mystic syllable AUM, the various Hebrew divine and angelic names, and certain artificial sound combinations. The use of such special word forms is what Hindus call *Mantra Yoga*, which plays an important part in Will development.

Such word forms are not to be experimented with by one who does not know what he is about. Such work demands the super-vision of a competent teacher. Of the power of sound, Madame Blavatsky says in *The Secret Doctrine* that it is "a tremendous force, of which the electricity generated by a million Niagaras could never counteract the smallest potentiality, when directed with occult knowledge." Therefore it is not exactly a plaything for the idly curious, who merely want to "see what will hap-pen".

The zodiacal sign Cancer, the Crab, is attributed to the let-ter Cheth and to Key 7. The crab is a shelled animal, hence has a direct relationship to the meaning of Cheth as a fence, and the meaning of 7 as denoting safety and security. According to astrology, Cancer rules the chest, the fence of bones that pro-tects the most important vital organs, and this is another point of agreement with the meaning of Cheth.

Cancer is ruled by the Moon, and the planet Jupiter is exalted therein. Our habitual subconscious mental states (the Moon, Key 2) have rulership over our expression of Will power. The fact that the power of Will always expresses itself in some form of cyclic activity has to do with the relationship of Jupiter to Key 7, as you will understand better when you have studied Key 10.

The title, *The Chariot*, sums up all that we have been considering. A chariot is a movable fence, a protection for its rider. But the key–word to the understanding of this title is the noun "vehicle". Buddha used to liken personality to a chariot, and so did Pythagoras. In the *Bhagavad–Gita* we find the same metaphor when we read: "The Self is the rider in the chariot of the body, of which the senses are the horses and the mind, the reins."

This is just what is meant by "Intelligence of the House of Influence". Right discrimination shows the enlightened that personality has no power of its own. Personality is a vehicle of power, an instrument through which power is made manifest. The place of personality in the cosmic order is that of an intermediating agency, through which the one Will power, itself the energy of superconsciousness, is brought to bear upon the states and conditions that constitute the environment of man. To see this, and to shape one's thought, word and action to agree with this right discrimination of the true significance of personality, is to adopt the right method for the highest possible development of Will power.

This week, as you are looking at Key 7 and coloring it, bring again and again to your mind the thought that your personality is the actual vehicle and instrument for the expression of the same limitless Will power that manifests itself throughout the entire universe as the power that marks out specific fields of concrete expression for the One Life. Remember that the number 7 is related to the idea expressed by the verb "to vow", and dedicate yourself to an ever–increasing measure of receptivity to the influence flowing into your field of personal consciousness from the superconscious plane above. Frame this vow of dedication in a sentence that will express the idea as briefly and clearly as possible. *And watch your habits of speech and thought, so that they may be brought into harmony with this dedication.*

The color instructions for Key 7 are:

Yellow: Background, chariot wheels.

Green: Trees and grass, wreath behind crown.

Blue: Stream, and faces in crescents on shoulders. Deeper shade on canopy. Panel behind charioteer and wings in front of chariot (not the disc between them) should also be of this deeper shade.

Gray: Chariot and chariot pillars, wall before city (on both sides of the chariot.)

Gold: Crown, belt (not figures), collar edging, ornament in square on breastplate, disc between wings, scepter in right hand (except the crescent at top of scepter).

Silver: Crescents on shoulders, and crescent on scepter, stars on canopy and back panel.

White: Cuffs, castles in city (not rooftops), shield on chariot, white sphinx, and stripes on headdresses of both sphinxes. Design on skirt of rider is also white, but very difficult to paint. It is advisable to leave it as it is.

Steel: Armor on arms of rider.

Brass: Breastplate (this is a greenish yellow, to simulate brass.)

Blonde: Hair.

Red: Roof–tops, symbol on shield in front of   chariot.

THE CHARIOT
(Cont.)

The title of this Key is directly related to the number 7, because the Pythagoreans, whose doctrine was known to the inventors of Tarot, called the number 7 the *vehiculum* of man's life. The symbolism of Key 7 is evidently an adaptation from the Pythagorean description of the Spirit as the rider in the chariot of personality. Plato gives this as a Pythagorean symbol; but Pythagoras probably learned it during his sojourn in India, for the *Kathopanishad* says:

> The Self is the rider on the chariot of the body, guided by the intellect as charioteer, drawn by the senses as powerful horses, controlled by way of the mind serving for the reins. Thus runs the vehicle over the course of experience. The Self thus conditioned by the senses and the mind is called the Enjoyer by those who know. He who is forsaken by the charioteer (intelligent discrimination) and has no idea of guiding the reins – his mind – in the proper manner, has no control over the senses, and is like a driver of restive horses. He who has the intellect for his driver and the mind for proper reins, is able to reach the other end of the course, the highest essence of the All–pervading. THAT ever concealed in all, is never manifest, but is grasped by the sharp intellect of those who are trained to minute observation.

This quotation emphasizes the importance of what Tarot represents by Key 1, the Magician, and that Key is associated with the letter Beth, the House. Hence in the background of Key 7 is shown a city, a collection of houses, to intimate that behind all that is shown in the foreground is the discriminative power of self–consciousness.

The structures behind the wall of the city have many towers surmounted by triangles or pyramids. These are red, and the towers themselves are masculine, or phallic, symbols. The true development of Will power, symbolized by Key 7, has behind it the constructive function of self–consciousness, and our exercise of that constructive function brings about a lifting–up, or sublimation, of the reproductive energies of the physical organism, accompanied by a release of that force in subconsciousness that analytical psychology calls *libido*.

The wall is a stone fence. In front of it is a wind–break of trees like those growing in the Empress' garden – a living wall. Then comes the river, a wall of water. In the foreground is the chariot, itself a portable fence, carrying a rider wearing armor, another kind of fence. Thus the Key contains repeated references to the letter Cheth.

The body of the chariot is a cube, like that on which the High Priestess is seated. Review what is said of the cubic stone in Lesson Eight and Twelve. See also the explanation of the noun Ehben (אבן), (A B N), "Stone", in Lesson Fourteen. To this may be added the fact that Qabalists associate the noun Ab, (אב), Father, formed of the first two letters of ABN, with that aspect of Reality they name Wisdom, and to which they attribute:
1. The forces of the zodiac; 2. the life–force of man. The wisdom of the Paternal Mind is expressed in the perfect order manifested by astronomical phenomena, and from the same source comes our life–energy, which, as modern science demonstrates, is directly derived from the radiant energy of the various heavenly bodies.

The cycles of transformation of this radiant energy within our bodies, and in the physical world that constitutes their environment, are the causes of all phenomena within our range of experience. These cycles are represented by the wheels of the chariot, which refer to the symbolism of Key 10, associated with the planet Jupiter, exalted in the sign Cancer, which is attributed to Key 7.

The direction East–Below, corresponding to the lower horizontal line at the rear of a cube facing an observer seated in the West, is assigned to the letter Cheth. This is a combination of the directions Below (assigned to Gimel and the High Priestess) and East (assigned to Daleth and the Empress).

This line of East–Below joins the lower and eastern faces of the cube of space mentioned in *The Book of Formation*. It connects the lower end of the north–east vertical line (assigned to the Emperor) and the south–east vertical line (assigned to the Hierophant). It is opposite to, and therefore complementary to, the horizontal line, East–Above, at the top of the cube, which is the line at the junction of the upper face (assigned to the Magician) and the eastern face (assigned to the Empress). This line of East–Above is the one assigned to the Lovers. Note that it connects the *upper* ends of the lines of the Emperor (North–East) and the Hierophant (South–East), just as the line East–Below, assigned to the Chariot, connects the lower ends of those same lines. What is intimated here is that the mental activities represented by Key 6 link together reason and intuition (Emperor and Hierophant) at the level of self–conscious mental activity represented by the Magician. Similarly, the functions represented by Key 7 link the powers of the Emperor and the Hierophant together at the level of subconscious activity represented by the High Priestess. *But note that the Empress is also related to Keys 6 and 7. The former has to do with conscious, and the latter with subconscious, mental imagery.*

What this means is that Key 7 refers primarily to operations of the Life–power that occur at the subconscious level, and are combinations of creative imagination (East: Empress) and memory (Below: High Priestess). These activities link together the subconscious consequences of reason (North–East: Emperor) and intuition (South–East: Hierophant). Specifically, these operations are those related to the sign Cancer, which governs nutrition and digestion. In these operations subconsciousness is the ruling power (Moon, High Priestess, governing Cancer); and the highest functions of what is known astrologically as Jupiter, working through the solar plexus or abdominal brain, are also brought into play.

This is important as showing that Key 7 has to do with the vehicle of personality, which is built by subconsciousness. Some have suggested that Key 7 ought to be named *The Charioteer*, but we do not agree with this opinion. The emphasis in this Key is all upon the *vehicle*, considered as the portable "House of Influence". Hence the body of the chariot is a cube, in order to indicate that the personal vehicle is actually no more than a particular shaping of the very same materials that constitute its environment. Those materials flow into the enclosure provided by the personal vehicle, as the river in the background of the picture flows into the scene, and, like the same river, flowing out of the picture, the various cosmic forces flow out of the personal vehicle after taking form in the personal activities. None of them *originates* in the vehicle. None remains within it.

Four pillars rising from the body of the chariot support a canopy. The number 4 is the number of order and measurement, and it also refers to the four elements: fire, water, air, earth. Each pillar is divided into two equal parts, reminding us of the Hermetic axiom, "That which is above is as that which is below." The point of division at the center of each pillar is surrounded by a ring.

This is a symbol of Spirit, for the rings are circles, or zero–signs. The idea symbolized is that each of the four elements is encircled by the One Spirit.

The starry canopy represents the celestial forces whose descent into the physical plane through the activity of the four elements is the cause of all external manifestation. This canopy represents the forces that surround the earth, and seem to be above us in the sky. It also represents the subtle metaphysical forces that are above the level of personality. It is therefore a symbol of what Eliphas Levi calls "Astral Light". (See Seven Steps in Practical Occultism.)

A shield on the face of the car has the same significance as the letter–name, the wall, the wind–break of trees, the river, and the chariot itself. The symbol on the shield is one form of the Hindu lingam–yoni, typifying the union of positive and negative forces.

Above the shield is a variation of the winged globe seen so often on Egyptian monuments. It is yellow, to represent the power of the solar rays, and the wings are blue to symbolize the moisture of the atmosphere that brings those rays to earth.

The crown of the charioteer is ornamented with three golden pentagrams. (See Lesson Seventeen, page 94.) Three are shown, because the mental dominion we can exert through right use of the power of speech does really extend over three planes or worlds.

The rider's fair hair is bound by a green wreath, like that on the head of the Fool, and having the same meaning. He is clad in armor, like the Emperor. The crescents on his shoulders refer to the Moon's rulership in Cancer. They are also symbols of the two aspects of the Life–power that Hebrew Wisdom calls Mercy and Severity. Hence there is a smiling face in the half–moon on the side of Mercy, and within the crescent on the side of Severity is shown a frowning countenance.

The charioteer's cuirass, or breastplate, is greenish–yellow to simulate brass, the metal of Venus, signifying the protection afforded by right use of the power symbolized by the Empress, who carries, it will be remembered, a shield as symbol of her protective function. The square on the cuirass symbolizes order and purity, while the three Ts of which it is made up refer to the limiting power of Saturn, which planet is attributed to the letter Tav. The skirt below the armor is divided into eight parts, and the units of its design are geomantic symbols, used in making magical talismans. The belt of the charioteer suggests the zodiac, and close examination will show the astrological symbol for Cancer in one of its square panels, and a crescent moon in another.

The charioteer's scepter is surmounted by a figure 8, which is combined with a crescent. This is a combination of the symbol over the Magician's head with the lunar crown of the High Priestess. Thus the charioteer's ensign of authority shows that his dominion is the result of a blending of the powers of self–consciousness and subconsciousness.

Key 7 is the end of the first row of Keys in your tableau, and is a synthesis of them all. It tells us that the chain of events leading to our ability to express Will power starts with the Magician. Acts of attention (Key 1) set going the associative function of subconsciousness (Key 2), and the result is creation of concrete mental images, which externalize as definite environmental conditions (Key 3). The observation and orderly correlation of these images, which present themselves to us as facts and circumstances, is what we call reason (Key 4). This enables us to test our intuitions (Key 5), with the result that we make discriminations between the real and the unreal, and with the further result that we become aware of the differences between self–consciousness and sub-consciousness, and perceive their relation to superconsciousness (Key 6). This discrimination, worked out by subconscious process-es of deduction and imagination, affects the bodybuilding activi-ties that give us our physical vehicles. Thus we become aware of the true nature of Will power, and perceive that the universal Self is the rider in every chariot of personality.

By the invisible reins of the mind, we *let* that Self guide the vehicle of personality. The result is that the motive–power of sensation is brought to rest, as are the sphinxes in this version, or the horses that draw the car in some of the older designs. The sphinxes are propounders of riddles, and so are the senses. By sensation we experience all the pairs of opposites – what we like, and what we dislike; what seems favorable to our aims, and what seems adverse. But when the One Self, through the intel-lect, guides the vehicle of personality, it controls the senses, and the result is the security, safety and peace represented by the number 7.

This week spend some time in a deliberate attempt to realize that your Inner Self is above and beyond your personality. Try to understand that this Self is the true actor in all that you do. Think of your personality as being merely a vehicle, having no power of its own, but only that flowing from the One Will as the en-ergy of the Astral Light. By repetition, this concept will become so habitual and natural that all you think and say and do will be influenced by it. Thus you will be taking an important step in the cultivation of your field of personality.

Above all, watch your words. Say what you mean, and mean what you say. Get the dictionary habit and begin to enrich your vocabulary with all the strong, positive words you can make your very own.

As an aid to this end we recommend the use of *Hartrampf's Vocabularies and Roget's Thesaurus*. These standard reference volumes are now published by Grosset and Dunlap, at the extremely low price of one dollar each. If you buy these books and use them daily, you will never make a better investment. It is not too much to say that by their aid you may take long strides toward the acquisition of truly magical speech.

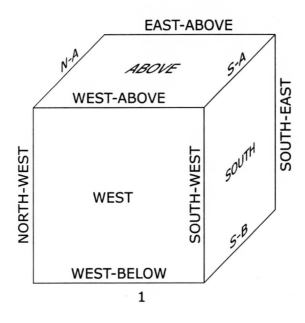

1

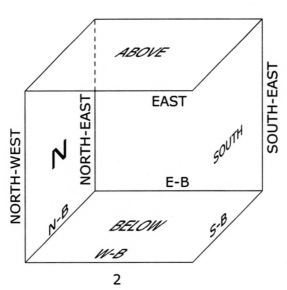

2

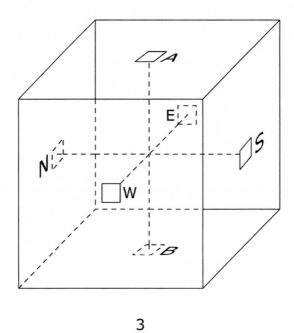

3

STRENGTH
(THE SERPENT POWER)

The Hebrew letter *Teth* (ט) means "snake". If you will study the form of the character in the corner of Key 8, you will see that the letter is simply a conventionalized picture of a coiled serpent. The serpent is one of the most frequently used, and one of the most important, symbols in occultism. It has been always a favorite device of the Wise Ones when they wished to compress their knowledge of the Great Magical Agent into a single emblem.

The Great Magical Agent is an actual force that is used every day by everyone. It is cosmic electricity, the universal life–principle, the conscious energy that takes form as all created things, and that builds all things from within. In human personality it is called *Kundalini*, the Serpent Fire.

Learning to control this Magical Agent is part of the daily work of every student of Ageless Wisdom. One step in that control is the establishment of a clear intellectual perception of the truth that all the varying forms of physical existence are merely transformations of this *one* energy. The world is full of a number of things, but they are all disguises of the *One Thing*. The essential nature of this One Thing is *Spirit*.

Here is a clue to the meaning of the old Hebrew name for the mode of consciousness associated with the letter Teth. It is called "Intelligence of the Secret of Works", but the noun translated "works" is sometimes rendered as "wages" or "reward". The secret of right work is making certain that whatever one does will bring about the desired result. What is the essence of that secret? The knowledge that the working power is the inexhaustible energy of the One Spirit. "I do nothing of myself: the Father that dwells in me, He does the works."

There is the secret. Compare it with what has been said about the word *Ehben*, (אבן), ABN, in the preceding lesson. To be absolutely certain of success, we must correctly identify the actual working power as being none other than the One Spirit. Only by so doing shall we be able to rid ourselves of concern as to the outcome of our works. Jesus taught his disciples to rid their minds of all anxiety concerning the future. The *Bhagavad–Gita* says that the secret of right work is to have no regard whatever for the results. Many have misunderstood this teaching, but it is perfectly sound, and easy to put into practice.

To be anxious about the future, to be concerned with results, is to be making mental images of failure, to be concentrating on mental patterns of some other outcome than the one we desire.

Such anxiety can be overcome by the realization that a perfectly adequate power is finding expression in all that we do. Having planted our seed of one single dominant desire, as explained in *Seven Steps in Practical Occultism*, we avoid all doubt as to its ultimate realization by our knowledge that the working power we are applying is more than sufficient for the perfect manifestation of that desire.

To that end, begin now to accustom yourself to think of *everything* as being a manifestation of Spirit. Perhaps you will be helped by thinking of everything as the direct expression of one radiant *mental* energy. The Great Magical Agent is a blind force to those only who fail to understand its nature. Learn to think of it as a conscious, intelligent force. *Practice* thinking this. Over and over again, as you look at things, remind yourself of their real nature. No matter if this idea is familiar to you, *make it second nature by repetition*.

The special form of the Great Magical Agent that is utilized for what are sometimes called "works of power" is dormant in the average human being. It is a tremendous force, as potent for destruction and debasement as it is for integration and illumination. It is a force not to be trifled with. No one should make any attempt to awaken it until he knows what he is about, for to do so is the most dangerous practice known to man. You will know what you are about if you study these lessons carefully, for they put you on the track of the true secret. The ability to control this force is not difficult to develop, once its nature is understood. The conditions under which it may be brought into activity safely are utmost purity of mind and desire, highest aspirations and ideals, utter unselfishness in action.

Every attempt to express these states of consciousness through right action will modify your bodily organism. When your organism is sufficiently altered, you will be brought automatically into the proper condition for awakening the SERPENT POWER.

Let us now consider some of the reasons for calling this force the Serpent Power. In Genesis we read that the serpent was more *subtle* than any other beast of the field. (And note that the "field" is the same field that is represented by the letter–name Cheth, corresponding to Key 7). The ordinary meaning of the Hebrew adjective rendered *subtle* in the English Bible is "cunning, dissembling, crafty". In addition to this, the same word, with different vowel–points, is the Hebrew adjective that signifies "naked, bare, uncovered". Here is a reference to the essential nature of the Great Magical Agent. *It conceals the true nature of things by seeming to expose them uncovered.*

This is to say that what we term the Great Magical Agent is that indefinable something that presents itself to us in various appearances. In each appearance it seems to show itself openly, without any concealment; but in reality every visible form is a veil of concealment for a hidden truth. Hence it is that those who call themselves "realists" are often, of all persons, farthest from having any notion of the true Reality. For them, *appearances* constitute the only truth. If they enter the field of art, they fairly wallow in what they call "naked truth", and their productions are usually characterized by extreme emphasis on unpleasant details of appearances.

A true "realist" is he who is not taken in by the apparent openness of external conditions. He understands the subtlety of the Serpent Power, and turns it to good use. Hence, in all ages throughout the history of mankind, great initiates have called themselves and their pupils "Good Serpents". The Christian admonition, "Be ye wise as serpents," is an echo of this ancient custom.

The motion of the Magical Agent is serpentine, that is, wavy or undulating. It is a coiling, spiral force, yet at the same time it is vibratory. This motion of the Serpent Power is one reason for assigning the number 8 to this Key, for 8 is a symbol of rhythm and vibration. To write it one begins at the top, and describes a letter S, which is serpentine in form, and is the alphabetical symbol of a hissing sound. The movement is then continued, so as to form the *reciprocal* curves to those first described. Thus in writing the figure 8 we make the same curved lines that are shown in the caduceus of Hermes by two intertwined snakes. These are also the lines of the movement of the Serpent Power within the human body. In this connection it is interesting to note that lightning (one expression of the Serpent Power) does not zigzag, but moves in sinuous, spiral curves.

8 is the only figure except 0 that may be written over and over again without lifting pen from paper. Thus it is a sign of endless activity, typifying the Life–power in rhythmic, vibrating, cyclic, spiral motion. In Christian occultism 8 is a symbol of the Holy Spirit, which has been described as a *feminine* potency. Hence the horizontal position in this connection. This is an esoteric conception with a world of meaning for the discerning student.

111

Again, 8 is a symbol of the ancient doctrine that all opposites are effects of a single cause, and that a balanced reciprocal relationship between opposites results in harmonious activity, symbolized by the number. Full understanding of this leads to the secret of controlling the Serpent Power.

The zodiacal sign Leo, ruled by the Sun, is attributed to Key 8. In the human body it governs the heart, the back, and the spinal cord, which is the main channel of the Serpent Power in the physical organism. Among the tribes of Israel Leo is represented by Judah, the tribe that had a lion for its standard.

In Hebrew the name of the sign Leo is Arieh, (אריה), A R I H, and the letters of this name are the same as those that spell the noun (ראיה), R A I H, Sight. Sight is attributed to the letter Heh, (ה), and is therefore associated with the sign Aries.

The numerical value of these two words, 216, is the same as that of the noun *rogaz*, (רוגז), R V G Z, which may be translated "trembling, vibration." This noun is particularly connected with the letter Samekh (ס) and the sign Sagittarius (Key 14). Furthermore, 216 is the number of the noun Geburah, (גבורה), GBVRH, Strength, which is actually the title of the eighth Key. Geburah is the name of one of the ten spheres of the Qabalistic diagram known as the Tree of Life, and this sphere is said to be the field of manifestation for the fiery planet Mars.

All these Qabalistic correspondences point in one direction. They intimate plainly that strength, or working power, is to be sought in a form of vibration that is fiery in quality, that is active in the sense of sight, and that also is connected in some way with the functions of the heart and spine. This power is the *light power* that makes vision possible. It is also the *life power* actually centered in the heart and coursing through the great main cable of the spinal cord, whence it is distributed by the nervous system to every part of the physical organism.

The color directions for Key 8 are:

Yellow: Background, lion's eye.

Green: Foliage, rose leaves, leaves in woman's hair, foreground (but do not extend all the way in right foreground, because the mountain range carries over to the right).

Violet: Mountain (both sides of background.)

White: Woman's dress, lion's teeth.

Blonde: Woman's hair.

Red: Roses, lion, flower in woman's hair.

Pay particular attention to this lesson and the next, for they deal with the force you are using for the regeneration of your personality. Use it, and you will attain the heights. Abuse it, and it will become an instrument of destruction. It is the cosmic *electricity*, of which Madame Blavatsky writes in *The Secret Doctrine*:

"Mighty word, and still mightier symbol! Sacred regenerator of a no less sacred progeny; of fire – the creator, the preserver, and the destroyer; of light – the essence of our divine ancestors; of flame – the Soul of things."

STRENGTH
(Cont.)

In your tableau, Key 6 is the first of the second row of Keys, which, you remember, represents the laws or agencies whereby the principles symbolized by the Keys numbered from 1 to 7 are carried into operation. Key 6 represents the law that is the means for expressing the principle of attention pictured by the Magician.

That law is *suggestion*. It is dealt with at some length in Lesson Three of *Seven Steps in Practical Occultism*, which should be reviewed in connection with this lesson. It is by means of suggestion that the force concentrated by acts of attention is carried into manifestation for the modification of external conditions. Remember that the force so concentrated is a perfect *Unity*, represented by the Hebrew noun Achad, (אחד), A Ch D, and that it is also Love–force, as indicated by the identity of number (13) between the Hebrew nouns *Ahebah*, (אהבה), A H B H, Love, and Achad, Unity. Ponder this in meditation, and you will have another clue to the *Secret of Works*. Note particularly that the number 13, which links these two Hebrew words, is the number of a Tarot Key that, as you will find in Lesson Twenty–nine, is definitely related to both unity and love.

The woman in Key 8 is the High Priestess, the Empress, and the woman in Key 6. She represents the human aspect of subconsciousness, which controls the functions of every organ in the body, and directs the currents of Prana, the vital energy or Life–Breath. The adjustment of the personality to the point where such direction brings about modifications of the bodily organism, to the extent that it becomes possible to make practical application of the high potencies of subconsciousness, is directly dependent on utilization of the law of suggestion.

Like the Empress, the woman is fair haired and crowned, but her crown is of flowers instead of stars. The hint here is that we are concerned with organic processes, rather than with the inorganic forces represented by the hexagrams on the Empress' crown. Furthermore, flowers are the reproductive organs of the vegetable kingdom, and any crown represents Will, because the technical name of the Primal Will in Qabalah is *Kether*, (כתר), K Th R, the Crown. Thus the crown of flowers means that the sovereignty of the human level of subconsciousness over the subhuman levels symbolized by the other details of the picture we are now considering is a sovereignty having to do with intelligent control of that aspect of the Serpent Power that manifests itself in reproduction.

Over the head of the woman is a horizontal figure 8, like that which hovers over the head of the Magician, for she partakes of his influence, and represents subconscious reaction to the principle he personifies. There is a sense in which all that is symbolized by Key 8 is a development of the symbolism of the roses and lilies growing in the Magician's garden.

The Empress and the High Priestess sit, but this woman, like the one in Key 6, stands. The High Priestess represents subconsciousness as the recorder and receiver of conscious impressions. The Empress typifies the *germination* of mental images through subconscious responses to conscious stimuli. The woman in Key 6 shows a more active function of subconsciousness, its direct reception of superconscious potencies and guidance. Now, in Key 8, the woman is shown controlling all the forces of nature below the human level.

Her robe is pure white, like the inner garments of the Fool and the Magician. This garment represents the purified aspect of subconsciousness, which it assumes as the result of intelligent application of the law that it is at all times amenable to control by suggestion. White also stands for the divine Unity, and is an emblem of purity and innocence, hence of regeneration that results in a personal realization of the truth that the ALL is ONE.

The chain of roses that goes round the woman's waist and encircles the lion's neck is intended to represent a figure 8, though this is far from being clearly indicated by this particular design. Roses represent desire; hence the chain is a systematic series of desires woven together. Desires, rightly cultivated and combined, are the most potent forms of suggestion. By definite formulation of desire, in harmony with the real nature of things, we are able to dominate the mighty forces of nature below the human level of activity.

As king of beasts, the lion is a symbol of the highest forms of development in the kingdoms of nature below the level of man. He is the ruling principle of the animal nature. He is also an alchemical symbol of one of the most important principles in the Great Work. That work is the transmutation of the gross forms of natural humanity into the Stone of the Wise, perfected man.

In alchemical books we read of the Green Lion, the Red Lion, and the Old Lion. The Green Lion is the animal nature before it has been ripened and purified. The Red Lion is the animal nature brought under control of the higher aspects of man's spiritual being. The Red Lion is the lion of Key 8. The Old Lion represents a special state of consciousness that becomes manifest after the work of purification has changed the Green Lion into the Red Lion. In that state of consciousness, one senses directly the identity of the personal life–force with the eternal radiant mental energy that, because it *was* before anything else had been brought into manifestation, is, in time relations, older than anything else.

Among the ideas suggested by the word *Lion* are: Rulership (since the lion is king of beasts), courage, bravery, valor (also symbolized by the color red), tenacity, resolve, fortitude, decision, will. We say that a person having these qualities has "backbone", and this ties up with the lion as symbol of the sign Leo, ruling the spine.

The direction attributed to the letter Teth, corresponding to Key 8, is North–Above. In the representation of the cube of space, touched on in Lesson Eighteen, this direction is assigned to the upper northern edge of the cube.

Thus it is the upper boundary of the north face, and the northern boundary of the top face. The north face is assigned to the letter Peh and Key 16, which we may say at this time is related to the force of Mars. The top face corresponds to the direction Above, assigned to the letter Beth, and to Key 1.

Thus in North–*Above* are joined the powers symbolized by Keys 1 and 16. Key 1 represents the self–conscious level of mental activity, and Key 16 represents the fiery energies that in Key 1 are symbolized by the red outer garment of the Magician. Key 8, then, suggests what happens when cosmic fire is controlled by self–conscious acts of attention. Furthermore, since Key 8 is North–Above we have here a clear intimation that what is pictured in this Key is a direct consequence of *intentional and conscious practice*. What is shown by this Key is not a spontaneous natural development. It is the result of deliberate decisions and purposes, consciously formulated, the outcome of knowledge consciously acquired, and the consequence of practice consciously undertaken.

To be sure, the law of suggestion is a law that works, whether we know anything about it or not. Key 8, however, shows the positive and constructive application of that law in the work of personal regeneration. Hence the situation pictured in Key 8 never occurs without the introduction of an impulse proceeding from what is represented by the Magician.

Here we approach one of the great difficulties of Ageless Wisdom. In order to perform the Great Work, the initial stages must be undertaken *as if* we were doing something of our own volition, and by our own power.

It certainly seems that way, and certainly involves a distinct sense of effort, a deliberate exercise of power, and careful selection of ways and means. The initial steps in the work, moreover, require no small amount of the strictest kind of self–discipline. No person who does not determinedly "take himself in hand" ever performs the Great Work of self–regeneration.

All this looks like the exercise of a very definite personal will, and, as said, *feels* like it in the earlier stages of the practice. The sages, nevertheless, assure us over and over again that this feeling is *illusive*, and part of their traditional discipline consists in mental practice that gradually builds up a realization that the work is not accomplished by personal effort at all.

By prolonged practice of this kind, pursued sometimes for months and years without any apparent result, those who follow the Way of Liberation effect in their subconsciousness the changes represented by Key 8, and produce at the same time the result shown in Key 16. When we come to the latter Key, the nature of this result will be more fully explained, but even here we may say that it is the *overthrow of a false conception of personal activity by a lightning–flash of true inspiration.*

It is because few persons have courage and persistence to continue the preliminary work in spite of its apparent fruitlessness; and also because not many are willing to practice the resolute denial of self–will required by all occult systems of discipline, that we have such a small number of adepts. And, all recent vaporings to the contrary notwithstanding, the time will never come when these first steps will be required no longer. No suspension of the discipline, for any reason whatever, can be made for the adherents of any school or teacher, because the discipline is not imposed by men or higher beings, but is the consequence of natural laws of physical growth and mental development that can never be changed *because they are part of the essential nature of all living beings.*

The line of North–Above, being the upper northern edge of

the cube of space, connects the upper end of the line North–East (assigned to Heh and the Emperor) to the upper end of the line North–West (assigned to Lamed and Justice). Thus Key 8 is shown to be the connecting link between Keys 4 and 11, *at the level of consciousness that is represented by the direction Above, the letter Beth, and Key 1, the Magician.*

You have not yet received the interpretation of Key 11, but one of its meanings is *Work* or *Action*, and another meaning is *Karma*. You already know that the Emperor represents *Reason*. Hence you will be able to understand that Key 8 is the connecting link that carries the power of Reason, or the Constituting Intelligence (Key 4) into the field of activity symbolized by Key 11.

That is to say, what is pictured in Key 8 is the agency whereby the power of control over the conditions of our external environment, symbolized by Key 4, is brought to bear upon all those complex operations of natural law that are designated by the word *Karma*.

In other words, *Karma is modifiable.* It is true that action and reaction are equal, and that today inevitably brings us into situations that are the consequences of past actions. We have to work with these situations as they arise; but it makes a great deal of difference whether we approach them ignorantly or intelligently. If we know the law, we can produce results not spontaneously provided by natural reactions to stimuli originating at some period in the past. And it is by bringing about the situation pictured as the taming of the Red Lion that the Cosmic Reason may be brought to bear in adjusting Karmic reactions.

Reference to the diagram of the cube that accompanies Lesson Eighteen will show you that the line corresponding to Key 8 is also the link between the line assigned to Zain, and that assigned to Samekh and Key 14. As the *northern* ends of these two lines are connected by the line assigned to Key 8, we know that Key 8 is to be considered as the link between that part of Key 6 that shows the woman, the Tree of Knowledge, and the serpent, and that part of Key 14 that shows the lion, the vase of water, and the mountains over which floats a crown. *For in all these Tarot Keys that part of the picture that is on the observer's left corresponds to the direction North. Similarly, that part of the design that is on the observer's right corresponds to South. This makes what is in the background correspond to the direction East, and what is in the foreground correspond to the direction West.* In other words, we look at the Tarot Keys from the symbolic West, facing East, just as we look at the diagram of the cube of space, which is one of the most important esoteric clues to the meaning of Tarot, hitherto unpublished.

Because you have not yet studied Key 14, it seems inadvisable to enter into an explanation of the meaning of Key 8 as connecting Keys 6 and 14. But the fact that these two Keys are linked in this manner by Key 8 needs to be mentioned at this time, and you will do well to pay close attention to this part of the present lesson. Remember, you *already know*, interiorly, the meaning of this and the fact that the correspondence has been brought to your attention will begin to have its effect on your subconsciousness. Thus, when you reach Lesson Thirty–two, you will find that the explanations given there are easier to grasp because, in the meantime, you will have been affected by the seed–idea now planted.

The scene in Key 8 is an open plain, in contrast to the city of Key 7. What we are considering here is the operation of a law that is always at work throughout nature, without being in any sense dependent on the artificial conditions of man–made civilization. The law of suggestion is always at work. It is the primary law of subconsciousness.

All the kingdoms of nature are represented in this picture. The woman represents the human kingdom. The lion is the chief of the animal kingdom. Flowers, grass and trees belong to the vegetable kingdom. They grow from the earth, consisting of disintegrated stone, and in the background a mountain like that in the background of Key 6 completes the representation of the mineral kingdom.

What is meant by this is that all the forces of nature are variations of the one Great Magical Agent, and are all subject to the law pictured here. The animal nature is subordinate to the human, the vegetable to the animal, the mineral to the vegetable. This control *does not need to be established*. It is in effect already, though the greater number of human beings experiences the consequences of its negative operation because they do not know how to reap the benefits of its positive use.

The difference between a tyro in practical occultism and a great adept is this: The tyro has little or no knowledge of the fact that subconsciousness at the human level automatically responds to the *predominant* suggestions originating at the conscious level. Hence he sets up activities whose reactions are negative and pain–bearing, and his subconscious *control* of the forces below his conscious level makes those forces take form as destructive reaction in his own body, and in the bodies of other persons.

119

Furthermore, this destructive reaction extends into the kingdoms of nature below the animal, and the net result is that the person finds his control of subconsciousness working *in reverse*, so that everything seems to be against him.

An adept, on the other hand, knows that the subtle power of the Great Magical Agent conceals the real nature of things by seeming to expose them uncovered. Hence he takes nothing at its superficial value. He looks attentively at the world reported to him by his senses. Thus he detects hidden relationships, and eventually he comes consciously and subconsciously under the guidance of the One Self symbolized by the Hierophant, the angel in Key 6, the charioteer in Key 7, and the angel in Key 14. Then his personal subconsciousness is purified, and wears the white garment of wisdom, as in Key 8. The consequence is that the reactions from the kingdoms of nature below the human level are favorable to the adept.

Yet there has been no change in the underlying law. Nor has the adept *gained* control that the tyro has not. The adept uses the already existing law *positively*. The tyro uses the same law *negatively*. That is all. But in that single difference is the difference between freedom and bondage, joy and misery, success and failure, perfect health and disease.

This week's practice work is highly important. Make every effort to carry it out. The most valuable lesson you can learn is that of *seeing through appearances*, and the consequent discovery of the One Reality veiled by them. Whenever you have anything to do with another person, try to keep in mind that it is not the appearance, not the external details of personality that you are speaking or writing to. Remember that his inner nature is *identical* with yours, and try to see with the mind's eye the real man behind the mask of personality.

At first this may seem difficult when you are dealing with those who, for one reason or another, are unpleasant or repulsive to you. Make the attempt, just the same, for this practice is more valuable than it would be in connection with somebody you like.

Don't make the mistake of being sentimental or emotional about it. This is an exercise in mental suggestion. Look deliberately for the good and the beautiful in every one. It is there, if you have eyes to see.

120

Don't gossip or discuss the unlovable things about any other person. Make an effort to see every human being as perfect in reality. Thus you will help yourself by telling yourself the truth about all men, and the power of your thought will be of great benefit to those on whom you turn it.

This exercise has far–reaching consequences. We purposely avoid a discussion of them now, because it is better and more interesting for you to find out for yourself. This is one of the most valuable, though simple, means of developing really pen-etrative vision, and he who has this insight possesses a key to limitless power.

LESSON TWENTY–ONE

THE HERMIT

The law attributed to Key 9 is *Response*. This law may be stated thus: *Every activity of human personality is really a response to the initiative of the Originating Principle of the universe*. The essential thought here is that no personal activity whatever has its beginning, source, or origin within the limits of the personality. All *personal* action is derived, reflective, and responsive.

To every one of us it seems as if our thoughts and actions express purely personal motives. This semblance of personal initiative affects the most illumined of wise men, except in rare instances of ecstatic identification with the Absolute, just as it does anyone else. A wise man, however, *knows* better, and thinks differently from those who try to live upon the assumption that personal thought, feeling and action are self–caused.

Personality is the mask of the true *Identity*. That *Identity* is superior to, and is not limited by, the conditions of personality. It is from this inner and superior *Identity* that all original impulse flows and all the activities of personality – the instrument or vehicle – are effects of this outward and downward movement of the energy, or working power, of the *True Identity* or I AM.

Ageless Wisdom teaches that there is but *One Identity* in all the universe. That *One Identity* is the single source of all forms of existence. Its presence is the substance of everything. The energy of the *One Identity* is what is released in any particular form of activity. The mental quality of the *One Identity* is what is manifested in any particular expression of consciousness. Your personality is but one of its innumerable forms of expression. Your real nature is none other than that *One*. Hence whatever laws and forces condition the activities of your personality must be laws and forces proceeding from your *True Identity*.

The Hebrew letter *Yod* (ʼ) resembles a tongue of flame. It is a component part of every letter of the ancient Chaldean alphabet now generally known as "square Hebrew", to distinguish it from the earlier script used by the Children of Israel before the Captivity. Because Yod is the foundation of the letters, and looks like a flame, this is often named "The Flame Alphabet". The Hebrew alphabet is in itself a symbol of everything that ever was or will be. Thus the letter Yod, as a component part of every letter, symbolizes the spiritual flame or energy that is present in every mode of the Life–power's self–expression.

Yod is a Hebrew noun meaning "the hand of man". Thus it is directly connected with the ancient doctrine: *The primary and fundamental reality of the universe is identical with the power that is expressed in the handiwork of human beings.* It is said that the upper point of Yod represents the Primal Will, while the rest of the letter is assigned to the aspect of the Life–power named Wisdom. This means that all mental activity is derived directly from the essential Will of the *One Identity*, and this mental activity, or volition, takes form as the Wisdom that is the basis of the entire cosmic order.

The hand of man is able to perform its manifold operations because it is the seat of highly organized centers of touch. Hence the sense of touch is assigned to the letter Yod. The hand of man is also a vivid symbol of that whereby the mind of man makes contact with that which is above. Thus, in Key 1, representing Mercury, it is the right hand of the Magician that holds aloft the wand by means of which he links the self–conscious level to the superconscious, and the uplifted wand represents the sublimation of the Serpent Power, the libido of analytical psychology.

The most intense forms of ecstatic union with the Absolute are almost always described in imagery closely approaching the erotic. Why? Because the most intense physiological sensation of pleasure is related to the sense of touch, and the higher forms of interior union with the *One Identity* are experiences of a bliss so intense that those who have them usually turn to erotic imagery, such as we find in the writings of Sufi poets, or in *The Song of Solomon*, in their endeavors to put into words what they have felt.

Key 9 represents attainment through union. This means that the end of the path is reached when the personality meets the inner Self in perfect contact. A graphic symbol of this is the slow, steady growth throughout the ages of stalagmites and stalactites in a cave. In that growth, the stalactite that grows downward from above is the active agent. It gradually extends itself downward, and the upward growth of the stalagmite is a response to the steady downpour of drops of the limestone solution from the stalactite. The stalactite is a symbol of the *One Identity*, ever moving itself nearer to union with the ascending personality, symbolized by the stalagmite. When at last they reach the stage of growth where they make contact, their united form is approximately that of the letter I, the Greek, Latin and English form of the letter Yod.

In writing the figure 9 in ordinary script, the first part of the character is a reproduction of the zero sign, and from the point where this circle is *closed*, a straight line, or figure 1, descends. In writing the circular part one describes a complete circuit, suggesting the completion of a course of action. Then the straight line is drawn, the figure 1, which is a symbol of *beginning*. The end of one cycle is always the beginning of the next. Attainment is never completed. After the union of personality with the *One Identity*, which is the goal of human attainment, there are still greater heights to scale.

The zodiacal sign Virgo is attributed to the letter Yod, and thus to Key 9. Virgo is ruled by Mercury, that is, by the power symbolized in Tarot as the Magician, and astrologers say that in Virgo Mercury is exalted also, that is to say, has its highest mode of expression.

Mercury represents the Life–power working at the self–conscious level through the brain. The physiological field of Mercury's brain–manifestation is the frontal lobe of that organ. Dr. Frederick Tilney, our greatest brain physiologist, calls the frontal lobe "Master of destiny". Here are the controls that determine all bodily responses. But the most important field of expression in which the controls exerted through the frontal lobe are manifested is the field that astrology assigns to Virgo.

This field is the abdominal region, and especially the upper part of the small intestine, where food is assimilated and sent to the various organs that transmute it into bone, sinew, tissue and the various secretions. At one stage of intestinal digestion, food is transformed into an oily, milky substance called chyle, from which the lacteals absorb nourishment for the bloodstream. When, under proper self–conscious direction, the finer forces always present in chyle are liberated into the bloodstream, these forces energize brain centers that function in the experience termed *illumination*. This experience is that of conscious union with the *One Identity*.

Pursue this thought as far as you can beyond this brief explanation. Consider the fact that in all legends of World–Saviors, the Great One is always born of a Virgin. Consider also that Jesus is said to have been born in Bethlehem, which means "The House of Bread", and that when the shepherds came to adore Him, they found the babe lying in a *manger*. The liberating power is born, or released, in the dark cave of the House of Bread.

Among the highest expressions of human self–consciousness are those that control the activities of the intestinal tract. This may seem strange, but it is perfectly true. We control the activities of the assimilative portion of the intestinal tract by carefully choosing what we eat, and by utilizing the law of suggestion to bring about the release of the subtle forces in chyle.

This last seldom happens unless one knows of the possibility, understands to some degree how such release of subtle force will bring about illumination, and definitely takes himself in hand for the sake of accomplishing the Great Work. It has been said that God chooses the weak things of the world to confound the wise, and certainly the fact that illumination depends upon the release into the bloodstream of a subtle force that is generated in the intestinal tract is not one likely to arouse any feelings of pseudo–aestheticism. But there it is, a stubborn fact, and there is real beauty in it for those with eyes to see. For is not anything that contributes to illumination something that makes for the perception of true beauty?

Ponder the ideas of this lesson during the coming week. Try to see in how many ways you can penetrate the veil of appearances, and see with the mind's eye that your personal activities are really responses to the impact of the Universal Will. See, if you can, how little by little, in the dark cave of the House of Bread, the Life–power is weaving the vesture of that finer vehicle through which you will eventually become consciously aware of your union with the *One Identity*. *Think* of these things daily, as you color Key 9.

COLORING INSTRUCTIONS

Yellow: Lantern rays between black lines.

Blue: Cap.

Brown: Staff, shoe.

Gray: Robe (not right sleeve of under–garment), foreground (not peaks).

White: Hair, beard, right sleeve, mountain peaks.

Gold: Star in lantern.

126

Indigo or Black: Background. Indigo is deep   blue, violet, and black. The scene is a night sky, so indigo is preferable to black, but far more difficult to apply. Do not attempt it unless you are an artist.

THE HERMIT
(Cont.)

9 is said to be the number of adeptship and prophecy. It is easy to see how the Hermit represents adeptship, for he stands on a mountain peak. His staff is in his left hand, which indicates that he does not need it for climbing. It is evident that he has reached the top, that he is supreme, and that he stands at the summit of the path of occult attainment.

It is not so obvious that he represents prophecy, though his white beard and venerable aspect suggest the traditional conception of what a prophet ought to look like. Yet the idea of prophecy is really suggested by this picture. In the first place, a prophet is not merely a person who makes predictions. If he is a true prophet his vision of the future is correctly founded on accurate knowledge, just as an astronomer can predict an eclipse hundreds of years ahead of its actual occurrence, because he knows the principles governing the movement of the heavenly bodies. A true prophet is one who understands and proclaims the laws of life. He knows the principles on which the self–expression of the Life–power is based. He has, so to say, been over the road, and this makes him competent to guide others.

The Hermit stands looking down over the path he has ascended. Others are climbing that path, and he watches their upward progress. He knows every step of the way. He knows what difficulties the climbers will encounter.

This is something we need to keep remembering. For the Hermit is a symbol of the I AM that is above every human personality. Thus Tarot intimates to us by means of this picture that we are in continual contact with a Reality that already knows all that we have thought, all that we have done, and knows also every step of the path before us.

127

This does not mean predestination or fate, as generally understood. No *outside force* is driving us remorselessly onward. An *indwelling Presence*, timeless because eternal, knows already every experience we must go through in terms of time and space for the fulfillment of its purpose. It guides us lovingly and sympathetically, and sends the light of its omniscience into our personal consciousness, to give us courage to continue the journey.

The Hermit is "He who stands *alone*". The title shows this, being derived from a root meaning *solitary*. Thus the name of this Key connects with the Hebrew noun *Jechidah*, (יחידה), I Ch I D H, meaning "the single, the indivisible", which in Hebrew philosophy is the term applied to the *One Identity*, just as *Atman* designates the same reality in Sanskrit. Jechidah is said to be seated in the first and highest aspect of the universal Reality, called Kether, the Crown, and corresponding to the number 1. The Crown is the Primal Will to which, as you learned in the preceding lesson, the upper point of the letter Yod is assigned.

The letter Yod is otherwise associated with Will, for the mode of consciousness attributed to this letter is called "Intelligence of Will".

In Hebrew "the Will" is *ha–ratsone*, (הרצון), H R Tz V N. This word has the value 351, the sum of the numbers from 0 to and including 26; and as 26 is the number of the name *Jehovah*, (יהוה), I H V H, the number 351, as the "theosophical extension" of 26, is a numeral symbol of the full manifestation of that which was, is, and will be, or Jehovah. Thus "the Will" is held to be a term that sums up all past, present and future manifestation of the Life–power.

The Hermit, therefore, is the representation of the Ancient of Days, or the *One Identity*, as the Will power in the universe. To that power all forms of its self–expression respond. It is the energy involved in all their activity. It has no support other than itself. Thus one book of Hebrew Wisdom says that the letter Yod is "above all (symbolizing the Father) and with Him is none other associated."

He who stands alone symbolizes adeptship also, because an adept, consciously identifying himself with all that is, by this very attitude sets himself apart from the rest of humanity, because he cannot share his knowledge with those who do not comprehend it. He will be always a hermit, by reason of his superior knowledge. His is not by any means the prideful separativeness of the egotist. There was no tinge of egotism in Einstein's remark that not twelve men in all the world could perfectly understand his theory of relativity. Superiority and loneliness are inseparable. Yet the loneliness of a sage is not as the lonesomeness of the unenlightened, because a sage has what the unenlightened do not enjoy – constant companionship with the Supreme Self, constant sense of union with the One Reality that is the sage's own *Identity*.

The scene in Key 9 is in direct antithesis to that of the Key preceding it. In Key 8 we see a fertile valley warmed by the sun. Here is an icy, wind–swept peak, wrapped in darkness.

This does not mean that they who experience the demonstration of the Primordial Glory receive for their pains naught but a sterile, icy perception of abstract truth. The Hermit himself is warmly clad, and *carries his own light*. The cold and darkness are but symbols of the latency of the fiery activity of the One Force, and thus are in direct antithesis to the lion of Key 8. The heights of spiritual consciousness *seem* cold and dark to those who have not scaled them; but they who stand upon these cold and lofty peaks endure no discomfort.

The ice at the Hermit's feet is the source of the river in the Empress' garden, the same river that flows behind the Emperor and the Chariot. Hence this ice is to be identified as the substance of the High Priestess' robe. That robe, as was said in Lesson Eight, symbolizes the *root matter* that underlies all form. In Key 9 the vibratory motion of the *root matter* is represented as being arrested and crystallized, that is, as ice, because the symbolism of Key 9 refers to THAT which does not, itself, enter into action, though it is the source of all activity in the universe.

The central figure of this picture is a bearded ancient. He is the "Most Holy Ancient One", identified in Qabalah with the Primal Will. He is clad in gray, a mixture of black and white, the colors of the High Priestess' pillars, of the wand and rose of the Fool, and of the sphinxes that draw the Chariot. Thus the Hermit represents the union and equilibration of all pairs of opposites.

His cap is shaped like a letter Yod. It is blue, the color of the High Priestess' robe, as if to intimate that the *One Identity* always perfectly recollects its own nature and powers. The cap, moreover, is a sort of crown, so that this bit of symbolism says to the initiated observer: *The Crown is Yod*. No comment is necessary, for those who are ready to receive the instruction compressed into these four words will perceive the tremendous import of the statement while those who are not yet prepared to understand it would find no additional light in our explanation.

The Hermit has brought his lantern and staff with him from the valley below, whence he came. The staff, a branch of a tree, is a product of the organic side of nature. It refers to the fiery activity of the Serpent Power of Key 8, which he has used to help him on his journey, and in several versions of Tarot the staff is drawn to look like a serpent. In other versions, but not the older ones, a serpent is shown on the ground in front of the Hermit;

129

but this is an unnecessary addition, as the staff itself is sufficient indication of the Serpent Power. The Hermit holds the staff in his left hand, to show that he no longer needs it for climbing.

The staff grew, but the lantern was made. It is of glass and metal, derived from the inorganic side of nature. The basic principles on which our understanding of cosmic law is founded are discoverable in the physical, chemical and electrical laws of the mineral kingdom, and our chief source of illumination (the lantern) is man's adaptation of those laws. We rely, however, on the Life–power's self–expression through organic beings to assist us in our efforts to rise above the limitations of self–consciousness to the heights of superconsciousness.

The light in the lantern is from a six–pointed star. This star is composed of two interlaced equilateral triangles, which from time immemorial have typified the union of opposites. One great Master of the Wisdom has written a statement to the effect that he who understands this symbol of the hexagram in all its aspects is virtually an adept.

The star, because it is a symbol of the number 6, has a special Tarot reference to Key 6. It intimates that discrimination is the source of enlightenment. Astrologically it refers to Virgo, *sixth* sign of the zodiac, which is attributed to the letter Yod.

To Yod also is assigned the direction North–Below, corresponding to that line of the cube of space in which the North (Peh, Key 16) and Below (Gimel, Key 2) are united. The intimation is that what is shown in Key 9 is something at work at the *subconscious level*, in spite of all the symbolism that suggests a high level of attainment. What is meant is that our contact with the One Identity symbolized by the Hermit is an *interior* contact, made in the *darkness* of subconsciousness. The subconsciousness is the instrument of our communion with superconsciousness. Note also that in the Tarot tableau (*See Lesson Two*) the number 9 stands *between* 2 and 16, as the agency that carries the power of 2 into the field of expression represented by 16. In other words, the power expressed by the Hermit is drawn from the source typified by the High Priestess, and applied to the activity symbolized by Key 16. *Through right recollection (Key 2) we come to know the One Identity (Key 9) and that knowledge overthrows all structures of separative illusion (Key 16)*. The lightning–flash in Key 16 is a ray from the Hermit's lantern.

The line of North–Below connects the lower ends of the lines of North–East (Heh, Key 4) and North–West (Lamed, Key 11). Thus we see that Key 9 represents cosmic forces working at sub-

130

conscious levels to bring to bear upon Karma (Key 11) the order-ing and controlling power of the Constituting Intelligence (Key 4). This is in accordance with the principle of antithesis, which makes every Key of Tarot a contrast to the Key that precedes it.

In Key 8 the emphasis was on personal effort, on *conscious* control, of the animal and other subhuman forces. The stress in Key 9 falls upon the doctrine that personal action is really a re-sponse to superconscious influence. The most important trans-formations are those of which we are quite unconscious. They take place below the level of conscious awareness, in the region of the organism governed by the zodiacal sign Virgo.

Yet they are direct consequences of the conscious effort repre-sented by Key 8. Just as the record on the scroll of the High Priest-ess is derived from the attentive observations of the Magician, so is the contact that is interiorly established with the *One Identity* shown in Key 9, a consequence of the working of the power of the Magician through the agency of the woman in Key 8.

Therefore Key 9 represents not only the rulership, but also the exaltation, of the planet Mercury. This astrological doctrine, as applied to practical occultism, means that man's power to take *conscious command* of the subtle processes in the Virgo region enables him to set a pattern for subconsciousness by which there is built a finer, regenerated vehicle of personality.

The actual building process is made possible by changes in the bloodstream, and it is in the Virgo region of the human body that these changes are initiated.

But they are never begun until one understands rationally the law that makes them possible. One must know that subconscious-ness is amenable to suggestion, that it controls body functions and structure, and that patterns impressed upon it from the self–conscious level will bring about alterations in the chemistry of the bloodstream, the function of organs, and even the structure of various parts of the body. One must know that the whole body is built from materials taken into the bloodstream from chyle in the small intestine. All this knowledge is really a participation in the Constituting Intelligence symbolized by the Emperor.

It is *head* knowledge, brought into our personal field of con-sciousness by the functions of the brain, ruled by Aries. It is a sharing of the vision of reality that is always present to the all–seeing eye of Universal Mind. Thus it corresponds to the Emper-or, and to the direction North–East.

Through the bodily changes occurring in the Virgo region, this head knowledge is actually incorporated into the bodily organism. And it is brought to bear particularly upon that part of the body that, as being under the astrological rulership of Libra, corresponds to the line North–West on the cube of space, and to Key 11 in Tarot.

Libra rules the kidneys and the adrenals. In the region under the influence of this zodiacal sign are organs connected with some of the most important functions of the physical organism. This lesson is not the place to discuss these functions, which will come in for more extended examination in our works dealing with alchemy. Yet here it may be said that the alterations in blood chemistry are completed by organs under the rulership of Libra, which controls that state of chemical equilibrium in the bloodstream upon which not only ordinary health, but also the special organic state peculiar to adeptship, *absolutely depends*.

The line North–Below connects also the northern end of the line East–Below, which is assigned to the letter Cheth and Key 7, to the northern end of the line West–Below, assigned to the letter Ayin and Key 15. This relationship, like that between Zain and Samekh mentioned in Lesson Twenty, must wait explanation until we study Key 15, but you will do well to note what correspondences you can. Take as your starting–point for this investigation the symbolism on the left–hand, or Northern, side of Key 7. This indicates the sources of the power that is expressed through the agency of Key 9, and brought to bear upon what is represented by the symbols on the left–hand side of Key 15.

In conclusion, we may say that the picture of the Hermit tells us that above the merely personal level of our daily experience there is a real Presence that now IS all that we aspire to be. That Presence, however far off it may seem to be, however inadequately we may understand it, however shrouded in darkness and obscurity its real nature, is friendly and definitely helpful.

Comprehend it we may not. Touch it we can, and as often as we remember to do so. For only by an illusion are we separate from it. In truth it enters into every detail of our lives. Actively present in all we think, or say, or do is this One Identity, the Ancient of the Ancient Ones, the fundamental and sole *Will*, whence all manifestation proceeds.

132

Key 9 has direct connection with each of the Keys preceding it in the series. As the number 9, it is the end of the numerical cycle, and includes within itself each of the preceding numbers. For instance, the Hermit is connected in many ways with the Fool. He is the Fool after the latter's re–ascent to the heights, after his descent into the valley of manifestation. The Fool is Spirit in its aspect of Eternal Youth. The Hermit is the same Spirit in its aspect of all–embracing experience. Yet both are the same, for both youth and age are but appearances of the No–Thing, which is at once the youngest and the oldest reality in the universe.

This week, try to establish a logical connection between Key 9 and each Key in the series preceding it. You will find this exercise of great benefit in your Tarot work, since it is essential that you learn to recognize the relationships existing among the various Keys. Skill in doing this comes from practice. It may seem difficult at first, but you will find it becoming easier and easier if you persist. Be sure to make the attempt. Write what you discover in your occult diary.

By the way, are you keeping that diary in accordance with our directions, and making a faithful record of your work and findings?

THE WHEEL OF FORTUNE
(ROTATION)

The number 10 is a combination of 0 and 1. In Lesson Two is a statement that 10 symbolizes the eternal creativeness of the Life–power, the incessant *whirling forth* of the self–expression of the Primal Will, and the ever–turning Wheel of Manifestation. Let us consider the meaning of this.

0 is a symbol of the One Force. 1 is a symbol of the Point where-in the One Force concentrates itself. Upon this symbolism review Lessons Three, Four and Five. It is at this Point that the One Force becomes active, and this, consequently, is the *Point where motion begins*. Concerning this initial motion, Judge Troward has written the following observations:

At this initial stage, the first awakening, so to say, of Spirit into activity, its consciousness can only be that of activity *absolute*; that is, not as related to any other mode of activity, *because as yet there is none*, but only as related to an all–embracing Being; so that the *only possible* conception of activity at this stage is that of *Self–sustained* activity, not depending on any preceding mode of activity because there is none. The law of reciprocity, therefore, demands a similar self–sustained motion in the material correspondence, and mathematical considerations show that the only sort of motion that can sustain a self–supporting body in *vacuo* is a rotary motion, bringing the body itself into a spherical form.

Now this is exactly what we find at both extremes of the material world. At the big end the spheres of the planets rotating on their axes and revolving around the sun; and at the little end the spheres of the atoms consisting of particles that, modern science tells us, in like manner rotate around a common center at distances that are astronomical compared with their own mass. Thus the two ultimate units of physical manifestation, the atom and the planet, both follow the same law of self–sustained motion that we have found that, on a *priori* grounds, they ought in order to express the primary activity of Spirit. And we may note in passing that this rotary, or *absolute*, motion is a combination of the only two possible modes of *relative* motion, namely motion from a point and motion to it, that is to say centrifugal and centripetal motion; so that in rotary or absolute motion we find that both the *polarities* of motion are included, thus repeating on the purely mechanical side the primordial principle of the unity including the Duality in itself.

—*The Creative Process in the Individual.*

Study this quotation carefully. It is full of meat. Build up in your mind an image of the initial whirling motion in the vast expanse of Limitless Light. The doctrine of Rotation is one of the most important in occultism, for it is the very embodiment of the principles of growth, evolution and involution, action and reaction, and the reciprocal relationship between every pair of opposites. It contains the secret of the manifested universe, for you will note that here we are dealing with things in manifestation, and not with the incomprehensible Absolute that is motionless, changeless, attributeless. Do not confuse *absolute motion* with the Absolute, for absolute motion is so called here simply because it is Self–derived and Self–sustained, and therefore unconditioned by other modes of activity.

The Hebrew letter Kaph (כ) printed on Key 10 represents a hand in the act of grasping, or a closed fist. Close your fist and turn it with the thumb toward you. Note how the forefinger and thumb suggest a *spiral*. The activity of the One Source is not simply circular in its form. It is spiral. Thus, and only thus, is growth possible, does evolution come about. The motion returns to its starting point, it is true, but always on a higher plane than where it began. Review what was said about spiral activity in Lesson Nineteen.

The basic idea suggested by Kaph is comprehension or grasp. As stated above, we are dealing in this lesson, not with the Infinite, but with a law of the Finite, which is within our mental grasp. What we are considering now is the series of manifestations, which is finite, however immense it may be. The principle of rotation that is at work in the entire series is intelligible. We can grasp it. It can be comprehended. This law, which can be understood and applied, is best represented by a *wheel*.

To Kaph, and thus to Key 10, the planet Jupiter is attributed. Jupiter is called in astrology the *Greater Fortune*. In mythology Jupiter is ruler of all the gods, and through their agency, of the destinies of man. In relation to the idea of comprehension that is represented by the letter Kaph, this intimates that it is possible to comprehend the underlying law that governs human destiny.

Jupiter is the planet exalted in the sign Cancer, which we have already considered in our study of Key 7. Thus the wheels on which the Chariot rolls represent the Law of Rotation in that Key.

A review of Key 7 should help you to see some of the practical applications of this law in your own life. When we *comprehend* the truth that even the least of our personal activities is a particular manifestation of some greater cycle of universal activity, we shall find that every detail of our personal life–expression is adjusted harmoniously to the sweep of the currents of cosmic manifestation.

Such comprehension gives man power over every disease, every misfortune and every semblance of restriction. The power of Jupiter, the sky–father, is *man's* power. Yet this must be comprehended truly. It must be more than mere intellectual apprehension of the meaning of the words employed in saying that whatever we do is part of the cosmic flux and reflux. It must be a *realization*. This may be arrived at by implanting the seed–idea in subconsciousness by aid of the Tarot Keys, used as starting–points for meditation. Then the seed–idea grows and bears fruit in the comprehension of which we speak.

Jupiter means literally "Sky Father". Thus he is god of clouds, rain, lightning and thunder. This is close to what modern scientists say concerning the nature of physical things. All the various things constituting this are forms of the manifestation of the electrical energy pervading the atmosphere. The *circulation of that energy produces all forms*. Here, also, we have a combination of the fiery energy that is directed by self–consciousness and the water symbolism used in connection with the *root matter*. All these are included in the symbolism of Key l0.

The mode of consciousness associated with the letter Kaph is named "The Rewarding Intelligence of Those Who Seek", or, more briefly, "Intelligence of Desire". What is meant is that comprehension of the Law of Rotation is the means to the satisfaction of every desire. Note, however, that this comes to those only who really *seek*. Truth is not grasped by the lazy–minded. Persons who have no definite idea of what they want never learn the inner significance of this law.

In some respects the Law of Rotation is one of the most obvious in nature. Yet it is one of the least understood. If humanity as a whole would realize that its future – not that of its children, but its very own future – is entirely dependent on its present actions, such a realization would mean the end of wars, of strife, of selfishness, of all that tends to separate. Do all you can to perfect your grasp of this law.

Your exercise this week should be an attempt to see this law in operation. Begin by thinking of all the instances you can where cyclic or spiral activity is apparent. Then examine yourself. Think back over your past life and note the cycles through which you have passed. Watch your moods, and you will discover that they have definite cycles. Think of your present activities, and try to picture their results in the future.

COLORING INSTRUCTIONS

Yellow: Serpent, eagle's eye, lion's eyes.

Blue: Background, sphinx (not head–dress.)

Brown: Animals. Lion should be tawny, brown and yellow mixed.

Orange: Entire body of the wheel.

Gold: Sword hilt.

Steel: Sword blade.

Gray: Clouds, but they are gray and white storm–clouds.

Blonde: Man's hair, eagle's beak (upper and lower).

White: In headdress, clouds as stated above, bull's horns, eye of Hermanubis, the rising figure.

Red: Hermanubis (jackal–headed figure, except eye); eagle's tongue.

THE WHEEL OF FORTUNE
(Cont.)

This version of Key 10 is an almost exact reproduction of the true esoteric design. From it Eliphas Levi adapted the illustration in his little volume, *The Ritual of the Sanctum Regnum*, which he called "The Wheel of Ezekiel", and of which he wrote:

> The Wheel of Ezekiel is the type on which all the Pantacles of the Higher Magic are designed.
>
> When the adept is in the blessed possession of a full knowledge of the powers of the Seal of Solomon, and of the virtues of the Wheel of Ezekiel, which is indeed correspondent, in its entire symbolism, with that of Pythagoras, he has sufficient experience to design talismans and Pantacles for any magical purpose.
>
> The Wheel of Ezekiel contains the solution of the quadrature of the circle, and demonstrates the correspondence between words and figures, letters and emblems; it exhibits the tetragram of characters analogous to that of the elements and elemental forms. It is a glyph of perpetual motion. The triple ternary is shown: the central point is the first Unity; three circles are added, each with four attributions, and the dodekad is thus seen. The state of universal equilibrium is suggested by the counterpoised emblems, and the pairs of opposites. The flying Eagle balances the Man; the roaring Lion counterpoises the laborious Bull.

The number 10, in Hebrew Wisdom, is called *Malkuth*, (מלכות), M L K V Th, the Kingdom. A kingdom expresses (or did, when this symbolism was devised) the will and authority of its rulers. The Tarot Keys from 0 to 4 inclusive add up to 10, and you need give only a few minutes to the inspection of these Keys to see that they represent all that is fundamental in the meaning of the noun "Kingdom".

One of the Greek names for the number 10 was *Pantelia*, meaning "all complete", or "fully accomplished". Westcott says: "Note that ten is used as a sign of fellowship, love, peace, and union, in the Masonic third token, the union of two five points of fellowship." Ten is also the number of complete manifestation say the Qabalists. A correct comprehension or mental grasp (Kaph) of the ten aspects of the Life–power represented by the statements numbered from 1 to l0 in *The Pattern on the Trestleboard* is what is required to place the ruling power in its rightful position. That ruling power is (יהוה), I H V H, *Jehovah*, identical in significance with the *Jove* or *Jupiter* of the Romans.

The title of Key 10 refers to Jupiter, the Greater Fortune in astrology. The perfection of good fortune is brought about by the functioning of a center in the human body known to occultists as the Jupiter center. This is the nerve center named the solar plexus. It is the point in the human organism through which we may synchronize our personal activities with the universal cycles of the Life–power's self–expression.

In the symbolism of the cube of space, the letter Kaph is assigned to the direction West. This is the face of the cube nearest to the observer in diagrams like that accompanying Lesson Eighteen. Hence, because nearest to us, the western face of the cube of space is representative of *those events and circumstances that, at any given moment, are in the immediate present.*

What is surrounding us at this moment is, however, the culmination of a stream of events having their origin in the past, so that *the present situation* represents always the end of various cycles of preceding manifestation. Hence the present moment is quite properly related to the direction West, the place of sunset, representing the end of a day, or time–period.

Key l0, therefore, by its space attribution, is in contrast to Key 3, the Empress, which is attributed to the direction East, the place of sunrise or dawn. Key 10 is a symbol of the culmination of a stream of events having its origin in the activity symbolized by the Empress. And because there is a sense in which a whole series of events is *continuous with its origin*, we may say that Key l0 is another aspect of the Empress. In the Tarot tableau, also, this correspondence is shown, because Key l0 represents the agency that brings into expression the principle symbolized by Key 10.

The *connecting link* between East and West, in the cube symbolism, is a horizontal coordinate line. This is attributed to the letter Mem, second of the three Mother letters, and associated with the element of water, and with Key 12 in Tarot. That is to say, it is the *root matter* of which water is a symbol, that links *origins* represented by the direction East to the *consequences* represented by the direction West. Of this more when we come to Key 12.

In the symbolism of Key 10 the bull, eagle, lion and man are supported by clouds, which are heavy thunder–heads reminding us that Jove and Jehovah are gods of lightning and storm. The animals are those mentioned in *Ezekiel* and *Revelation*. The lion represents Yod (I), the first letter of I H V H; the eagle is the first Heh (H); the man is Vav (V); the bull is the final Heh (H). In astrology these are the four fixed signs of the zodiac: Leo (lion), Scorpio (corresponding to the eagle), Aquarius (man), and Taurus (bull). These are the 5th, 8th, 11th and 2nd signs. Their numbers in the zodiacal series add to 26, the number of I H V H, *Jehovah*. These four creatures are shown also on the arms of Freemasonry.

On Key I0 they are placed at the corners of the design to illustrate the Biblical statement: In him we live, and move and have our being. This statement was used by St. Paul in his sermon on Mars Hill at Athens, and was directly connected by him with a saying in Cleanthes' *Hymn* to *Jupiter*. The same thought is in these lines from the *Kaivalya Upanishad*:

> Within me the universe come into being;
> Within me the universe is established,
> Within me the universe passes away –
> This Brahma, without a second, I myself am It.

The solution of the quadrature of the circle is indicated by the total value of the eight letters on the wheel. Reckoned according to their Hebrew values, they add to 697, and the sum of the digits in this number is 22. From very ancient times 22 has been taken as the number representing the relation of the circumference of a circle to its diameter. The ratio is that the circumference is as 22 to a diameter of 7.

This is not exact, but is so close an approximation that it is satisfactory for most practical purposes. Furthermore, the fact that it is only an approximation has meaning. We cannot measure exactly any manifestation of the Infinite, because the Infinite itself is immeasurable, but we can make *practical approximations*. The relation between 22 as circumference and 7 as diameter is a key to many occult formulas of great value. It occurs in the Bible, in Egyptian hieroglyphics and architecture, in ancient magical medals, and in many other places. As you progress in your occult studies, it will come up again and again.

The tetragram of characters mentioned by Levi is shown in the middle circle of the wheel. At the top, under the letter T, is the sign of alchemical Mercury. At the right, beside the letter A, is the symbol of alchemical Sulphur. At the left, beside the letter O, is the barred circle, symbol of alchemical Salt. At the bottom, above the letter R, is the symbol of alchemical Dissolution, which is also the astrological symbol for the zodiacal sign Aquarius, representing Man as the dissolver of the phantasms of illusion.

Mercury, Sulphur and Salt, the three Principles of the alchemists, correspond closely to the three *Gunas*, or Qualities, of Hindu philosophy: *Sattva*, Wisdom (Mercury); *Rajas*, Passion (Sulphur); *Tamas*, Inertia, (Salt). They correspond also to the three planes of consciousness: superconsciousness (Mercury); self–consciousness (Sulphur); subconsciousness (Salt).

The symbol of dissolution, which stands also for the sign of Man, Aquarius, reveals a great truth. The Great Work (in alchemy and yoga) is an operation whereby man dissolves the various forms of appearance that surround him, extracts their essence, and assimilates it to himself.

The symbol of Spirit, the alchemical Quintessence, the *Akasha* of the Hindus, is shown in the smallest circle. It is an eight–spoked wheel, like that repeated ten times on the robe of the Fool. The center of this circle, as Levi says, represents the First Unity, whence all motion originates. The central point is the *Archetypal World* of the Qabalists, also represented by the knobs at the top of the staff and crown of the Hierophant. The smallest circle, surrounding this center, stands for the *Creative World*, or mental plane, corresponding to the upper bar on the Hierophant's staff, and also to his upper crown. The next circle, within which are the alchemical symbols, stands for the *Formative World*, represented by the middle bar of the Hierophant's staff, and by the second of his three crowns. The outer circle containing the letters, and thus suggesting the manifestation of the WORD, stands for the *Material World* or *World of Action*, represented by the lower bar of the Hierophant's staff, and by his third, or lowest, crown.

The eight segments of the smallest circle divide its circumference into arcs of 45 degrees. Since 45 is the number of the name Adam, (אדם), A D M, in Hebrew the generic name of Man, what is suggested here is that the essential spiritual being, or Quintessence, is the same Life–power that is in man. And since the number 8 is indicated by the eight radii of this circle, and we know that 8 is the number of Hermes and of Christ, this indicates that the secret of mastering circumstance is to be sought in the fact that the innermost spirit of Man is inherently and eternally the ruling power (Christos, the Anointed) in the cycles of manifestation that bring the universe into being.

This dominion is expressed in the *Formative World*, through the combination of the three alchemical Principles in the Great Work of dissolving all seeming obstacles by right knowledge, or true comprehension, which is suggested by the meaning of the letter–name, Kaph, the grasping hand. This dissolution is what makes available for human use the various energies locked up in form.

The letters in the outer circle form the words *Jehovah*, (יהוה), I H V H, in Hebrew, and *Rota*, Wheel, in Latin. The letters of *Rota* may be arranged to form a sentence in rather barbarous Latin: *Rota Taro Orat Tora Ator*. It means: The Wheel of Tarot speaks the Law of Ator (Hathor, the personification in Egyptian mythology of Mother Nature, also of Venus). Note that the law is the Law of Hathor, represented in Tarot by the Empress. The letters also remind us that the *Material World* is really the plane of the uttered Word of the Indwelling Spirit.

The serpent on the descending side of the wheel is yellow, to represent light, and its wavy form represents vibration. It is a symbol of the descent of the Serpent Power, *Fohat*, into physical manifestation. Thus it represents the involution of Light into Form.

Hermanubis, the red figure rising on the right side of the wheel, represents the evolution of form, and specifically typifies the average level of the present human organism. He has a human body, with a jackal's head, to show that humanity as a whole has not risen above the intellectual level. His ears rise above the horizontal diameter of the wheel, to show that through interior hearing (Intuition, Key 5) man is beginning to gain some knowledge of the segment of the cycle of evolution through which he is destined to rise.

The segment of the wheel between Hermanubis and the Sphinx contains the letter Yod, represented in Tarot by the Hermit. That which completes the unfoldment of man, and develops powers beyond his intellectual level of consciousness, is an organic change. To effect this change is to accomplish the Great Work, and the letter Yod is a symbol of that accomplishment. For the perfection of the Work is the identification of the personal "self", the Ego seated in the heart, with the Ancient of Days represented by Key 9.

The Sphinx represents the perfection of this identification. She

143

carries a sword, the weapon corresponding to the element of air, to the *Formative World*, and to the letter Zain, symbolized in Tarot by Key 6. Thus her sword represents conquest in the formative world, or world of subtle forces of the Life–Breath, and that conquest is effected by right discrimination.

The Sphinx combines the two principal elements in the symbolism of Key 8. She has a woman's head and breasts, combined with the body of a male lion. She is the union of male and female powers, the perfect blending of forces that, at lower levels of perception, seem to be opposed.

A brief summary of the meaning of this Key is: *All cycles of natural manifestation are cycles in the orderly expression of One Power that is identical with the innermost life of man.*

LESSON TWENTY–FIVE

JUSTICE
(ACTION–EQUILIBRIUM)

Equilibrium is the basis of the Great Work," says an ancient occult maxim. This is the doctrine behind all the meanings of Key 11 in Tarot.

Consider the number itself. Its digits equal each other, so that it is, in itself, a glyph of balance, of equilibrium. Thus the number typifies equality, balance, poise, and so on. The number 11 is also somewhat similar to the zodiacal sign Gemini ♊ and the Roman numeral II. For the idea of equilibration implies that of duality. Balance is the result of equalizing two opposing activities or forces.

The Law of Equilibration, then, is rooted in the Law of Polarity. Its application consists in the alternated use of contrary forces. Thus Eliphas Levi says:

> Equilibrium is the result of two forces, but if these were absolutely and permanently equal, equilibrium would be immobility, and consequently the negation of life. Movement is the result of alternated preponderance — warmth after cold, mildness after severity, affection after anger — this is the secret of perpetual motion and the prolongation of power. To operate always on the same side and in the same manner is to overload one side of a balance, and the complete destruction of equilibrium will soon result. Everlasting caressing quickly engenders disgust and antipathy, in the same way that constant coldness or severity alienates and discourages affection in the end.

The *Kybalion* states the same law thus: "To destroy an undesirable rate of vibration, put in operation the Principle of Polarity and concentrate upon the opposite pole to that which you desire to suppress." The same book gives this excellent summary of the Principle of Polarity:

> Everything is dual; everything has poles; everything has its pair of opposites; like and unlike are the same; opposites are identical in nature, but different in degrees; extremes meet; all truths are but half–truths; all paradoxes may be reconciled.

146

Give a great deal of thought to these quotations. They set forth basic principles. They will do much to give you clear insight into the meaning of Key 11.

The Hebrew letter printed on this Key is Lamed (ל). It means "ox–goad". Thus it suggests the idea of control. He who understands and applies the Law of Equilibrium may gain perfect control over the forces of his world.

An ox–goad urges or incites an ox into action, and keeps him on the road chosen by the driver. In the Hebrew alphabet the ox is Aleph, corresponding to the Fool, and though it is not really true that we incite the superconscious Life–power to enter into action, nor true that we may in any way control or determine its perfectly free and spontaneous activity, we *seem*, nevertheless, to do both these things.

What really occurs is that the Life–power directs itself through the functions of personal consciousness that are represented by the letter Lamed and Key 11. So far as we are concerned, the functions *appear* to originate within us. Those who have not had instruction naturally suppose these activities to be something peculiar to themselves. For all practical purposes, furthermore, those who know the truth of the matter act just as if they were directing the Life–power. They know better, but they act "as if", just as a man who knows that the sun does not revolve round the earth may reckon the hour by the sun's apparent position in the sky.

The shape of the letter Lamed is that of a serpent. Thus it represents the same force we discussed in our study of Teth and Key 8. Teth represents a coiled serpent. Lamed is the same snake, uncoiled and active.

The zodiacal sign Libra is attributed to Lamed. Libra means "scales", hence the correspondence between this sign and Key 11 is obvious. Physiologically Libra rules the kidneys, whose function it is to maintain the chemical equilibrium of the blood. Note that the kidneys are organs whose functions are both eliminative and balancing, so far as those functions affect blood–chemistry. The ruler of Libra is Venus, and Saturn is exalted in this sign.

You will remember that Venus, Key 3, is connected with creative imagination. All occult practice calls imagination into action. The books on yoga are full of exercises in the use of mental imagery. The books of alchemists and magicians abound in similar instruction. Modern metaphysical teachers make extended application of the same principle. The school of analytical psychology headed by Carl Jung employs mental imagery in the treatment of neuroses. And creative imagination is, of course, the basis of all our practical work with Tarot.

Imagination builds faith. True imagination — not mere fantasy — rests on the firm foundation of science. The *Arabian Nights* give us a fanciful notion of flying in the tale of the Magic Carpet; but from Leonardo da Vinci to the designer of the China Clipper, true creative imagination has justified man's faith in his power to fly. With every advance in exact knowledge, in exact weighing and measuring, creative imagination grows clearer and sees farther. Leonardo had his faith, though he never flew. So he collected facts and classified them, and made valuable contributions to the science of aviation. The Arabian storyteller contented himself with flights of fancy. He rendered no service to the cause of the conquest of air, because he had no real faith in the possibility of human mastery of that element.

Faith is a prime requisite for the accomplishment of the Great Work. Without faith you can do nothing. You must have confidence in the principles by which you operate. You must have faith in yourself. Hence all occult schools make their pupils familiar with the lives and achievements of adepts who have completed the Great Work. Study the lives of Jesus and Buddha. In what they said and did, the principles of the Great Work are explained and exemplified.

Saturn, the planet exalted in Libra, represents the power of limitation, which makes possible the manifestation of specific forms. This power of limitation is the active power at work in Karma, which expresses itself to us as undeviating justice. Hence the Saturn power has its highest manifestation in the Great Work that enables us to control Karma.

Man can make full and complete conquest of his future. He can make whatever Karma he chooses. Some persons are so afraid of "making bad Karma" that they do nothing at all to improve the conditions in which they live. Others are afraid of interfering with Karma. Don't worry about that. It can't be done.

You can generate fresh Karma, but you cannot change immutable law, nor interfere with it. You must reap what you sow, but you can select your seeds, and so determine the nature of tomorrow's harvest. As for today's tares among the wheat, use your discrimination. You can put even bad Karma to good use if you are ingenious.

There is also the type of person who "invites his Karma", and immediately thereafter begins to have all sorts of unpleasant experiences, which he usually "bears" with a proper facial expression of uncomplaining martyrdom! What has really happened is that he has had the silly notion that Karma is identical with sorrow and disaster. Thus he has more or less definitely imagined evil forms of experience, and subconsciousness faithfully reproduces his imaginations in the materials constituting his environment. These self–deluded martyrs have not called down their

Karma from a Pandora's Box of afflictions in the custody of the Lords of Karma. They have simply indulged their imaginations in making patterns of evil, and they get just what they have made.

There is no escape from Karma, because in all the universe there is no such thing as inaction, and the literal meaning of Karma is *action*. The same meaning is behind the Hebrew noun translated *Work*. This is attributed to the letter Lamed. The fruit of what we call "inaction" is loss of faculty and function, because that which is not used atrophies; but this very loss of power is action in the wrong direction. Thus Madame Blavatsky wrote: "Inaction in a deed of mercy is action in a deadly sin."

The truth of the whole matter is found in the admonition "Whatsoever your hand finds to do, do it with your might." This does not mean that you should exert as much force in picking up a pin as you would use to lift a crowbar. "With your might" means that you must apply your *whole* power to whatever you do, whether the expenditure of energy is great or small. This takes concentration, and concentration is basically limitation, the power of Saturn, for concentration eliminates every distraction that will take force away from the work you have in hand.

In connection with this lesson, read, if you can procure it, Walter Pitkin's *More Power to You*, published by Simon & Schuster in New York City. Pitkin is not an occultist. He would probably scoff at Tarot. But he is a careful scientist, and has given some valuable hints in this little book on the right use of human energy. Own a copy if you can afford it.

COLORING INSTRUCTIONS

Yellow: Between curtains in background.

Green: Surrounding square on crown, cape over shoulders.

Blue: Sleeves (same shade as canopy on chariot in Key 7).

Indigo: The letter T on chest.

149

Violet: Curtains (not ropes, tassels or fringe), oval round neck, veil connecting pillars of throne (a light violet for this veil).

Gray: Throne and dais.

Gold: Balances, sword hilt, rings holding ropes on curtains, outline and peaks of crown.

Steel: Sword blade.

White: Shoe, square on crown, panels beside T on chest inside violet oval.

Blonde: Hair.

Red: Circle in square on crown, garment (not cape or sleeves), ropes, tassels and fringes on curtains.

LESSON TWENTY–SIX

JUSTICE
(Cont.)

The background of Key 11 is the same yellow that is shown on Keys 1 and 8. The Law of Equilibrium is brought to bear through the directive activity of self–consciousness and by means of the Serpent Power symbolized by Key 8.

The two curtains suggest duality and polarity, and their symmetrical arrangement typifies balance. Their folds are reminiscent of the drapery of the High Priestess, and suggest vibration. Their color, violet, is complementary to the yellow background. It is also the color associated with the letter Kaph and Key 10. This means that the mechanical aspect of universal manifestation symbolized by the Wheel of Fortune veils the living, conscious *Identity* behind.

The throne repeats the symbolism of the pillars of the High Priestess, and the veil between them. Here the pillars are part of the throne, and are surmounted by pomegranates, instead of lotus buds, to show that the activity represented by Key 11 has arrived at the stage of fruition.

The crown is surmounted by a triple ornament. It has reference to the letter Shin, printed on Key 20, which is in close correspondence with Keys 2 and 11. This triple ornament represents the Serpent Power, which, in its highest manifestation, releases human consciousness from the limitations of three–dimensional interpretations of experience.

The circle and square on the front of the crown refer to the movement of Spirit within physical form. This little detail of the symbolism is also connected with Key 10, which shows a wheel or circle moving in space bounded by the four mystical animals corresponding to the four fixed signs of the zodiac and to the four elements constituting the forms of the physical plane.

The ornament on the breast of Justice combines a T–cross with an ellipse. The cross is indigo, the color associated with Saturn. This detail foreshadows the mathematical elements combined in the composition of Key 21, and is also a reference to the exaltation of Saturn in Libra, the sign corresponding to Lamed and Key 11.

The pointed blade of the sword has the same basic meaning as the ox–goad. The blade is of steel, the metal ruled by Mars, in reference to the fact that whenever the Venus force dominant in Libra comes into manifestation, the Mars force is active also, because these two are complementary and the operation of the one invariably excites that of the other.

The hilt of the sword is in the form of a T–cross. Thus the up-lifted hilt of the sword is another reference to the exaltation of Saturn in Libra. The handle is golden, relating it to the Sun, whose metal is gold. Here is a hint of a profound alchemical se-cret having to do with the transmutation of lead into gold; but there is also a simpler meaning. Saturn represents limitation and form. The Sun stands for light and radiation. When the power of limitation is used positively, it is combined with the radiant energy of the Sun. Thus enlightenment exalts form.

In the alphabet, Zain is the letter corresponding to the sword. A sword cuts off. Thus it symbolizes the eliminative processes, physical and mental. Here is another correspondence to Libra, which governs the kidneys, which maintain chemical equilibrium in the body by eliminating waste. Psychologically, the practical meaning of the sword is: "Use right discrimination to rid your-self of everything useless, to free yourself from attachment, from prejudice, and from resentment and regret."

The scales represent weighing and measuring, or the exercise of powers of consciousness related to mathematics. The pans of the scales are semicircular; hence each semicircle stands for the number 11, since 22 is the number representing a complete circle. Thus the pans of the balance represent the equilibration of the 11 pairs of complementary activities represented by the 22 letters of the Hebrew alphabet and the 22 Tarot Keys. The pans of the balance are golden, to show that all these pairs of activities are modes of the single force, radiant energy, physically manifested as solar force.

The length of the cross–bar of the scales is the same as that of each of the lines supporting the pans. Thus seven equal straight lines are shown. They refer to the seven aspects of the Life–pow-er represented by Keys 1, 2, 3, l0, 16, 19 and 21 — the Keys cor-responding to Mercury, the Moon, Venus, Jupiter, Mars, the Sun and Saturn. These seven heavenly bodies correspond also to the seven alchemical metals, and to the seven centers in the human organism, which bear the same names. Again, the seven Keys just mentioned correspond, through their respective Hebrew letters, to the six sides and interior center of the cube of space. (See the diagram accompanying Lesson Eighteen.)

The seven equal lines of the balance also refer to the relationship of Key 11 to the sign Libra, which is the seventh sign of the zodiac. This is the same sort of hint as is given in Key 9, where the six–pointed star in the Hermit's lantern is, among other things, a reminder that Virgo is the sixth sign of the zodiac.

The seven equal lines also remind us of the seven–sided figure, or heptagon, which appears so often in alchemical diagrams, and is implied in the description of the seven–sided Vault, given in the Rosicrucian *Fama Fraternitatis*. Note also that the arrangement of these lines shows the symbolism of a square combined with two triangles. The number of the square is 4, and the two triangles are twice 3, or 6. Hence the seven straight lines give a hint of the number l0 by their arrangement, as well as a direct presentation of 7 by their actual number, the result of adding the digits of 28, the sum of the numbers from 0 to 10. What is weighed and measured by the scales of Justice is the activity of the cosmic energy, which expresses itself in the cyclic motion represented by Key 10.

The direction assigned to Lamed and Key 11 is North–West. This is the line of the cube of space connecting West, the face assigned to Kaph and Key l0, and North, the face assigned to Peh and Key 16. The latter face is related to Mars, while the Western face is in correspondence with Jupiter.

Now look at Key 11. On its left–hand, or North side, you see the uplifted sword of Mars, and on the right–hand, or West side, is the pair of balances, whose two semicircular pans, if fitted together, would make a wheel. Thus it is evident that the arrangement of the symbolism on Key 11 is related to the two faces of the cube of space with which the Key is connected.

The line North–West also connects the West end of the line North–Above (assigned to Key 8 and Teth) to the West end of the line North–Below (assigned to Key 9 and Yod). Since the general meaning of *West* is, as explained in Lesson Twenty–four, *the completion of a cycle of activity*, it follows that Key 11, as linking the West ends of the lines of Keys 8 and 9, represents the culmination of the activity symbolized by those two Keys. Key 8 has to do with *conscious* and Key 9 with *subconscious* activities, which reach completion in what is represented by Key 11. In other words, *the modification of Karma, by right discrimination and right judgment applied to work or action, is the outcome of the processes typified by Keys 8 and 9.*

Key 11, as related to the line North–West, also joins the North

153

ends of the lines West–Above (assigned to Samekh and Key 14 and West–Below (assigned to Ayin and Key 15); but the explanation of this must wait till we come to the interpretation of these two Keys.

The cape of Justice is green, the color attributed to Venus. Green is also the color associated with Libra in one occult scale of color correspondences.

The robe is red, complementary to green. It symbolizes the Mars force, which energizes the muscular system. This force has much to do with the function of the adrenals, ruled by Libra, because the adrenals control the tonicity of the entire muscular system. The general symbolic meaning of the robe is thus (sic).

The dais and throne are of stone, meaning that the law of equilibrium is operative throughout the physical plane. For many persons the physical plane is the only one directly sensed. Tarot means to say here that if we interpret correctly our experience of the physical plane, we shall learn all that is necessary to know in order to begin to utilize the Law of Equilibrium. "That which is above is as that which is below." We do not have to sense the higher planes in order to see the law at work. If we interpret correctly what happens to us here we shall gain the fundamental right knowledge, which will serve us everywhere.

This week consider your actions more carefully than you have ever done before. Go about your daily tasks earnestly, no matter how trivial they may seem. No one ever did great things well who had not first done well with small things. This does not mean that you should drive yourself unmercifully. That is wrong action, because it puts a strain on mind and body.

Go about your work in a poised, quiet manner. When you sit down to study, sit still. Teach your body the meaning of balance. This is not only highly necessary training for an occultist, but it is also a most potent suggestion to subconsciousness that you wish it to set to work to equilibrate your whole organism.

Fear not. Be free from anxiety. Banish the mood of haste. Whatever you try to do, remember that every personal activity really is a particular expression of the perfect Life–force. Above all, train yourself to fashion clear, definite forms for your desires, and to look upon these mental images as *present realities*. Thus counsel the Wise Ones of the Inner School.

154

LESSON TWENTY–SEVEN

THE HANGED MAN
(REVERSAL)

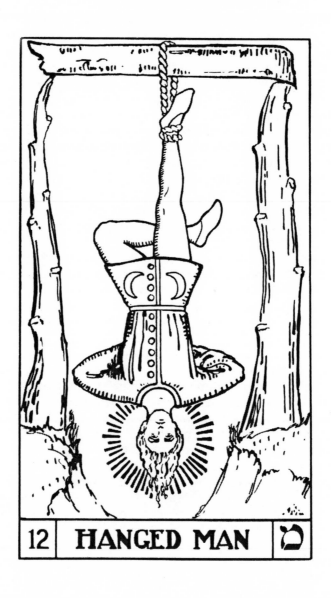

The symbolism of Key 12 is as obviously related to the Law of Reversal as is that of Key 11 to the Law of Equilibrium. The application of this law finds expression in the mental attitude of the truly wise, which is the exact reverse of popular opinion. That on which the wise set high value is accounted as nothing in the estimation of the average man. This is one reason that the first picture in the Tarot series is named *The Fool*.

The whole series of Tarot Keys is intended to effect a reversal of the superficial, deluded interpretation of the universe, which holds the ordinary human being in bondage. Hence Key 12 is a symbol of the state of absolute freedom, as experienced by the wise, but this state is indicated by a combination of symbols that looks like a picture of bondage and suffering.

The Hebrew letter Mem (מ), printed on this Key, means *waters* or *seas*, and the letter–name is the generic Hebrew noun corresponding to our word *water*. It refers also to the metaphysical substance, which is called water in the various texts of occultism.

Water symbolizes the Law of Reversal because it reflects everything upside down. More than this, no one but the person who has experienced the reversal of consciousness pictured in Key 12 can understand what is really meant in occultism by the word "water". Others may approach the truth intellectually, but only they who have actually experienced reversal can fully comprehend the Water of the Wise, as alchemists call it.

In connection with the symbolism of the High Priestess you learned to identify water with subconsciousness. You learned also that subconsciousness is actually the substance of every form in the universe — that it is the One Thing from which all things are made. Consequently it will be easy to recognize the letter Mem as signifying the *Mother Deep*, or *Root of Nature*. This is further carried out by the fact that this letter is one of the three *mother* letters of the Hebrew alphabet, the other two being Aleph and Shin. These three letters represent three aspects of the Absolute, or the ALL.

The universal subconsciousness is also your personal subconsciousness. Its creative powers are those which you govern by means of suggestion, as explained in *Seven Steps in Practical Occultism*.

One thing, which makes all forms of mental and occult practice seem difficult, is the supposition that what we have to do demands an exertion of some intangible mental power against the inertia of a very tangible physical reality. This "matter" surround-

156

ing us seems to be so dense, so resistant, so hard to move, that most persons think it preposterous to believe that mere *thinking* can have any power over it.

A wise man is not taken in by this surface appearance. He sees himself surrounded by things that have neither the solidity nor the inertia his unaided senses report. He understands that the densest forms of physical substance, as well as the lightest gases, are really *forms of energy*, built up from infinitesimal, widely separated drops of the fluidic "water" of the occultists. Thus, when he begins to attack the practical problem of changing conditions by changing his thinking, he does not face the difficulty that besets everyone who believes what his senses report concerning the things in his environment. A practical occultist knows that there is no difference between the energy that takes form as thought and that which takes form as a diamond, a piece of metal, or any other physical object. He knows, moreover, that thought–forms are centers of more intense and lasting activity than any physical thing.

Thus the occult teaching about water as substance that, in many respects, is precisely the same as the modern scientific conception of the electrical constitution of matter, enables an aspirant to effect a *reversal* in his mental attitude toward the conditions of his environment. By means of this reversal he is enabled to free his mind from that subjection to appearances that prevents most persons from using mental imagery to change conditions for the better.

The number 12 is almost inexhaustible in its meanings. In this respect it is like the number 7, and it is also related to that number. 12 is the product of 3 and 4, and 7 is their sum. You are already familiar with 12 and 7 as representing the number of signs of the zodiac and the number of heavenly bodies known to ancient astronomy. 12 is associated with the idea of completeness, because there are twelve months in the year and twelve signs in the zodiac.

Since 12 is composed of the digits 1 and 2, and we read digits in a composite number from right to left, 12 expresses the idea of the manifestation of 2 through the agency of 1. In Tarot, the High Priestess is 2, and 1 is the Magician, so that this reading of 12 suggests the outpouring of the powers of subconsciousness through the fixation of the self–conscious power of attention.

This is precisely what the Hanged Man typifies. When concentration is prolonged, the effect produced is what Hindus term *Samadhi*, or the direct experience of superconsciousness. It is the perfect union of personal consciousness with the universal, attained by practices that quiet the mind and suspend the formation of chains of associated ideas.

The title of Key 12, *The Hanged Man*, refers to the result of such practices. Without changing its meaning we might call it *The Suspended Man*. The Sanskrit root of our noun "man" is *manas*, meaning mind as the thinking principle. Hence this title suggests to the initiated the idea of the suspension of personal mental activity. This suspension is achieved by concentration. It is then that those marvelous powers of subconsciousness are released that manifest themselves in the mighty works of an adept.

As a result of even momentary experience of the superconscious state, one's whole attitude toward life becomes the reverse of that of the average human being. He who has had this experience knows himself to be merely a vehicle, or instrument, of the cosmic Life–Breath. Gone forever is the delusion that personality is, or can be, separate from the sum–total of cosmic activity.

The words of Jesus: "Of myself I can do nothing," express the mental state reached by all who have this experience. Yet this is not in the least degree a confession of weakness. It is simply the recognition that there is not the least personal activity that is not an expression of universal forces and laws. Instead of lessening the importance or value of personality, this consciousness tremendously enhances one's estimate of the worth of the personal vehicle, by showing that personality, though it can do nothing of itself, is the indispensable agency whereby the powers of the One Life find expression in the conditions of relative existence.

The planet Neptune is the astrological correspondence to Key 12. Though this planet was not discovered by exoteric astronomers until long after these Keys were invented, it was known to occultists, so that we find a place for it in the Tarot series. One has only to know that astrologers call Neptune the planet of *inversion* to understand that it must be related to Key 12.

Neptune is said to rule inspiration, psychometry and mediumship. It is also connected with the gases and drugs that produce unconsciousness. It is an established fact that some of these drugs and gases effect chemical changes in the blood, which make possible an imperfect perception of higher forms of consciousness.

Be on your guard here. You may have read of the many cases on record in which a narcotic drug or gas has opened temporarily the gateway to the higher consciousness. Never experiment with such dangerous things. No intelligent occultist ever uses drugs for this purpose. Though such chemical substances, when introduced into the blood, do stimulate the action of brain centers through which the higher consciousness is experienced, the active principle in them that produces this result cannot be separated by any process known to modern chemistry from certain other substances that are terribly destructive to the delicate tissues of nerves and brain.

Yet the fact that narcotic drugs do enable one to experience a measure of superconsciousness points to an important conclusion. He who experiences the Divine Consciousness does so because of a chemical change in the composition of his blood. This change, however, must be effected from within the bodily organism, and not by outside agencies.

Since the bodily processes are completely under the control of subconsciousness, it follows that the alteration of bodily states is also effected by subconsciousness. The necessary chemical changes in your organism are being brought about by the work you are doing in connection with this instruction. When you look at these Tarot Keys, and carry out the other directions given in these pages, you give subconsciousness certain definite patterns on which to work. Subconscious response to these patterns brings about the required modifications of your body chemistry in a perfectly normal and safe way. Ultimately you will, as a result of these changes of chemistry and nerve structure, experience the kind of consciousness represented by Key 12.

COLORING INSTRUCTIONS

Yellow: Slippers; halo round head.

Blue: Coat (not crescents, buttons, belt or stripe down front and round neck), same as canopy on Key 7.

Green: Grass.

Brown: Scaffold, hill slopes at base of trees.

Gray: Background.

Silver: Crescents, belt, buttons and front stripe.

White: Hair of man, and rope by which he is suspended.

159

Red: Hose.

In many respects this is one of the most important Keys of Tarot. As you color it this week, and during your regular periods of study, be sure to make note of any impressions you may receive.

Do not forget that many highly advanced human beings are at all times using Tarot as the focus for their meditations. Because they are illuminated men and women, they are like high–powered broadcasting stations. As you work attentively and receptively with Tarot, you are likely to pick up some of the ideas sent forth by these illuminated members of the Inner School. You will soon learn to distinguish these thoughts from the ideas developed through the deductive process in your own field of subconsciousness. You may even get a very distinct impression as to the personal source from which these flashes of illumination come to you. Always have pencil and paper at hand as you work with the Tarot Keys. Then you will be ready to make a record
of anything you may get in this way.

THE HANGED MAN
(Cont.)

The gallows from which the Hanged Man is suspended is shaped like a Hebrew letter Tav (ת). Each upright line of the letter is a tree–trunk, having six lopped branches. They correspond to the twelve signs of the zodiac, and thus they typify the twelve astrological types of personality. The intimation is plain. In the state of mental reversal symbolized by Key 12, personal peculiarities are reduced to a minimum (the branches are lopped) and the emphasis falls on the inner Self, the true spiritual Reality.

The correspondence of the gallows to the letter Tav takes us ahead in the Tarot series to the last Key, bearing the number 21, for that Key represents the esoteric significance of Tav. In the state of Samadhi, or the suspension of *personal* consciousness, an adept in concentration becomes aware of the real nature of the universe, as depicted in the symbolism of Key 21.

To reverse one's mental attitude is to have a new world–view, which sees the universe as a dance of life, full of joy and freedom. Furthermore, the suspension of the Hanged Man from the letter Tav intimates that in the state of consciousness represented here, one realizes the utter dependence of personality on the universal life. That universal life, moreover, is understood to be the perfectly adequate support of personality.

Here we may note also that since Key 12 is related to water, the first mirror, which reverses the images thrown upon it, even the number of the Key is a reversal of 21, to indicate that the state of Samadhi, as the *reflection* of the perfect freedom of the Self depicted as the World Dancer in Key 21, appears in Key 12 to be a state of restriction or bondage. That is to say, the appearance shown in Key 12 is the reverse of the inner reality.

In Samadhi, the personal vehicle is in a state of motionless trance. The physical body is cold, the heartbeat slow, and the respiration almost imperceptible. All the organic functions are in a state of suspension. But this is only the outward seeming. Interiorly an adept in this state experiences the bliss of union with the Central Reality of the universe, and that Central Reality is a focus of intense activity, though itself at rest. Here the limitations of language force us into the use of paradox, but what has just been said is the report of the wise who have had the experience no words can describe.

Again, the letter Tav is associated with the direction *Center*. It is said to be the Temple of Holiness, which stands in the center as the support of the six dimensions of space represented by the six faces of a cube. Thus Key 12, showing the Hanged Man supported by a letter Tav, indicates that the state of Samadhi is one of union with the supporting Center of all things.

As one of the three mother letters, Mem is attributed to one of the three co–ordinate lines defining the cube of space. This line is the one that connects the center of the Eastern face with the center of the Western face. Mem is attributed to this line because it represents the element of water, the stream of substance that flows from the mental origins represented by the direction East and Key 3 into manifestation as the system of related events constituting the mechanism of the cosmos represented by Key 10 and the direction West.

Here we touch on another occult doctrine. It is often objected that the practice of concentration leading to Samadhi is a selfish procedure. Persons who labor under the impression that nobody does anything unless his body is in more or less violent motion sneer at the motionless recluse, seated in his retreat, and accuse him of heartless escape from the responsibilities of life.

It must be confessed that a certain type of quietist mysticism is open to this objection. There are persons who seek escape from reality by mystic practices, just as there are other persons who avoid reality by rushing madly from one form of occupation to another. But the true adept is not idle, though his outer physical body may be in motionless trance. True Samadhi is union with the sustaining principle of all manifestation, and a sage in this condition is actually sharing the burden, the responsibility, and the joy of *cosmic administration*. Thus we find that to the letter Tav is attributed the Administrative Intelligence that directs and associates the motions of the planets, directing them all in their proper courses.

Furthermore, in relation to the cube of space we must consider the *final* form of the letter Mem (ם). This is the special form of the letter used always at the end of words. In the cube of space this final form of the letter is assigned to the center, along with the letter Tav.

Now, as this is the final form of the letter, its combination with

Tav at the interior center of the cube must be represented by the Hebrew noun (תם) Th M, *tome*, signifying "completeness, wholeness, fullness; soundness, welfare, prosperity; integrity of mind, uprightness, innocence." Is it not evident that all these meanings apply to the state of consciousness symbolized in Tarot by Key 12? It may be noted also, in this connection, that *concentration* means literally a state of being "one with the center", as anyone may see who will consider the derivation of the word.

The legs of the Hanged Man form an inverted figure 4, which here refers to Reason. His body and arms form with his head an inverted triangle corresponding to the number 3. The symbolism here is a correct statement of the situation depicted by the Key.

The practices, which lead to mental reversal, are based on rational grasp of certain principles of Reality, among them being the necessary real presence of the Universal Life, or God, at the center of human personality. This is a reasoned consequence of the truth that God must be present at every point in space, since He is omnipresent. No person who has not grasped this principle as the result of rational thinking will ever undertake the practices, which bring about the actual realization of the indwelling presence of the Life–power.

This realization is the fruit of subconscious response to the seed–idea that the Divine Presence must logically be thought of as central in human personality. This idea is a suggestion that subconsciousness elaborates, and in response to which are effected those subtle physiological changes that set going the functions of the higher brain centers. Through the activity of these brain centers, what begins as no more than a rational grasp of principle develops into an ecstatic experience of the Real Presence of the I AM. To the glory of this experience the great mystics of all ages have borne witness.

The 4 over the 3 also shows the subordination of imagination to reason. Most persons permit reason to be dominated by imagination. A few have discovered that reason can determine what mental images shall occupy the field of attention. These few imagine creatively and their imagery is governed by their mental vision of the place of human personality in the cosmic order.

Most persons merely rationalize their uncontrolled imaginations, which are at the mercy of race thought and suggestions engendered by external appearances. Not so the adept pictured in Key 12. His subconsciousness is always under the control of the reasoning self–consciousness. He is not the slave of moods, nor swayed by race thought. He remains unmoved when others are tossed about by tempests of passion. The Constituting Intelligence pictured in Tarot as the Emperor is the ruling principle in every detail of his life–experience. By clear mental vision he sees:

1. That there is only ONE POWER;
2. That the ONE POWER is centered everywhere;
3. That the ONE POWER is therefore the central fact behind every mask of personality;
4. That, consequently, whatever is done apparently by any person is really done by the ONE POWER, acting through that person; and since the same power is the energy that takes form in all the immensity of manifestation we call "The Universe", it must be true that whatever seems to be done by a person is actually performed by the sum–total of cosmic forces, *through* that person.

The Hanged Man's jacket is blue, the color attributed to the element of water. The lunar crescents forming the pockets of the coat represent the forces of subconsciousness, and are shown as pockets to emphasize the idea that subconsciousness is the container of the powers and stored–up experience that are the equipment of personality. The ten buttons of the jacket represent the ten aspects of the Life–power, called Sephiroth or *numerations* by Qabalists. In Hebrew Wisdom, the aspect of the Life–power associated with the letter Mem and the Hanged Man is said to be "the source of consistency in the numerations". The belt and trimming of the jacket suggest the combination of the circle and cross, with the cross uppermost, so that the symbol is that of the planet Mars. Here is a hint that what appears to be absolutely motionless suspension of activity is really a form of intense expression of force.

The radiant halo surrounding the Hanged Man's head suggests that he is an embodiment of the One Light. To carry out this suggestion, his hair is white, like the hair of the Emperor and the Hermit, hinting that he is to be identified as the Ancient of Days, even though his face is young.

Below his head the ground is hollowed out, as though by a watercourse. This is a further reference to the letter Mem. All that part of his head from the eyes to the top of the skull is actually below the surface of the soil from which the trees spring. Thus we are shown that his vision and his brain functions are active *below the surface*.

This is what differentiates an adept from most persons. He sees through the surface of things, and discerns laws hidden below the illusive appearances on which the unenlightened base their judgments and their actions.

The whole figure represents a pendulum at rest. Thus the tree–trunks are like the pillars of Key 2 and the sphinxes of Key 7. The Hanged Man is unmoved and immovable. He knows that no *person* ever thinks anything, or says anything, or does anything. He knows that the *One Identity* is the only Thinker, the only Speaker, the only Actor. He realizes his identity with that One, and sees that his personality is perfectly and wholly supported by the Central Principle of the universe, symbolized by the Tav–shaped gallows.

This week, use as an exercise the practice of checking your thoughts to see how many times the reversal of your first thought is more nearly in line with the teachings of the Ageless Wisdom. Be on your guard against rationalizations. One of the commonest forms of rationalization is that which makes some course of action seem to be reasonable when in reality it is just the opposite. An overworked example is the desire for something that reason says one can't afford. As often as not, one proceeds to rationalize himself into the firm conviction that he cannot do without the object of his desire. Thus, he places imagination above reason and deludes himself. Maintain alert watchfulness against this and other forms of rationalization.

LESSON TWENTY–NINE

DEATH
(TRANSFORMATION)

So many superstitions are connected with the number 13 as a symbol of bad luck and disaster that you will not be surprised to find it connected with the Tarot Key entitled *Death*. But, like so many things in occultism, we shall learn that 13 and *Death* have other meanings for those who know than for the masses of mankind.

Both the number and the title symbolize the Law of Transformation, which brings about change and dissolution. Minds dominated by race thought fear change, not because change is usually adverse, but because its outcome is unknown. Such persons fail to realize that without continual change life could not exist, and that even if it could, its monotony would be unbearable.

13 is the number of two Hebrew words, (אחד), A Ch D, *Achad*, meaning "unity", and (אהבה), A H B H, *Ahebah*, meaning "love". The Unity, the One Power from which all things proceed, is also the Love Power that is the cause of all attractions and affinities.

We generally think of the Love Power as chiefly concerned with reproduction. Thus to Key 13 is attributed the zodiacal sign Scorpio, which governs the reproductive organs. This sign is the natural ruler of the House of Death in any horoscope, and what is hinted at is that the same Love Power is what controls those physical changes, which include dissolution or death. The Love Power governs both the beginning and the cessation of our bodily activities.

This is important, and you will do well to ponder it. There are not two antagonistic powers, one making for life and the other for death. There is only a *single* power, which has a twofold manifestation. Grasp of this truth is the first step toward right understanding.

Man fears death because he does not know the meaning of this transformation. "Dissolution is the secret of the Great Work." The dissolution of form is imperative for growth. When forms break down, energy is released and is utilized for further development.

Stone disintegrates to form soil, and from soil the vegetable kingdom springs. Animals eat the vegetables, and incorporate their essences into a higher type of organization. Man eats both animal and vegetable forms, and builds the chemical energy of their cells into his own body and, if he learns a secret that is available for all who have ears to hear and are willing to work, man does more than this. He liberates himself from the conditions of physical existence, and by so doing becomes master of the energies that build his organism.

When he has achieved this mastery, he is able to maintain his physical body for many years beyond the ordinary span of human life. Furthermore, in the full perfection of this mastery, a man is able to disintegrate his physical body at will, and able also to reintegrate it. For such a man, death as the world knows it is at an end.

This is an amazing statement. To the average person it sounds utterly preposterous. Possibly it is expecting too much to suppose that you will accept this teaching at this stage of your progress. Whether you accept it or not, be sure you know what the teaching is, because when you have put yourself in a position to examine the evidence for the doctrine, you will undoubtedly be fully persuaded that it is no extravagant or fanciful claim. More than this, you will ascertain its truth at first hand by performing the experiments that demonstrate its accuracy.

In fact you are beginning these experiments now, with this instruction. You have been taught the importance of forming the right kind of mental images. You must visualize yourself as having a body that readily responds to the Will power you express. Your clear image of a changed organism, which will be a perfect and beautiful body, both in function and appearance, has suggestive power that subconsciousness accepts.

In response to that suggestion, subconsciousness is even now-beginning to set in motion processes that lead to the desired transformations. You do not need to tell subconsciousness *how* to do these things, for it already knows. Tell it what you want accomplished, and make your picture as clear and concrete as you can.

Thus will man triumph eventually over physical death. Actually he has already triumphed over death, because man does not die. It is impossible to present the tremendous accumulation of concrete evidence now available in proof of man's survival of the death of the physical body. Suffice it to say that this is an ascertainable fact, which any interested person may prove to his own satisfaction. Those who are prejudiced will not examine the evidence. Those who are lazy will not look for it. Yet the evidence is abundant, and thoroughly convincing. Man does not die.

Man is immortal and can never die. Though his bodies change and disintegrate a thousand times, *he* remains. You are approaching a time when you will *know* this as others know it, who have gone this way before you.

The Hebrew letter–name, *Nun* (נ), as a noun, means "fish". As a verb it signifies "to grow" or "to propagate". For centuries the fish has been a symbol of Christ, the immortal principle present in every one of us. It is only as we grow "to the measure of the fullness of the stature of Christ" that we approach anything like true comprehension of life. The first moment of superconsciousness, of true Self–realization, is mystically called the "birth of the Christ–child" in human personality.

The idea designated by the noun "fish" is closely related to that of "propagation", since fish are among the most prolific breeders. It has been estimated that the progeny of a single pair of codfish, if they arrived at maturity, would fill the Atlantic Ocean from shore to shore. This idea of propagation is fully intimated by the attribution of the sign Scorpio to the letter Nun and Key 13.

Scorpio governs the reproductive organs. Here is the strongest possible hint that the force used in reproduction has much to do with the liberating, transforming power of dissolution discussed earlier in this lesson. Do not be misled by this intimation. It has nothing to do with the pseudo–occultism that is responsible for the formation of free–love cults. We are speaking here of a *force*.

This force is ordinarily utilized in the reproduction of the species. It may be applied to much higher purposes. It may be used to change your consciousness so that you will *know* yourself to be immortal. It may be used also to control the metabolism of your body so that you can renew it continually or, if you so desire, dissolve it instantly and as quickly reconstitute it.

Be careful not to get any false notions concerning this. We are suggesting no abnormal restraint of the sex functions, nor do we recommend celibacy. Special instructions in the higher occult direction of the Scorpio force are reserved always for those who have demonstrated their fitness to receive such information and use it wisely. They will come to you when you are ready for them. The information you are receiving now aims to aid your subconsciousness in bringing you to the stage where you are competent to undertake more practical work. Purity of thought and action are essential. For the rest, the instruction you are receiving now is all you need at this time.

Scorpio is ruled by Mars, and it is the Mars force in the human organism to which we have been referring. Mars is also the ruler of Aries, represented by Key 4, the sign that governs the head and brain. Aries is called the *day house* of Mars, while Scorpio is its *night house*. When the Mars force, working in the darkness and concealment of Scorpio, is raised by occult practice so that it energizes brain centers in the region ruled by Aries, it brings one into the daylight of that clear vision of Reality symbolized by the Emperor.

According to modern astrology, Uranus is exalted in Scorpio. In Tarot, Uranus is typified by the Fool, representing superconsciousness. The highest expression of the Uranian influence in human life is that which results in first–hand knowledge of immortality. This is brought about through the activity of the Love Power.

Both death and inheritance are connected with the eighth house of the horoscope, and this house is related to the eighth sign, Scorpio. *Our most precious heritage is the power that ordinarily manifests itself in bodily death.*

The very power that, because we misunderstand it and misapply it, results in disease and death, is the power whereby we may experience perpetual health and immortality. That power is the power of life and growth to all who know and obey its law. Only to those who disobey it is it the instrument of death and destruction.

Ponder well the connection between the eighth sign of the zodiac and what is shown in this 13th Key. As you color the Key, ask for light, and listen for the messages of the Hierophant. Note particularly that 13 is the expression of 3, the Empress, through 1, the Magician. Then you will begin to understand the Love Power.

COLORING INSTRUCTIONS

Yellow: Sun; band on man's crown.

Green: Leaves and rosebush.

Blue: Stream.

Brown: Scythe handle.

Steel: Scythe blade.

White: Skeleton, rose, cuff on hand in center.

Blonde: Woman's hair.

Gold: Points on man's crown.

Red: Background.

This week, give a great deal of thought to the idea of dissolution and change. Note how much it is a part of your daily life. Learn to welcome change and overcome any fear of it. The future holds only that which you have earned, in strict conformity with your past actions and the patterns you are now making. Face it without fretting about it. The ultimate is only good.

D E A T H
(Cont.)

The skeleton of Key 13 is, on the surface, the conventional representation of the "Grim Reaper". Actually it conveys to the eye of the initiated a reminder that the bony structure of the body is the foundation of its every motion. It is because our muscles are attached to our bones that we can walk, move our hands and feet, and so on. Even the involuntary muscles have their connections with the skeleton, and could not move otherwise. Thus what is shown here is really the basis of all our bodily activities. Symbolically, therefore, it stands for that which is the indispensable basis of all function and of all growth and development.

That something is the *One Power* specialized in the reproductive functions of the body. This power is the *seed power*, and it is to this that the conventionalized picture of a seed placed in the upper left–hand corner of the design refers. Note that this little seed is composed of two ovals, that is of two zeroes.

From the smaller oval, five rays extend toward the limits of the larger one; the two ovals are united, or really one. Here is a simple hieroglyphic of the whole process of manifestation. The inner and smaller oval is the source of radiant energy, differentiated as Ether, Fire, Water, Air and Earth. (You will learn more about the inner meanings of these elements in later instruction.) This energy fills the space enclosed by the larger oval that, remember, is one with the small oval. Here we have expressed a fundamental doctrine of Ageless Wisdom, namely, that the *Inner Power* projects itself, or a seeming extension of itself, as *Space* (the large oval), and fills that space with forms of energy whose combination constitutes the body of the universe.

Write that idea in your notebook and spend some time with it. Eventually you will come to a point where you will understand that it is a concise and accurate statement of the way the universe comes into being.

Two details of this skeleton will probably arrest the attention of any artist or anatomist who sees the picture. The figure is twisted at two points, one just above the pelvis, the other at the neck. This would be obvious if the skeleton were covered with flesh, for it would then be in a position few contortionists could imitate. The meaning of this strange position is that the force here symbolized must be twisted, or reversed, in order to perform its highest function.

The skeleton walks from north to south, from the darkness of ignorance to the light of perfection. It represents the framework of all progress — the disintegration of form for the sake of release of energy.

The handle of the scythe is shaped like a letter T. Thus it has the same fundamental meaning as the gallows from which the Hanged Man is suspended, and refers to the ideas represented by Key 21. The blade of the scythe is formed like a crescent, and refers to the powers of subconsciousness, of which the moon is a symbol. Thus the blade is related to Key 2. Yet it is made of steel, a metal assigned to Mars. The influence of Mars in Scorpio is symbolized also by the red background of this Key.

The river flows toward the sun. It starts in the North and makes a bend, so that it flows eastward. The bend in the river has the same significance as the twist in the skeleton's spinal column. It intimates a change of direction in the current of energy.

The sun itself is another important detail. Ordinarily the idea of death is associated with sunset. But in this Key the sun is in the East, and is therefore rising. Here is a clear intimation that the power men see as death is really the power of life. Every dissolution of form brings about the birth of new ones.

The rising sun is particularly connected with the letter Daleth and with all the Symbolism of Key 3, the Empress. A little thought on this relationship will give you deeper insight into the meanings of Key 12, preceding the one we are now studying. In this connection, notice that the digits of 12 add to 3. The rising sun refers to the dawn of higher consciousness in the state of Samadhi typified by the Hanged Man. It is this dawn of a new order of knowing that is behind the transformation shown by Key 13.

The white rose refers to the planet Uranus, and has the same meanings as that in the hand of the Fool. Review what is written concerning it in Lesson Four. Remember also that the rose is related to the number 5, and review what is said of it in Lesson Six. The key thought is that mastery of the subtle forms of the Mars force is a work of adaptation, symbolized by the number five, and by the five–pointed star or pentagram, explained in Lesson Thirteen.

The woman's head at the left of the picture is a symbol of Understanding, for reasons that will become evident when you take up the study of the Qabalistic Tree of Life. In the Qabalah, the Sephirah named Understanding is usually called the Mother, but we are told that in the perfection of the Great Work the Queen and the Mother are made one.

The man's head represents Wisdom and also Beauty, for it is a Qabalistic symbol of that which, as Father, is termed Wisdom, and as Son, is called Beauty. Yet remember that the Father and the Son are *One*, and their unity is intimated here.

Three hands are shown. Two are active, springing up from the earth. The third is passive, resting palm downward on the surface of the ground. The active hands represent the new works that result from the transformation indicated by Key 13. The passive hand is a reference to Yod, the Great Hand, of which we become aware in the higher order of knowing.

Only one foot is shown, because this picture refers to the end of the Piscean Age, and the zodiacal sign Pisces rules the feet. That is to say, we are in the latter end of the Piscean dispensation.

These details of the three hands and one foot are in strict conformity with the esoteric Tarot, which has never been published. They agree also with the early exoteric Tarot shown in Court de Gebelin's *Monde Primitif*, and reproduced in Papus' *Tarot of the Bohemians*, and in *The Key of Destiny*, by Dr. and Mrs. Curtiss.

For good reasons, much has been left to your intuition with respect to this Key. Lessons like these are not the proper medium for practical instruction in the reversal of the currents of the Mars force. Yet we believe that enough has been said to put you on the track of principles. If you follow this lesson through, with Key 13 before you, many valuable intimations should present themselves to you in your periods of meditation.

In the language of pictorial symbolism, perfectly understood by your subconsciousness because it is the one truly universal language, Key 13 tells the secret of secrets and passes on to you our great inheritance from the wise men who have gone this way before us. It is a secret that kills out the old mistaken conceptions of the place of personality in the scheme of things. It is a secret that truly makes one free from the "last enemy", because it gives us, as we realize it, direct perception of life eternal.

174

As you progress in the path of practical occultism, this will become to you more and more an open secret. As you begin to understand it, you will understand also the reasons for the careful reserve concerning it that is characteristic of all truly wise instruction, ancient and modern. He who knows it has in his hands a power that could be used to overturn the world. Yet no person learns it until he is truly prepared, and more than anything else, this means such *ethical* preparation that no temptation to the misuse of this power could ever succeed in turning one from the path of strictly constructive application of the forces involved.

For the present, then, school yourself to know that change is never your enemy. Strive to become one of those of whom the *Bhagavad–Gita* says: "The wise in heart mourn neither those who live, nor those that die. Nor I, nor thou, nor any of these, ever was not, nor ever will not be, forever and forever afterwards. All that doth live, lives always! To man's frame, as there come infancy and youth and age, so come there raisings–up and laying down of other and of other life–abodes, which the wise know, and fear not."

TEMPERANCE
(VERIFICATION)

14   TEMPERANCE

The Hebrew letter Samekh (ם) means, as a verb, to prop, bear up, establish, uphold, sustain. As a noun it means a tent peg that makes firm the tent, or dwelling–place. Both as a verb and a noun, its meanings are closely allied to the principle of *verification* which is the keynote of this lesson.

Most of the instruction you have been given thus far consists of theory. This is an essential part of your training, because it is an occult maxim that the pupil must be grounded in theory before he can begin to practice. It is necessary for you to learn the terms, the alphabet, so to speak, in which your working instructions are written. Nevertheless, these theories must be *established* and *supported*. They must be verified before they can become part of your working equipment. They must be *tried*; their *temper* must be *tested* to the utmost. APPLICATION IS THE TOUCHSTONE BY WHICH ALL KNOWLEDGE MUST BE TESTED.

This point is precisely where the teaching you are now receiving, and will receive, differs from many systems of occult instruction. It is *practical*. You will be given very precise directions as to how to apply these theories. Already you have made a start, if you have faithfully carried out the exercises given with these lessons. They are intended to have their principal effect in shaping your attitude toward yourself and your brothers here on earth, since a realization of the nature and true unity of all mankind is an *absolute essential* for the successful practice of magic in its truest, highest forms. These exercises are intended also to accustom you to linking up the various ideas depicted by the Tarot Keys, both with one another and with your experience of life.

You must, however, see one thing clearly in this connection. The foregoing does not mean that in order to practice the magical art you need nothing more than a recipe, or set of directions that you can follow as mere routine. The magical art includes a transformation of your personality, and the raising and expansion of your consciousness, until you perceive clearly the principles and laws whereby you operate. The great trial and testing is a testing of yourself. Tarot represents *your* states of consciousness. The principles it depicts are those that govern *your* life. They emanate from the ONE IDENTITY, which is your *innermost Self*.

The letter Samekh, consequently, represents the trial, the probation, the purgation and purification of your personality, that it may, in time, become a fit channel for the expression of the One Force, a fit Temple of the Most High, a pure and holy habitation for Spirit. Only thus does the Law of Verification bring about the *establishment* or *foundation* of the House of God. As you progress with your studies and perform the practical work given to you, you are at the same time undergoing subtle tests that prove your fitness to carry on the Great Work. See to it that you take this enterprise seriously. You have announced yourself as a candidate for Truth. Truth will be revealed to you when you have proved yourself ready for it. Your first test is the earnestness with which you apply yourself to this preliminary instruction,

In its meditation on Samekh, *The Book of Tokens* says:

> Thus am I as one who testeth gold in a furnace
> And this aspect of my being
> Presenteth to the unrighteous
> A face of wrath
>
> Yet by the purgation of fire
> Do I uphold and sustain thee
> In every moment of thy life.
>
> Behold, I am he who trieth thee
> With many subtle tests.
> Wise art thou if thou knowest
> That the subtle serpent of temptation
> Is in truth the Anointed One
> Who bringeth thee to liberation.

Note that this quotation refers to wrath and to a serpent. These are both closely connected with the letter Samekh and the underlying meaning of Key 14.

In Key 8 we see the serpent coiled, symbolized by the letter Teth. In Key 11 we see, in the letter Lamed, the serpent uncoiled and active, its head erect, and its tail pointing downward and to the left. The letter Samekh shows the completion of the upward movement of the tail toward the serpent's mouth, and is therefore a reversal of the symbolism of Teth. In other words, Teth shows the serpent power as it is before it comes under control. Lamed shows it at the half–way stage of our mastery over it. Samekh shows the result of perfect control. The serpent biting its own tail has been for ages a symbol of eternity and of wisdom. It suggests circular movement by its shape. This establishes a connection between Key 14 and Key 10, to which Jupiter is attributed.

That connection is verified by the attribution to Samekh of the sign Sagittarius, ruled by Jupiter. Sagittarius means "archer," and its symbol is an arrow. It is a sign of the fiery triplicity, Leo and Aries being the other two fire signs. It is said to be ruled by Jupiter because the fiery power, which it manifests is directed and controlled in accordance with the Law of Cyclicity or Rotation pictured by Key 10.

That fiery activity is a form of intense vibration, and the Hebrew noun for "wrath" also means vibration. The serpent power is vibratory. It is the desire force, which is the energizing principle behind all that we do. It can be terribly destructive when not under control, hence fully justifying the use of the noun wrath in connection with it. Yet it is the power that leads to freedom, the force that destroys limitations and impediments to free expression. It is really the tempering, cleansing power that gets rid of all impurity and error in our personal consciousness. To the objects of its disintegrating activity it is terrible, but the wise perceive its beneficence.

The number 14 represents the principle of reason (4) expressed through the agency of concentration (1). The verification of hypotheses arrived at by the use of reason is carried out by means of concentration. Remember that concentration is the focusing of the vibratory activity of the serpent–fire at a definite point in the brain. The means whereby concentration is accomplished is typified by Key 1.

The digits of 14 add to 5, the number of the Hierophant. Thus we arrive at the conclusion that the goal of verification is reached by following carefully the instruction imparted by the "still, small voice" of intuition. 5 is also the number of adaptation and desire, and proper adaptation of the tremendous force of desire, through intelligent control, results in the attainment of the higher consciousness. This process of adaptation is involved in most of the tests you will be called upon to meet.

The clue to the inner meaning of all this lies in the word spelt (דבח), D B Ch, which has a numeral value of 14, and signifies sacrifice. Nobody ever attained to perfection without sacrifice. To be sure, he who knows the value of his objective feels no sense of loss in ridding himself of all encumbrances that interfere with his progress. In the earlier stages of the Great Work, however, one is often called upon to make decisions that appear to involve sacrifice. Experience demonstrates the falsity of such appearances, for it shows that every bit of wise elimination makes possible the expression of a greater degree of power. At first, though, some of the tests are difficult to meet.

Those who fail in them are usually the persons who are readiest to assert that there is nothing in the promises of Ageless Wisdom. Nor is there anything in these promises for the lazy, the double-minded, or the fearful. There never will be for persons who have not the courage to face periods of seeming failure. He who would seek the highest must have burning zeal. He must be in fiery rebellion against the limitations and bondage of ignorance. To carry on against apparently hopeless odds, he must be filled with intense, one-pointed desire to demonstrate by actual experience that he is really and truly what every one of these lessons has declared concerning the inmost nature of man.

Zeal, however, is not enough. Nor was any person ever liberated just because he had a flaming desire for freedom. The fiery force of the desire nature must be directed intelligently. To this the title of Key 14 refers. *Temperance*, here, is not restricted to the meaning now in common use, though it does, of course, include the thought of control over appetites and desires. It is to be understood in its ancient signification as "the act of tempering or mixing." The object of tempering is to impart strength. This object is attained in the Great Work by the proper mixture of opposite forces, that is, by applying the Law of Equilibration. This meaning is apparent on the surface of the symbolism in Key 14.

Consider that symbolism carefully as you color the Key this week. By this time, Tarot should begin to speak to you even before you have read the detailed analysis of its symbols. Remember, too, that no analysis can exhaust the meanings. What is written in these pages is intended to put you on the track of correct interpretation, but in every Key there is for you a special personal message, because in the age-long development of your personality to its present stage of growth, you have accumulated a store of experience. That treasure is below the surface of your consciousness, but through psychological laws, which have been utilized in the construction of Tarot, these Keys can evoke from subconscious depths just exactly what each student most needs to know.

So write out, this week, what you feel Key 14 means for you. Then compare your findings next week with the analysis of the symbols given in Lesson Thirty-two.

COLORING INSTRUCTIONS

Yellow: Crown over mountain peaks, Yods over eagle, torch flame (interspersed with red to show that it is fire), lion's eyes, path from mountains.

Brown: Lion (see instructions for Key 10), eagle (except beak and legs), torch handle.

Blue: Pool, and stream from vase.

Green: Grass.

Orange: Ornament on head of angel, vase.

Violet: Mountains in background. Dilute the color so that the mountains will not be a violent purple tint.

Gold: Background, star on the angel's breast. (Use yellow if not gold.)

White: Dress.

Blonde: Angel's hair; beak, legs and talons of eagle.

Red: Angel's wings. These are high–lighted with blue.

The rainbow is a succession of bands of color. Begin at the upper side of the arc with violet, and apply in succession blue, green, yellow, orange and red.

LESSON THIRTY–TWO

TEMPERANCE
(Cont.)

The central figure of Key 14 is the angel Michael, angel of the sun and archangel of the element of fire. He is also the angel of the direction South. All these attributions connect him with the sun pictured in Key 19. His name means "Like unto God."

He is neither male nor female. The pronoun "he" is used solely for convenience. Neither is he a person. In Psalm 104:4 we read, "Who makes his angels spirits; his ministers a flaming fire." Michael is a personification of the fiery Life–Breath of the One Identity.

On his brow is a solar symbol, and light radiates from his head. One foot rests on water, symbol of the cosmic mind–stuff. The other foot is on land, symbol of concrete manifestation.

This angel is a symbol of that, in every human being, to which the term Higher Self is applied. He is not the ONE IDENTITY, but the Life–Breath of that ONE IDENTITY, centered in the heart of personality. The greater number of human beings, when they use the pronoun "I," think only of the personal self, and regard it as being a separate, independent entity. Others suppose themselves to be guided or overshadowed by some divine or angelic presence that they look upon as being separate, on the one hand, from the ONE IDENTITY, and separate, on the other, from the personal ego. The true esoteric doctrine is that one's feeling of "egoity," (if we may use this term,) is due to the focusing of a ray of the fiery Life–Breath of the ONE IDENTITY within the personal organism. That fiery Life–Breath is in continual circulation between its personal center of manifestation and the ONE IDENTITY whence it originates, just as the electricity lighting a lamp is in continual circulation between the lamp and the dynamo at the power station. Hence when Ezekiel saw this with his higher vision, he said: "And the living creatures ran and returned as the appearance of a flash of lightning."

On Michael's white robe is the Great Name, יהוה, *Jehovah*, written in Hebrew characters. This definitely identifies the angel as belonging to the order called *Melakim*, "Kings," in the books of the Qabalists. Thus it also places him in relation to the Sephirah named Tiphareth, or Beauty, on the Tree of Life, This is the sixth aspect of the Lifepower, and to it the name יהוה is particularly referred.

Among the names of Tiphareth are בן, *ben*, the Son, מלך, *Melek*, the King, and אדם, *Adam*, Man. In Qabalistic psychology, Tiphareth is called the seat of the personal ego. It is the point of manifestation for our essential humanity (Adam), which is truly the Divine Son (Ben) of the ONE IDENTITY or Father, even as Jesus knew and taught out of his own firsthand experience. It is also called King, because it is made manifest in order to rule all things below the human level of the Life–power's self–expression. Thus, in answer to the question, "What is man?" the Psalmist wrote: "You made him to have dominion over the works of Your hands; You have put ALL under his feet."

To exercise this dominion, however, we must be purged of all sense of personal separateness, must be rid of all notion that we are personally independent. The I AM that we feel within us as the ego is actually the Life–Breath of the ONE IDENTITY, in continual circulation between ourselves and its source. This we must know theoretically at first, and then prove it by practical experiment. In the course of establishing that proof we come to have first–hand knowledge of that wonderful presence that the Greeks called the *Augoeides*. This experience is mentioned also in certain works on magic, and is termed "The Knowledge and Conversation of the Holy Guardian Angel."

The seven–pointed star on the angel's breast is a figure that can only be drawn by actual experiment with a pair of compasses, for the regular heptagon whence it is derived is not an equal divider of the 360 degrees of a circle, and does not occur spontaneously in nature. Thus the seven–pointed star is one of the most striking symbols of the work of man, the result of the development of skill in the use of the compasses. Freemasonry has preserved a tradition of the older esoteric schools when it tells us that the compasses are to circumscribe our desires and keep our passions within due bounds. In other words, the compasses are the Masonic symbol of the control of the fiery desire–force, which is represented by the circular form of the letter Samekh, as explained in the preceding lesson.

183

Now, Albert Pike tells us: "The compass is an instrument that has relation to spheres and spherical surfaces, and is adapted to spherical trigonometry, or that branch of mathematics that deals with the Heavens and the orbits of planetary bodies. The compass is a natural and appropriate symbol of the Heavens, and of all celestial things and celestial natures." (*Morals and Dogma*)

Can you take this hint? Skill in wielding the compasses is represented by the seven–pointed star. But that star is on the angel's breast, as if to remind us that the requisite skill in the control of the desire–nature depends on "Knowledge and Conversation of the Holy Guardian Angel." To obtain this skill, we must have the higher instruction of the angel. This results from one–pointed devotion to the work of making experimental verification of the fact that the real presence of the Higher Self may be known at the heart of our personal lives. Such single devotion brings us into harmony with the universal order, which is exhibited in the laws that are expressed by the cycles of the heavenly bodies, or celestial spheres.

The Great Work, which completes the expression of the laws of nature, is an artistic adaptation of those laws by man. Without man, that work comes never to its full fruition. "Nature unaided," says an ancient occult maxim, "always fails." Although all human activity is a series of transformations of the One Energy, it is only when that Energy is expressed through intelligently directed human speech, thought and action that fulfillment is possible. The Great Art of the occultist requires the active agency of human personality.

The wings of the angel are fiery red, with blue highlights, to indicate the fiery quality of the sign Sagittarius and its color attribution, which is blue. Remember that the symbol of Sagittarius is an arrow, suggesting aim, will, purpose, intention. Bear in mind, too, that as the natural sign of the ninth house of the horoscope, Sagittarius has to do with distant journeys (those "travels in strange countries" mentioned in Masonic rituals), and with dreams, visions, religion and philosophy. With the systematic formulation of ideals, that is, and with the quest for knowledge that is implied by the word "verification." Hence Sagittarius is connected with those high aspirations of the human heart, which lead man away from "this world" of false appearances into the country, strange, alas, to many, which is his true home.

184

The torch is a symbol of fire, and from it fall five Yods upon an eagle. The Yods refer to the five differentiations of the Life–Breath into the five subtle principles of sensation. Thus they have the same meaning as the radiating lines in the oval shown in Key 13. Furthermore, since they are Yods, they indicate a connection with Key 9 and the Hermit. The fire is the subtle fire that is generated in the Virgo region of the human organism. (See Lesson Twenty–one)

Here the flame is directed toward the head of an eagle, symbol of the sign Scorpio, because the Great Work has to do with the modification of a specific phase of the Life–Breath, which is concentrated in the nerve centers connected with Scorpio. Here is a hint of one of the most carefully protected secrets of alchemy. Its full meaning cannot and must not be put into plain words, lest the unprepared misuse the knowledge. But if you verify in your own experience the teaching of Tarot, you will be able to develop this seed–thought fully, and with your comprehension of the secret will come also full understanding of the necessity for *keeping* it as a mystery undisclosed to the profane.

The vase represents what alchemists call the "Vase of Art." In Philalethes' *Fount of Chemical Truth* we read: "When we speak of our vessel, and our fire, we mean by both expressions, our water, nor is our furnace anything diverse or distinct from our water. There is then one vessel, one furnace, one fire, and all these make up one water. The fire digests, the vessel whitens and penetrates, the furnace is the bond that comprises and encloses all, and all these three are our Mercury." This cryptic language refers to *personal consciousness*, which is threefold, to wit, spirit, the fire; Soul, the vessel, Body, the furnace. These three constitute "our Mercury," or human *self–consciousness. This is what is represented by the vase, which is held in the hand of the angel as an indication that the Great Work cannot succeed unless human personality is taken in hand by the Higher Self, or Holy Guardian Angel.*

The water pouring from the vase is a reference to the letter Mem, and to the doctrine represented by the Hanged Man. (See Lessons Twenty–seven and Twenty–eight.) When the purified water, or reversed personal consciousness, is poured out on a lion, as in Key 14, the meaning is plain. Through suspension of the false notion of personal independence, one comes to understand the true function of personality as the instrument of the Divine Will. This change in consciousness is carried into subconsciousness, as shown in Key 8, which represents, like the lion in Key 14, the zodiacal sign Leo. *A change of heart is brought about.* More than this, a definite activity is instituted at the heart center of the physical body, and this is to be understood just as it is written. Here are no blinds or figures of speech. This is the change to which another alchemist, an anonymous German philosopher, alludes when he says: "Fire and flowing water are contrary one to another; happy thou, if thou canst unite them: let it suffice thee to know this!"

The rainbow represents the differentiation of the vibratory activity of light into color, by means of water suspended in the upper air. When the water of consciousness has been mingled with the cosmic Life–Breath, then is manifest the rainbow of promise. The colors of the rainbow are the colors of the planetary centers. In the instructions for coloring given in the preceding lesson, no mention was made of indigo, the color of Saturn, because it is hard to show it clearly in painting the cards. This deep blue–violet is between the violet at the top of the rainbow and the blue you were told to place beneath the violet. Thus the rainbow represents the harmonious combination of the alchemical "metals," which are the same as the planetary centers, and the same, too, as the chakras of the Yogis. The rainbow refers also to the occult use of color, which is a powerful means for bringing power into our human field of operation. By means of color, we are able to use vibratory activity to modify external conditions. This subject will be treated more extensively in later instructions, when you will receive many exercises in its practical application. Finally, the rainbow confirms the attribution of Key 14 to the letter Samekh and to the sign Sagittarius, for the name of this sign, in Hebrew, is *Quesheth*, the Bow.

The path in Key 14 rises between the twin mountain peaks of Wisdom and Understanding, and ends beneath the Crown of the Primal Will. Note that it has its beginning in a pool, which represents what the Qabalists call Yesod, or *Foundation*, designated also by them as "The Sphere of the Moon." In this connection, remember that all representations of water in these Keys begin with the robe of the High Priestess, and bear in mind what was said in *Seven Steps in Practical Occultism* to the effect that mind–stuff at subconscious levels is the basis of all forms of embodiment.

In Lesson Thirty no mention was made of the direction assigned to the letter Nun and Key 13, because we wished to bring this into closer correspondence with Key 14.

The direction corresponding to Nun is South–West, the vertical line at the south side of the western face of the cube of space shown in Figure 1 of the diagram accompanying Lesson 18. This line is opposite the line South–East, corresponding to Taurus, just as the sign Scorpio is opposite to Taurus in the zodiac.

As the southern boundary of the western face of the cube it corresponds to the ascending side of the wheel in Key 10, and to the rising figure of Hermanubis. For one of the fundamental meanings of Key 13 has to do with the ascending scale of organic evolution, or bodily development, which is an expression of the reproductive forces under the rulership of Scorpio. Through the operation of these forces, first of all in the laws of chemical affinity, and later in the sexual activities of plants and animals, the Life–power provides itself with finer and finer vehicles of expression. At last the human organism appears, and it also goes through progressive refinements, from race to race. The continuation of the process is due to the manifestations of the reproductive function, and few of the human personalities who are the agents of this progressive development are aware of what is really at work behind the compelling urges of the *libido*.

Finally, there appear on earth those men and women, a few in every generation, who are sufficiently receptive to the impact of the Life–power's higher levels of awareness to begin to register in their brains some measure of knowledge of what is really the true significance of this universal mating urge. The earlier forms of this knowledge seem to have been comparatively imperfect, and were expressed in a phallic symbolism that seems crude and offensive to modern taste. Yet the truths discovered in those long–ago ages were not less true because all their consequences were not perceived by their first discoverers. What has been learned since does not cancel or contradict the awareness so strangely expressed by the phallic symbolism of the ancient wise men. Fundamentally, it is just as true as ever it was that man's progress to the goal of Illumination is conditioned by his understanding of the significance of his sex life.

It is by controlling the *drive* of the libido that one goes beyond the position of Hermanubis in Key 10, and rises to the point of conscious union with the Higher Self. And thus the cube symbolism shows the ascending line of South–West terminating at the end of the line of West–Above, which is assigned to the letter Samekh and Key 14.

This line of West–Above begins at the upper end of the line of North–West, which is assigned to Lamed and Key 11, and the current of energy represented by it moves from North to South. But we are informed that the current of energy on the line North–West moves from Above to Below. Consequently, although the line of West–Above joins the upper end of the line North–West to the upper end of the line South–West, *it receives no influence from the line North–West*, corresponding to the letter Lamed and Key 11. On the other hand, the current of energy in the

187

line North–Above, corresponding to the letter Teth and to Key 8, moves from East to West. At the Northwest upper corner, where the lines of Teth, Lamed and Samekh meet, the current flowing in the line North–Above is divided. Part of it flows downward, through the line North–West. Part flows southward, through the line West–Above. (Here observe that the letters Teth, Lamed and Samekh, by their serpentine form, all symbolize the serpent–fire.)

Observe, too, that as the current of energy in the line South–West moves *upward*, it does not communicate anything to the current in the line West–Above. The latter receives an impulse from the line corresponding to Teth, but none from the line corresponding to Nun. Note, also, that in the symbolism of Key 14, the lion of the sign Leo (Teth) is on one side of the angel, and the eagle of the sign Scorpio is on the other side, so that the angel, or principal symbol of the Key is between the lion and the eagle, whose relative positions are like those of the corresponding lines on the cube. Only the head of the lion and his forepaws are shown, and his body rests horizontally, with the hindquarters nearer the East than his head. But the eagle's whole body is shown, and stands in a *vertical* position. Thus the positions of the bodies of the lion and the eagle correspond to the positions of the lines on the cube to which these animals are assigned through the astrological symbolism. By such careful attention to detail does Tarot demonstrate that it must have been worked out by men who were truly great adepts, familiar with all the correlations of the mystery language of Ageless Wisdom.

These details about the cube of space are among the most important bits of occult wisdom given in this course. We realize fully that at first they may seem extremely abstract, and out of relation to any practical concern of the average student. Yet just the contrary is actually true. For this cube symbolism is not only a key to all the deeper meanings of Tarot, but also a key to practical application of the most potent forces at the disposal of man.

Another point that should be considered in connection with the line West–Above is that it is the *western boundary* of the *upper face* of the cube. That is to say, it represents an activity carried on at the level of selfconscious awareness (Above) and this activity is the goal or objective completing the work symbolized in Tarot by the Magician. Knowledge and conversation of the Holy Guardian Angel is what the Magician aims to accomplish or, to put it another way, the end toward which all the activities of human self–consciousness are directed is experimental verification of the truth that the personal life of every human being is actually under the guidance and direction of what is pictured by the angel in Key 14.

Understand, this verification does not at all bring such guidance and direction about. The most ignorant man, utterly deluded by the illusion of personal independence, is just as certainly under such guidance as the most illuminated sage. Every human being is led and aided by the Holy Guardian Angel. Only a few are *consciously aware* of this wonderful truth. To the mass of humanity the Holy Guardian Angel presents himself under the forbidding and dreadful aspect of the central figure in Key 15, which we shall begin to study in the next lesson.

This week test yourself in various ways. Test yourself with respect to your own earnestness in this work and philosophy. Ask yourself such questions as: "Does my belief actually support me in the various crises of my daily experience? If not, what does? Who does what I do, thinks what I think, feels what I feel? Is my study and work transmuting the base metal of my personality into the gold of real attainment? Are my desires becoming purer, my mental processes clearer, my intuitions better defined? If not, am I applying myself to the work as earnestly as I ought, in order to give it a real testing?"

It cannot be repeated too often that Ageless Wisdom is not a creed, not a system of beliefs, not an escape from reality into a mirage of glittering generalities. Nor is it a doctrine that puts aside until after death all verification of its fundamentals. Plainly and specifically it declares that its basic principles have been matters of human experience in other days, and are now matters of tested knowledge for many of our living contemporaries.

Just as plainly and specifically it avers that such experience is not miraculous, that it may be repeated, as to its fundamentals, by any person willing to undertake the training of body and mind that makes it possible. It warns all who approach even the beginning of the Path of Attainment that this ancient way is not for cowards, not for the lukewarm, not for triflers. To the courageous, the zealous, the persevering, it offers evidences that admit of no denial. It points out the way to attaining first–hand knowledge and shows how to follow that way.

At the same time it steadfastly refuses to communicate the higher aspects of that knowledge to those who have not made ready their bodies and minds to receive such communication. It never attempts the impossible feat of transmitting to those who are not duly and truly prepared any part of those inner mysteries that must always remain hidden by the veil of ignorance from such as are unready to partake of the feast of wisdom.

LESSON THIRTY–THREE

THE DEVIL
(BONDAGE)

The first thing to get into your consciousness in connection with Key 15 is that the condition that manifests as bondage is an illusion, a wrong construction put upon the principle of limitation, making that principle *take on the appearance of the Devil*. Be warned at the very beginning that you must look behind the gross and repellent surface of this Key in order to discover its true meaning.

Let us begin by examining the number 15. In Roman numerals this is XV. X and V are the last two letters of the word L.V.X., designating the One Force, which we concentrate by acts of attention. In other words, XV suggests L.V.X. *minus* the L. The L is Lamed, which means "to instruct" when used as a verb, and "ox–goad" when used as a noun. Thus L.V.X. minus L suggests the absence of the equilibrating and directive quality symbolized by Key 11. Thus we have an intimation from the number XV that the Key now before us represents the One Force as it operates apart from human knowledge (Lamed as a verb) and human direction (Lamed as a noun).

Yet XV is composed also of the numbers X and V. In the Tarot series, the first of these numbers is that corresponding to the Wheel of Fortune, which Key symbolizes the *mechanical* aspect of the universal manifestation of the One Force. Man's conception of the universe as a mechanism has been built up from his observation of the cycles of the seasons, and from the study of astronomical phenomena. That study is largely devoted to the realms of the Life–power's manifestation *below the human level*. In those realms the One Force seems to be a fatal force, working by blind necessity, according to the law of averages.

We see this law of averages operating in what is known as the survival of the fittest, and we find that law becoming increasingly less dominant as evolution progresses. A poet once wrote of the Life–force: "How careful of the type it seems, how careless of the single life!" In the lower forms of life, countless numbers are apparently being wiped out of existence, only the strongest and most fit surviving. Thus nature perfects her types.

But behold how different this is among men. Here the survival of the individual takes on increasing importance, because a new principle is in operation. That principle is what Tarot represents by Key 5, or V. It is the *principle of consciousness* veiled by the mechanical appearance of the universe. Key 10, or X, shows the conception of the nature of the One Force that man builds in his mind as a result of examining the outside world of his environment. Key 5, or V, represents the indwelling presence of the

Great Revealer, discoverable by man when he turns his attention to the inner world, at the center of his own being. Thus X in XV represents the objective world of appearances, through which man gains experience of the outer aspects of the manifestation of the One Force; and V in XV stands for the subjective world of consciousness whence man derives all his knowledge of the *significance* of the whirling cycles of change that surround him.

Through the working of these two aspects of the operation of the Life–power, X and V, man learns to control his environment. He is waging a successful war against sickness, poverty and death. Successful, that is, where he has developed the conscious unfoldment that enables him to act as a channel for the superior powers whereby the automatic forces of nature, below the human level, may be controlled. Slowly, but surely, man is learning how to exorcise the Devil. He is adding the L to XV, and making the V *central*, as in the word L.V.X.

There are several other points in connection with the number 15 that may help you to establish connections between this Key and others in the series. 15 adds to 6, and you need only compare Keys 15 and 6 to see that they are in contrast, but contain similar details. It is as if Key 15 were a caricature of Key 6. The number 15 is also the sum of the numbers from 0 to 5, so that, strange as it may seem, we ought to find in Key 15 a summary of the Keys just mentioned. You have learned also that the number 14 is related to the number 5, because 1 and 4 add to 5. Now, since 15 is the "theosophic extension" of 5, there ought to be a direct connection between Keys 14 and 15. There is such a connection. See how much of it you can work out for yourself, after comparing the two Keys.

The letter printed on Key 15 is Ayin (𝒱). Its primary meaning is "eye." It also signifies "a fountain" and has as a third meaning "outward show, or superficial appearance."

The All–seeing Eye has been a symbol of Deity in all parts of the world for ages past. This tells us at once that, no matter how strange to unaccustomed minds may be the symbolism of this Key, everything connected with it has something to do with certain aspects of the One Power that theologians call God. Add to this the ideas related to "fountain," and you will begin to understand that this Key has to do with occult doctrines concerning God as the fountain of manifestation, or source of creation. Add now the third meaning, and you will see that Key 15 ought to be interpreted as a symbol of the One Identity, *as the source of the forms and appearances of relative existence.*

The human eye, as the organ of vision, establishes a relation-ship with Key 4, because Key 4 represents sight, and eyes are the means whereby the sense of sight is exercised. It is a common-place that the sense of sight, important as it is, is nevertheless a source of manifold illusions and deceptions. Every student of elementary psychology is familiar with the phenomena of optical illusions. We all know that we must make mental adjustments in order to interpret correctly the things we see. If a man standing on the observation platform of a train accepted the report of his sense of sight at face value, he would be under the delusion that the parallel tracks over which the train had just passed had somehow become welded together as they receded into the dis-tance.

The eye deceives us, however, only if we let it. Hence we find a direct connection between the meaning of the letter Ayin and the title of Key 15, for *Devil* is derived from the Greek διάβολος, *diabolos*, meaning "a traducer, a slanderer." An old proverb says that appearances are deceiving, and Jesus wisely counseled his disciples to avoid judging by appearance. In the New Testament, also, the Devil is called the "father of lies," that is, the progenitor, originator, cause, source, or principle of falsehood, deception, perversion of truth, delusion, error, fallacy, mental disorder and confusion. The Devil represents the fundamental error whence all other falsehoods proceed — the error of supposing that a *re-ality* called "matter" is opposed to another reality termed Spirit. Or the error that the only reality is matter, and that all man des-ignates by the word Spirit is actually no more than an intellectual abstraction.

In Sanskrit matter is called *Maya*, which means "illusion." In contrast to the Occidental mind, which has a tendency to accept the world of appearances constituting the objective universe as the *only* reality, the philosophers of the Orient are inclined to interpret the objective, phenomenal world as an unreal phantas-magoria of ever–shifting appearances. Ageless Wisdom reconciles these opposing interpretations by saying that the term *reality* applies to *both* worlds. The outer world may be *Maya*, or illusion, in one sense of that term. But because what we call "matter" is actually the "appearance" of what we term "Spirit", as the latter makes itself manifest in the field of name and form, we do not see how it is possible to separate the reality of the *appearance* from the reality of the *One Identity* that is making the appear-ance. According to Ageless Wisdom, the error consists precisely in attempting to establish such a separation between the appear-

194

ance and what we may term the "Appearer." The seeming two are really one, and they are not in opposition to each other.

Thus in the Qabalah we find that the letter Ayin is attributed to the 26th path on the Tree of Life. (The Tree of Life is a Qabalistic diagram showing the various relations between the different aspects of the Life–power.) The *number* assigned to this path is striking because 26 is the numeral value of the Divine Name, יהוה, I H V H, *Jehovah*. Moreover, the aspect of the Life–power corresponding to the 26th path is called the Renewing Intelligence, and *The Book of Formation* says it is so called "because by it the Holy God renews all that is begun afresh in the creation of the world."

Consider this in connection with the meaning of Ayin as "fountain." A fountain is a spring, from which flows the water, which nourishes the growth of plants and makes waste places fertile. Wherever there is a fountain in a desert there is an oasis, and when an oasis is viewed from a height, it looks like an eye in the face of the desert.

In a magical manuscript of the sixteenth century, quoted by Eliphas Levi in the introduction *to Transcendental Magic*, we read that among the powers and privileges of an adept, those connected with the letter Ayin are: "To force nature to make him free at his pleasure." We find, moreover, these startling words in the first verse of the fourth chapter of the Gospel of St. Matthew: "Then Jesus was led up into the wilderness by the Spirit to be tempted by the devil." This is the literal rendering of the Greek original. It provides us with an important clue to the whole mystery of Key 15. Note that the Spirit did the leading, for the specific purpose of *testing* Jesus by the temptation. And bear in mind what you have learned from the two preceding lessons concerning the importance of verification. Consider also that in the first

chapter of Job, at the sixth verse, we read: "Now there was a day when the sons of God came to present themselves before Jehovah, and Satan came also among them."

Observe, first of all, that there is no hint that Satan is prohibited from coming into Jehovah's presence. He comes, too, as one of the "Sons of God," or "Beni–Elohim." In the Qabalah the Beni–Elohim are said to be a choir of angels associated with the Sphere of Mercury, or sphere of Mercurial influence. That is, they have to do with the phase of consciousness we have learned to associate with Key 1, the Magician. That Key represents human self–consciousness, making contact with its environment through the senses, among which the sense of sight is chief.

What are we to conclude from all this? First of all, that the appearances that deceive us are *necessary* to the manifestation of the Life–power. Furthermore, that to attain our full stature as human beings, so that we are in a position to force nature to make us free at our pleasure, we must be subjected to tests and trials of our faith, and these trials are imposed on us by appearances. The whole book of Job is an elaboration of this theme. So are the four Gospels. The "mystery of evil" is no mystery to those who have met and passed the trials of faith. Every person who has left a report of his experience of the higher order of knowing has testified that in that experience all consciousness of evil disappears.

"All very well," you may say, "but I am acutely aware of the economic, political and social evils of the present day. I have some shortcomings myself, and most of the people around me are simply dreadful. No amount of fine theory will erase the slums, raze the hospitals, empty the insane asylums and the prisons."

Granted. But the way of life that leads to realization of man's true place in the scheme of things does more than banish consciousness of evil. It brings with it power to transmute all semblances of evil into manifestations of positive good. Thus the magical manuscript already quoted ends with these words:

"The wise man rules the elements, stills tempests, cures the diseased by his touch, and raises the dead... The initiates know, and as for others, whether they deride, doubt, or believe, whether they threaten or fear — what matters it to science or to us?"

Until we experience the higher order of knowing, we may have difficulty with the various appearances of evil. We may wonder why appearances are so often deceiving. But even without that higher knowledge, reason will take us far. Logic forces us to attribute the manifestation of the visible universe to a power, which is essentially good. A power, moreover, that is wholly wise. Thus it follows that even if appearances are deceiving, appearance itself is necessary for the perfect manifestation of the Life–power. The manifest universe, as Oriental philosophers assert, may be Maya or illusion, but on the hypothesis that it proceeds from an all–wise, all–good, all–powerful Source, then, whether we can explain it or not, we are forced to conclude that this power to deceive the human mind and originate all sorts of delusion is somehow useful, somehow part of the universal order.

This involves no denial whatever of the various appearances of relative evil. Nor does Ageless Wisdom narcotize us into indif-

196

ference to those appearances. Precisely those persons who have done most to banish sickness, sorrow and pain from the lives of their contemporaries are the persons who bear witness to the reality of a higher order of knowing in which all consciousness of evil disappears.

Tarot here affords us a clue by the attribution of Key 15 to the zodiacal sign Capricorn, which is ruled by Saturn, the planet of limitation and restriction. In Capricorn, moreover, Mars is exalted, or has its highest field of expression. Thus we may expect to find in Key 15 a symbolic presentation of a power, which both binds and liberates.

In its binding aspect it creates form. All form has definite limitations. All release of energy, as we saw in our study of Key 13, which also represents an aspect of the Mars force, requires the dissolution of form. In Capricorn, then, these opposite aspects of Reality are brought together.

As applied to the keyword of our lesson, the meaning is this. Form necessitates limitation and in our experience limitation is bondage. Yet the very limitations that gall us may become the spurs to action that release us.

See how clearly this is indicated by the first column of Keys in the tableau given in Lesson Two. The exercise of concentration (Key 1) puts into operation the law of suggestion (Key 8), which results in a renewal of consciousness that releases us from bondage (Key 15). When the force of Mars, represented by the red robe of the Magician, is brought to bear through concentration, it brings about a regeneration, which dissolves the appearances of limitation.

Through Ayin, again, Key 15 is associated with the idea of Mirth. Laughter is caused by perception of the incongruous. It is but a step from this to the truth that joy results from the perception of the incongruity between the appearance of limitation and the truth that man is the immediate agent of the One Identity. Experimental verification of this truth brings an experience of the most intense bliss, far beyond, yet comparable to, the most ecstatic sense–experiences known to man.

Finally, to return to the title of Key 15, there is an old saying, "The Devil is God as He is misunderstood by the wicked." This means that the monstrous figure in Key 15 is a symbol of man's ignorance of the true nature of Reality, and more especially of man's ignorance concerning his own place in the scheme of things. That ignorance is the real Devil, and because it may be overcome, those who set their feet upon the ancient Way of Lib-

197

eration learn how to banish the Devil and destroy his works.

As you color the Key this week, notice particularly that this hideous figure is an impossible combination of incongruities. This nightmare shape never did, and never can, exist outside the realm of disordered fancy. Notice also that it is a caricature of Key 6, and compare it, detail for detail, with that Key.

COLORING INSTRUCTIONS

Yellow: Insignia above cross below navel of devil. The hair of the male and female figures, the torch flame, and the tail of the male figure are yellow, shot with red.

Green: Tail of female figure.

Brown: Feathers, legs and horns of devil, torch handle, foreground, body and wings of devil (this is more effective if a little gray is mixed with diluted brown to give a dull, earthy color.)

White: Star, beard, horns of male and female figures.

Steel: Chain and ring.

Red: Cross on devil's body, grapes on tail of female figure, devil's eyes. (Also note under yellow.)

THE DEVIL
(Cont.)

The black background of Key 15 represents darkness. It is therefore a symbol of ignorance. It also refers to Saturn, the planet ruling Capricorn, which is often represented, especially in heraldry, by the color black.

The central figure is that of an androgyne goat, with the wings of a bat, the arms and hands of a man, and the legs and feet of an eagle. The wings refer to the fact that the Devil is called "prince of the power of the air." They indicate a subtle energy contained in the atmosphere, which is one of the forces controlled by practical occultists. The eagle's legs and feet refer to the sign Scorpio, ruled by Mars, which planet is exalted in Capricorn. For the Scorpio forces must be purified in the fires of test and trial if we are to be released from bondage. The arms and hands of the monster are shown in a gesture like that of the Magician, but the uplifted right hand is open, and bears on its palm the astrological symbol of Saturn, signifying limitation. The position of the fingers of the Devil's right hand is a contrast to the gesture of esotericism made by the Hierophant. The Devil's gesture means, "What is visible, what can be grasped by the senses, is all there is."

This is the basic fallacy of materialism. In the symbolism of the Devil's hand it is associated with the astrological sign for the planet Saturn, because materialism is the cause of man's worst limitations.

The inverted torch in the Devil's left hand burns wastefully and gives little light. It is typical of the false light of pseudo–science. It also represents the blazing torch of revolution and rebellion.

The symbol of Mercury on the Devil's body, just below the navel, refers to the activity at work in the subtle processes of digestion and assimilation. These processes, under the influence of Mercury in the sign Virgo, are brought under control in the work of practical occultism. That work is a combination of mental processes, indicated by the yellow upper half of the Mercury symbol, and of bodily responses or reactions, represented by the red cross forming the lower half of the same symbol.

The Devil's eyes are red because Mars, corresponding to that color, is exalted in Capricorn. They emphasize the meanings of the letter Ayin, and refer also to the fact that sight is attributed to the letter Heh, and thus to Aries, a sign ruled by Mars.

The inverted pentagram between the horns of the Devil is the most evil of all signs of black magic. The essence of black magic is mental inversion, and the root of that inversion is the belief that the Self of man is dominated by the elements composing his physical environment. Thus the inverted pentagram is a symbol of essential falsehood, for it is never true that Spirit can be dominated by matter. All appearances to the contrary are delusive. Furthermore, since the pentagram is a symbol of man, to reverse it is to deny the truth that man has power to control everything below him in the scale of creation.

This inverted star is a clue to the meaning of the whole design. Man's false notion of himself is the source of his belief in a Devil. Primitive man, afraid of his environment, imagined that every stick and stone held a malignant goblin that must be propitiated. In time all these little demons were merged into one big Devil, just as, on the other hand, all good spirits were merged into one God. A synthetic Devil opposed to a synthetic God! Small wonder that intelligent men and women reject exoteric theology.

The pedestal is a half–cube, representing imperfect understanding of the physical world because the cube represents that world. At the front of the pedestal is a large ring. To it are fastened chains, which bind the two smaller figures. These typify the human conscious and subconscious minds. The bondage of delusion, which affects them both, has its origin in man's erroneous interpretation of the nature of the physical universe. The horns, hoofs and tails of these little prisoners intimate that delusion bestializes man.

On the cube of space, Key 15 is represented by the line West–Below, shown in Figs. 1 and 2 of the diagram accompanying Lesson 18. This line connects the lower ends of the lines North–West and South–West. Hence it designates an activity working at the *subconscious* level. It is the *lower* boundary of the western face of the cube, and at the same time the *western* boundary of the lower face. Considered under the first of these two aspects, it represents the operation of the law represented by Key 10 at *subconscious levels*. Considered under the second of these two aspects, it represents the *subconscious element* in the Law of Rotation. Actually, these are simply two ways of describing one and the same activity. Hence they are represented on the cube by the same line of West–Below. In terms of Tarot, then, we may say that the Key numbered 15 shows how the power represented by the High Priestess manifests itself in the Law of Rotation, and shows also those aspects of the Law of Rotation that operate in the universe and in the life of man below the level of conscious awareness.

The current of energy in this line moves from North to South. It combines the current passing from East to West along the line of North–Below with the current passing from Above to Below along the line North–West. In terms of Tarot therefore, Key 15 represents activity, which combines the forces of Key 9 with those of Key 11. Here is an important clue to the *practical* meaning of Key 15, for it shows us that whatever is represented by the symbolism of the Devil combines the secret forces of Virgo and Libra.

Note also that the line West–Below is opposite to the line East–Below. The latter is related to the Chariot and to the sign Cancer, which is the zodiacal opposite of Capricorn, the sign corresponding to the line West–Below. Furthermore, the line West–Below is *diagonally* opposite to the line East–Above, and we have already seen that there is a hint of this opposition in the symbolism of Keys 6 and 15.

In practical occultism, Key 15 represents a force that combines the energy released into the physical organism through the functions of the Virgo region, (as explained in Lessons Twenty–one and Twenty–two,) with the force specialized by the adrenals, governed by Libra.

In one sense, of course, all these forces are really phases of the operation of the One Force. But each phase is distinct, and has its own peculiar characteristics. As an illustration of the same general principle we may think of the One Force as electricity that may be specialized, through appropriate instruments, into various kinds of activity. Passing through the filament of an electric bulb, it manifests as light. Sent through the coil of a stove it becomes heat. One manifestation enables us to read at night. The other warms a room, or cooks a meal. But we do not try to read by the light of a stove, nor cook a dinner over an electric lamp.

To speak of anything so obvious may seem out of place in a course of lessons meant for the instruction of intelligent men and women. Yet it seems advisable, because so many persons appear to believe that one needs only to make contact with the central source of the One Force in order to accomplish all things. Again and again we have been asked what good there is in "all this technical knowledge." And not seldom has the question been put by a person describing himself as an "advanced student," who has spent years in reading occult literature, and has been a member of a number of "very occult" societies.

Failure to grasp this principle accounts for the lack of success attending the efforts of many genuinely earnest students. It needs to be said often that *practical* occultism is just as full of inevitable technicalities as *practical* exoteric science. Our conquest of the inner world of occult forces is made by the same kind of procedure that has brought about our conquest of the outer world of forces, which actually, are just as occult. There is no short–cut to mastery, other than the road of exact knowledge that, however long and arduous it may seem, is really the shortest path to the goal of attainment.

In *Seven Steps in Practical Occuitism*, Lesson 1, is a quotation from Eliphas Levi, describing the Astral Light. Add to it these words from the same author:

> This electro–magnetic ether, this vital and luminous caloric, is represented on ancient monuments by the girdle of Isis, which twines in a love–knot round two poles, by the bullheaded serpent, by the serpent with the head of a goat or a dog, and by the serpent devouring its own tail, emblem of prudence and of Saturn. It is the winged dragon of Medea, the double serpent of the caduceus, and the tempter of Genesis. Lastly, it is the devil of exoteric dogmatism, and is really the blind force that souls must conquer, In order to detach themselves from the chains of earth.

Now in Genesis, the tempter is called נחש, N Ch Sh, and this noun *Nachash* is also closely related to the word translated in the Authorized Version as "brass," though it really means copper, the metal of Venus. The number of the word Nachash is 358, and it is the same as the number of משיח, M Sh I Ch, *Messiach*, signifying "the anointed," and referring to the Christos.

What is hinted at by this numeral identity? This, that the agency of temptation and that of release are really one and the same. In other words, the Life–power is the cause both of bondage and of liberation. When we do not understand it, the laws of the Life–power's self–expression seem to be our adversaries. When we come to know that all manifestation proceeds from the One Identity, we discover that a reversal of relationship is possible, so that what seems to be against us is transformed into the means for our release from all restriction.

When Eliphas Levi speaks of the Astral Light, the force symbolized by Key 15, as "blind," he employs a subtlety of language. The force is blind only so long as we are unaware of its true nature. When we ourselves see the truth, that force becomes the vehicle of our vision. Hence it is connected with Ayin, the Eye.

The whole secret of release is to get the pentagram right side up. Man's monstrous imaginary creation, the Devil, is really none other than God, as God seems to men who have an upside–down conception of the I AM. To *know* what the Self of man really is dispels the delusion that Spirit is dominated by the elements. When this delusion is overcome, the powerlessness of evil becomes self–evident, and the works of the Devil are soon destroyed.

Learn to laugh at appearances. Laugh at the notion of a Devil. The most effective resistance to error is ridicule. Laugh at the Devil, and he and all his angels will flee. And keep in the front of your mind, whenever you are beset by false appearances, that whatever in your experience now takes on the form of a veritable monster of adversity is really your opportunity for demonstrating the utter freedom of Limitless Spirit.

LESSON THIRTY–FIVE

THE TOWER
(AWAKENING)

16   THE TOWER

Wwe come now to the second stage of spiritual unfoldment, which is the awakening from the dream of sense,
from the nightmare of bondage. The first stage, represented by Key 15, is that of the realization of the nature of bondage, and the perception that it is, after all, only a dream.

Key 16 is obviously a picture of destruction, but it is important
to notice that the source of the destructive power is the sun, and
that the disintegrating force comes forth as a flash of lightning.
This refers to the flash of superconsciousness, which constitutes
the first awakening. It is the first moment of clear vision, after
which the person to whom it comes is never again quite the same
as he was before. It is like the hatching of a chick from an egg.
Once the shell is broken, the chick can never return to the egg. It
has entered a new phase of existence. Another life opens before
it. So it is with man. At the moment of sudden illumination pictured by Key 16, he receives an initiation, and from then on he
belongs to a new order of creatures.

In The Book of Tokens, the meditation on the letter Peh (פ)(to
which Key 16 is attributed) says:

> Verily destruction is the foundation of existence
> And in the tearing–down thou seest
> Is but the assembling, of material
> For a grander structure.

A little observation will convince you that destruction is the
foundation of existence. Our entire lives are spent in the disintegration of forms for the sake of building up other forms. Power
is released by disintegration. The food we eat, the clothes we
wear, the automobiles we ride in, are all in process of destruction
from the very first moment we put them into use. In the very act
of destruction itself lies all the utility that can be extracted from
any of these things.

In the experience of spiritual unfoldment, awakening is distinctly a destructive process. All the customary wrong thinking
and wrong acting must go. The false sense of personal will, of
personal autonomy, of personal self–action, must be destroyed.

This is not a comfortable process. When one is forced to recognize the truth that some of his most cherished beliefs are false,
the consequent readjustment is not easy. Yet the wise in every
age have testified that this destruction is essentially a *gathering
of materials for a grander structure.*

The first chapter of the Gospel of St. John says: "In the beginning was the Word, and the Word was with God, and the Word was God. All things were made by Him; and without Him was not anything made that was made. That which has been made was life in Him, and the life was the light of men." This passage refers to the power, which you have been studying since the first lesson of *Seven Steps*. You have learned that this power is not only the source of the forces used in reproduction, integration and creation, but that from it spring also the forces manifest in the opposites of these.

Hence *The Book of Tokens*, in the meditation on Peh, (which means literally "the mouth of man as organ of speech") states:

I am the Mouth, whence issueth the breath of Life;
I am the all–devouring one
Whereunto all things return.

This is the power that is active in the disintegration of the old forms of personal consciousness. It rends the veil, which hides truth from our eyes. The teaching that this breaking down of form is fundamental in the process of the Life–power's self manifestation is very important. The practical occultist has to learn that he cannot hope to reach any goal he may have set for himself without first breaking down the conditions in which he finds himself when he formulates his desire. In occultism, as in everything else, we cannot have our cake and eat it too. Before we can find release from the chains that bind us, we must learn how to break them.

The time to begin this process of breaking down the old limiting forms is NOW, not some time in the future. You have already made a good start. You are aware of your limitations. You are making an effort to transcend them. This is witnessed by the fact that you have followed this instruction thus far. As you proceed with it, other practical methods for combating your limitations will be given you, and things of splendor will unfold within you. Your first step is to apply in your daily life the principles represented by the Tarot Keys, so as to build those principles into the structure of your own being.

206

The number 16 says as much. Right discrimination, the principle represented by Key 6, is essential to the work. Apply this principle through acts of concentration, typified by Key 1, and you will find that each day's experience brings you some measure of the awakening so strikingly pictured here. Superficial observation will not suffice. You must give attention to the meaning of your thoughts, desires and actions. Thus you apply the principle of limitation to overcome limitation.

He who is proficient in concentration rarely places himself in embarrassing situations by rash and unconsidered action. He thinks before he acts, and then acts wisely. The planet Mars is related to Key 16 through the letter Peh, and in exoteric astrology Mars is the planet of war and rash action. Yet it is also the planet of the driving force behind all successful activity. The way the Mars force manifests in us depends, therefore, on whether we control it and make use of its driving power, or whether we permit it to control us, thus inducing rash and foolish activity.

The Mars force is the driving energy of desire force. Control of desire is not repression. No man without powerful desires and emotions ever attains to the heights of mastery. When one tries to repress the Mars force, it sooner or later breaks loose in a burst of terrific destruction. Books on analytical psychology tell of many horrible examples of human wreckage caused by the repression of desire.

The channels through which the desire force finds expression are, however, *normally* under our conscious control. It is perfectly natural to effect this control. Key 1, the Magician, shows how. Formulate your desires, using intelligent discrimination, and then bring them into manifestation by concentration. Make your mental images of the desired results sharp and clear, so that subconsciousness will receive definite impressions. Then the activity of the dynamic Mars force will make your dreams come true.

Some very old versions of Key 16 are named "The House of God." Others are called "The Fire of Heaven." Still others bear the title, "The Lightning–struck Tower." The title on our version is a short form of this third variant. There is a tradition that it refers to the fall of the Tower of Babel, at which time human speech is said to have become a confusion of tongues.

Thus this title is related to the notion of speech, which is connected with the letter Peh. The old Bible story indicates that it is a mistaken use of language to try to reach heaven by means of a structure of words. The correct use of language is to control the forces of nature by making words the tools of organized thought. When we try to use words to define superconscious states, which are actually beyond words, confusion is the inevitable result.

This week, as you color Key 16, observe its details closely. Try to get some hint of its deeper meaning, and make notes of any ideas that may come to you.

COLORING INSTRUCTIONS

Yellow: Two bands on crown that look like rope, star, crown of woman. The Yods are yellow, with a tongue of red in the general shape of a Yod in the lower right corner of each. A preponderance of red, shot with yellow, makes them more realistic.

Blue: Dress of woman, hose of man.

Gold: Crown, except yellow parts; lightning flash.

Gray: Tower, clouds (heavy storm clouds, as in Key 10).

Brown: Cliff. Top of cliff is made a lighter brown.

Blonde: Woman's hair.

Red: Boots and coat of man, shoes of woman. (See also under yellow.)

THE TOWER
(Cont.)

The lightning flash in Key 16 is a reference to the words of *The Book of Formation* (1:5): "The appearance of the ten spheres out of nothing is like a flash of lightning, being without an end. His word is in them when they emanate and when they return." The point most noteworthy is that the lightning flash represents the power of the Word, so that it corresponds to the letter Peh, since the letter–name means the mouth as the organ of speech.

The flash comes from a solar disk, to show that the active force at work in the picture is, in spite of the seeming destruction wrought by it, a phase of the working of the Life–power. Note that the disk is in the same corner of the picture as the sun in Key 0, and review what is said in Lesson 4 concerning this. Remember that the force in question is the Mars force, so that this is a link with the attribution of Mars to the letter Peh.

The form of the lightning flash is also important. It is so drawn that it is a diagram of the complete expression of the ten aspects of the Life–power, which are mentioned in *The Pattern on the Trestleboard*. This symbolism is borrowed from a diagram familiar to Qabalists.

In relation to the second stage of spiritual unfoldment, the lightning indicates the sudden illumination or flash of inspiration that comes to us when we have faced our particular problem boldly, and have concentrated the full force of the Life–power on it by means of prolonged acts of attention. Notice that the end of the flash is formed like an arrowhead, which is a symbol for the letter Beth, attributed to Key 1.

The tower is built of bricks, laid in twenty–two courses. Thus it represents a structure of human speech, for the components of speech are the letters of the alphabet, and in Hebrew these are twenty–two. This tower is a structure of human error and ignorance, yet it is at the same time a House of God. Nothing is truer than that these physical personalities of ours, even though they are structures that incorporate our false notions, are at the same

209

time Temples of the Living God. The ugliness and inadequacy of our bodies, their want of grace and comeliness, are caused by the influence on subconsciousness of our false thinking, expressed in erroneous words. Hence the lightning flash of true perception always makes itself felt in the physical body, because there must be a period of physical readjustment before our bodies can be vehicles for the expression of the higher levels of consciousness.

The crown, which is knocked off the top of the tower is a symbol of will power, because the Hebrew noun *Kether*, meaning "*crown*," is a synonym for "will." The crown here is a false crown, and its nature is exposed by the four letters M with which it is ornamented. In Hebrew, M is Mem, and 40, the numeral value of Mem, multiplied by 4 is 160, the value of the proper name קין, Q I N, *Cain*. Cain, the first murderer, is a personification of the false idea of will power, the notion that every person has a will of his own, separate from the will power of other persons, and separate also from the Cosmic Will.

Right knowledge begins with a flash of perception, which makes us realize that no detail of our personal experience can be separated from the total expression of the Life–power's activity. However brief this flash of realization may be, it overthrows the notion of separate personal will, and it also disrupts mental structures based on the error that we are living our lives in perpetual antagonism to the universe and to the lives of our neighbors. This lie is behind every murder. It is eradicated by even the briefest perception of the fundamental unity of all that exists.

The falling figures represent the two modes of personal consciousness. The man is self–consciousness, the woman is subconsciousness. The flash of inspiration upsets all our former conceptions of the nature of personal consciousness, and reverses our former ways of thinking. In Key 16 the figures are clothed, because they hide their true nature from each other while man remains in the state of ignorant separateness. In this connection, remember that clothes are symbols of shame and sin.

Twenty–two Yods are shown, suspended in the air. Ten are on one side of the tower, so disposed that they form the Qabalistic diagram of the Tree of Life. The twelve on the other side are also arranged symmetrically. These letters really stand for the twenty–two letters of the Hebrew alphabet, because every Hebrew letter is said to be some aspect of the letter Yod. Thus these Yods floating in the air represent the sum–total of cosmic forces, and they also represent the elements of the Creative Word, as well as the elements entering into the consciousness of human personality.

They are shown hanging, as it were, in space, in order to present symbolically the idea that none of these forces has a physical foundation. This idea is just the reverse of that suggested by the rocky, isolated peak on which the tower is erected. Note that this peak is the same color as the Devil's body in Key 15.

The average person thinks of his life as having a physical basis. He supposes it to be sustained by food, air, water, and the various physical forces of his environment. Ageless Wisdom says just the opposite. It declares explicitly that the One Life–power is the basis of all manifestation whatsoever, physical or otherwise. It by no means denies the importance, much less the actual existence, of the physical plane; but it does say that the physical world is a manifestation and expression of the powers of spiritual life. Thus it declares that instead of life being supported by the conditions of the physical plane, these conditions are supported by life.

It is undoubtedly true that certain definite physical conditions must obtain in order that the functions of human personality may be exercised here on earth. It is not true that these conditions either *cause* or *support* those functions. The true cause is the Life–power itself, and it is the Life–power that manifests itself in the physical conditions in question. The latter are the effects, not the causes, of manifestation.

In other words, Ageless Wisdom holds causation to be vital, rather than physical. In our day this conception of causation is not in fashion, any more than the conception that the earth is round was in fashion in the days of Columbus. It is true, nevertheless, and it is *demonstrably* true. Nor is it any less true because relatively few persons are at present able to make the demonstration.

Not every person can play a concerto. Those who have sufficient musical talent, and have devoted themselves to piano practice, are able to do so. Similarly, there are persons on this planet today who are sufficiently acquainted with the laws of life, and sufficiently skilled, because they have practiced, so that they can control physical conditions to an extent that seems miraculous to others.

Such virtuosi in the art of living have a command of their bodies and, *through* their regenerated bodies, of their environment, which enables them to do many extraordinary things. Yet they all bear witness that at one stage of their development they were just as ignorant of the laws of life as are most persons today. They met the same problems that we are meeting, faced the same difficulties. At one time in their experience they were as

211

much in the dark as we seem to be. They supposed that causation was physical, and they thought they were "going it alone." Their house of personality, like the Tower, was a structure reared on a peak of personal isolation, and crowned with the usurper's diadem of belief in "personal" will.

But there came a day when, like lightning, all their former opinions were reversed in a flash of clear perception. Darkness closed round them again, for at this stage of spiritual unfoldment the light is not continuous. Yet they remembered what they had seen, and the consequence of that recollection was a radical change in the fundamental conception on which their whole conduct of life was based.

We must make the same change, but before we *can* make it, we have to pass through the same experience. If you have had this experience already, you will understand all the deeper implications of Key 16. If you have not had it, this lesson will help prepare you for the sudden, wonderful, yet terrible awakening, which will end your dream of separation and bring you near the beginning of the Way of Liberation.

In the directional attributions of the Hebrew letters the letter Peh is assigned to *North*. This is the place of the greatest symbolic darkness. Thus in Masonic lodges there is no station in the North because it is said that the sun never shone on the north side of the temple at Jerusalem.

Compare this darkness symbolism with the color of the pillar on the left side or north of Key 2, and with the color of the sphinx on the same side of Key 7. Note that this pillar marked with Beth is associated with the idea of *strength* and that, in Hebrew wisdom, the word translated strength may also be rendered as *severity*, which is suggested by the forbidding aspect of the black sphinx in Key 7.

The idea behind this association of darkness and the North with strength is the idea that those powers that are, to the average mind, veiled in darkness, are the powers that bring release and enlightenment. The occult forces are the liberating forces. What inspires fear and terror in the mind of a savage is just what a civilized man employs to set himself free from a thousand limitations that restrict the freedom of the savage.

212

Nothing in nature inspires man with greater fear than lightning. Yet the civilized man annihilates distance by telephone, telegraph, cable and wireless. He sends words and pictures round the world by this willing servant of human intelligence. He makes in hours journeys that took days and weeks a few years ago, and it is the lightning flash in a gas engine that makes this possible.

It is for this reason that the Emperor is shown facing North. Human reasoning is always concerned with the unknown, with what is hidden from the mind of the average person. He who has conquered his fear of darkness is able to discover the secrets hidden there, and bring them and himself to light.

In Job 37:22 we read, "Fair weather comes from the north," but the margin in the King James Version substitutes "gold" for "fair weather," and this is the more accurate translation. In Hebrew it reads מִצָּפוֹן זָהָב יֶאֱתֶה, and the numeral value of this phrase is 696, which is the numeral value of אֵשׁ הַשָּׁמַיִם, A Sh H Sh M I M, *Aysh Ha–Shamaim*, "Fire of Heaven," which is the same as the French title of Key 16, *Le Feu au Ciel*.

This passage from Job is the text for a long alchemical commentary in Aesch Metzareph, *The Book of Purifying Fire*, but discussion of this Hermetic doctrine must be reserved for our texts on Hermetic Science. The point to be brought out now is that here is rather more than a hint that by "Mars" and "North" the wise men of old hinted at their knowledge of the same force that men now call electricity. What is more, they knew that the occult force, which they sometimes symbolized by a flash of lightning, is the basis of those inner modifications of the personal vehicle that result in enlightenment. This aspect of the cosmic vital electricity they usually represented by a serpent. Hence in Key 10 we see a serpent descending on the north side of the wheel.

Thus we may interpret "Gold comes from the north," as meaning "Enlightenment has its origin in the hidden sources of power that arouse the emotion of terror in the minds of the ignorant."

Remembering that a fundamental activity of the Mars force in human personality is the stimulation of desire, devote yourself this week to a study of your desires. Most of us are beset by a veritable mob of miscellaneous desires. Many of them are unimportant, weak, and ephemeral. An enlightened man is a man of comparatively few desires, but they are deep, powerful and one–pointed. Such a man shoots straight for his mark, permitting nothing to turn him aside from his purpose. His thoughts dwell upon it. His activity is directed to its attainment.

Select your most important desire. Do not allow less important ones to interfere with it. Yielding to the influence of small desires dissipates energy, which should be applied to truly important work.

This practice is difficult, easy as it is to describe. It might easily take a lifetime of effort to bring the desire–nature under control.

Hence you are not to drop this practice at the end of this week. Practice desire control continually. It is the basis of all mastery.

LESSON THIRTY−SEVEN

THE STAR
(REVELATION)

17   THE STAR

The third stage of spiritual unfoldment, as represented by Tarot, is Revelation. By revelation is meant *unveiling, disclosure, discovery*. The discovery is not made by the seeker for truth. It is made to him. He *receives* the revelation. He does not lift the veil of Isis. It is she who unveils herself. Thus Key 17 pictures something that operates from above the level of human personal consciousness. The disclosures made at this stage are not perceived by the physical senses. They are not something arrived at by the reasoning mind, engaged in external observation. Quite the reverse. These revelations come when the reasoning mind is completely stilled and the senses sealed.

The Hebrew letter assigned to Key 17 is Tzaddi (**צ**). Its name means "fish–hook". A fishhook is a symbol of angling. Thus it is related to our ideas of experimentation, quest and research. The quest is for something not yet definitely realized. It is a sort of groping, a feeling one's way, a "fishing" for something. What is clearly indicated here is that a fish–hook represents an agency or instrumentality whereby one attempts to solve problems or enigmas. It typifies a means for discovering secrets, a method whereby one follows a more or less faint trail leading to the understanding of a mystery.

This agency symbolized by a fishhook is meditation, which is the human function attributed to the letter Tzaddi, and thus to Key 17. Patanjali defines meditation as "an unbroken flow of knowledge in a particular object." We shall see that the symbolism of Key 17 agrees with this definition. Meditation is close, continued thought. It is *deep reflection*. It is a continual dwelling on one *central* idea, a diving down into the depths of the mind for the ideas associated with the main thought — that is, a fishing for truth.

You will note that such associations of ideas are the basis of Tarot practice. You will find this carried out even further when, later on, you come to the detailed study of Qabalistic correspondences and the Tree of Life. Keys 1, 2 and 3 symbolize the fundamentals of the process. First, the selection of some definite object, on which attention is focused (Key 1). Second, the associative process, represented by the meaning of the letter Gimel (Key 2). Third, the development of mental imagery, the basis of true understanding (Key 3).

These are the *mental aspects* of the meditation process. What should not be overlooked is the fact that meditation has specific physical results, and employs physical energy in the organism of the person who engages in meditation. The letter–name Tzaddi, "fishhook," gives a hint as to this physical part of the meditation work, because in the Hebrew alphabet the idea "fish" is represented by the letter Nun, and the idea "hook" by the letter Vav. (Note, also, that in the Hebrew letter–name נון N V N, *Nun*, the letters Nun and Vav are used.)

The letter Nun, represented by Key 13, is associated with the zodiacal sign Scorpio, and with the secret force governed by that sign. The letter Vav, represented by Key 5, is associated with the sign Taurus. Scorpio and Taurus are opposites, but complements, in the zodiac. The centers corresponding to them in the human body are also opposite and complementary.

In meditation, the force which ordinarily expresses itself through the Scorpio field of the human body is *raised*, and made to express itself through the Taurus region, which includes the hearing centers in the brain. It is by the stimulation of these centers in the work of meditation that one becomes aware of the Inner Voice represented by the Hierophant. The Hierophant, then, is the Revealer, and in Key 17 we have a symbol of the Revelation.

The numeral value of the letter Tzaddi is 90. This is also the value of the letter–name מים, M I M, *Mem*, which is associated with Key 12, the Hanged Man. This numeral correspondence indicates the probability of a cross–correspondence between the two letters and the ideas represented by them. Such a correspondence is evident even in the meaning of the letter–names. For certainly a fishhook makes one think of water. It is, in fact, an instrument for lifting fish out of water. Water, you will remember, is the occult name for the universal subconsciousness, which is the substance from which all things are made, the Great Sea in which all things have their origin.

You will recall that the title of Key 12, The Hanged Man, is synonymous with "Suspended Mind," and signifies the suspension of the activity of personal consciousness as a result of profound meditation. In the Sanskrit writings on Yoga this suspension is called Samadhi. In these books the practice of meditation is said to lead to the revelation of the highest truths.

In meditation, by keeping the stream of consciousness flowing in relation to some particular object, we gather impression after impression from that object. Our minds take the form of that object. We become more and more identified with it. Thus we become aware of the object's inner nature. It reveals itself to us.

The object of meditation is usually some sort of problem. Just as one must have the right sort of bait before the fish will bite, so must one have a definite object for meditation. The solution of the problem is the reason for meditating. Because it is a problem, it appears to be the adversary of the person who is meditating. It may look like the very Devil himself, but a practical occultist knows that this is but the first appearance, and thus he disregards it. He knows the solvent power of consciousness, and how to apply it.

The first thing to do in meditation is to silence the superficial activity of personal consciousness. Just as a fisherman sits quietly, so must one in meditation learn to wait patiently until the fish of thought takes the hook. The hook is always a specific question. They who imagine they are meditating when they sit passively, imitating a jellyfish by their mental attitude of utter emptiness, are sadly mistaken.

True as it is that we ourselves do not discover truth, it is also needful for us to understand that our mental attitude must be one of *active* quest. We must not be content merely to sit still, in hope of enlightenment. Still we must be, but at the same time intent on receiving light on our problem. The right mental attitude is one of quiet but alert *receptivity*. We must *invite* the soul, as the poet says. In this attitude we are able to hear the Voice of the Hierophant, and he will speak distinctly and definitely.

As we become skilled in the practice of meditation, we find that about all we have personally to do with the disclosure of new aspects of truth is the selection of a specific problem as the pivot for our meditation. In old Egypt there used to be a statue of Isis, with an inscription asserting that no mortal had ever lifted her veil. This continues to be true. Yet the veil of Isis is lifted again and again for those who are duly and truly prepared for the vision of her lovely presence. Nature does not hide herself from us. The veil that conceals truth is the veil of human ignorance, the veil of man's foolish belief in his own separateness and mortality, and that veil may be removed by the practice of meditation.

The number 17 is composed of the digits 7 and 1, with 7 standing for the power that is expressed, and 1 for the agency through which that power is manifested. In Tarot, the number 7 refers to the Chariot and, consequently, to the receptivity that is indispensable for success in meditation. He who seeks this must be keenly aware that personality is but the vehicle for the Life–power, and he must also understand that the Life–power, being the WORD or Creative Speech, finds expression in *all* forms.

It is because the WORD is actually seated in our hearts that we are able to receive its disclosures of truth. The mental attitude symbolized in Tarot by the Magician is the means whereby truth so disclosed may be put into practical application. Man is the transformer of his environment, in accordance with his perceptions of reality. He IS that, whether he applies his power wisely or unwisely. We are all magicians, projecting our own magic circle of circumstance by our mental imagery. When we understand this truth about ourselves and act upon it, we find release from every kind of bondage.

The zodiacal sign Aquarius, the Water–bearer, is attributed to Tzaddi, and thus to Key 17 also. Its symbol is the same as one of the alchemical symbols for dissolution. Thus it is directly connected with ideas we have considered in our study of Key 13. It is apparent that this Key is related to Key 17, since the letter Nun, associated with Key 13, means "fish." In the symbolic representation of the fixed signs of the zodiac, in the corners of Key 10 and 21, the sign Aquarius is represented by the Man. Man is the great fisher for new forms of truth. Man is the possessor of the Universal Solvent mentioned in the alchemical books. That solvent is human consciousness, focused in meditation. It is the most potent force at our disposal, and will solve every problem.

Aquarius is jointly ruled by Uranus and Saturn. These two planets are represented by the first and last Keys of Tarot. Uranus is the Fool, and Saturn is the World. Here is a hint that the practice of meditation will eventually bring about answers to every question, from the most abstract to the most concrete. Many other interesting ideas may be found in this co–rulership of Aquarius. See if you can follow some of them out by meditating on them.

The title, *The Star*, refers directly to the universal Light–energy which condenses itself into stars as the Reality behind their physical forms. There is a more recondite meaning to this title, but its explanation must be deferred to another place.

This week, develop the exercise you began last week. Formulate your desires into specific problems. Give them your complete attention. Focus the spotlight of your consciousness upon them. Make every detail clear and definite. Then, with this as a basis, begin the fishing process of meditation. Do not try to think about your problem's probable or possible solution. Rather let the stream of consciousness flow, as it were, past your point of observation. Watch all the ideas that seem to rise to the surface of themselves, and reject them unless they show some definite relation to the central idea of your meditation. Keep your object always in view.

COLORING INSTRUCTIONS

Yellow: The central star.

Green: Grass, tree leaves.

Blue: Background, pool, water from vases. Deeper shade in ovals on vases and stripe round necks.

Violet: Mountains. (Note that there are rising hills before the peak.)

Orange: Vases (except stripes and ovals and handles).

White: Smaller stars, vase handles, stripes across ovals on vases, except stripes colored red, highlights on water.

Brown: Tree trunk.

Blonde: Hair (this can be done beautifully by putting a little darker shade over the shading lines).

Red: Top band over oval on vase at left of card; lower band over oval on vase at right; the bird on the tree.

LESSON THIRTY-EIGHT

THE STAR
(Cont.)

The great yellow star is the Blazing Star of Masonic symbolism. It is also a symbol of the Quintessence, or Fifth Essence, of the alchemists. This is clearly indicated by the fact that the star has eight principal rays. The eight-spoked figure on the dress of the Fool, the Wheel of Fortune, and this eight-rayed star are all emblems of the Quintessence, which is Spirit, the essential power behind the energy transmitted to their world-systems by suns. Note that the star has also eight very short secondary rays. You will find these rays fully developed in the symbolism of Key 19.

The seven lesser stars are also eight-pointed, to show that they are manifestations of the same Quintessence. They also represent the seven alchemical metals: Lead, Iron, Tin, Gold, Silver, Copper and Mercury. These correspond to the seven astrological planets: Saturn, Mars, Jupiter, Sun, Moon, Venus and Mercury. Thus the stars of Key 17 are symbols of the seven interior stars, or chakras, which are centers through which the One Force manifests itself in the human body.

This last is a forerunner of teaching you will receive in later lessons. Then you will be told much more concerning these centers, and will learn practical methods for utilizing the forces that work through them. For the present this is not a necessary part of your instruction.

Much teaching is extant with regard to the development of these centers. A great deal of it is very dangerous, because it either gives technical knowledge to persons who are not really prepared for it, so that they often do themselves grave injuries, or else fills the mind of the student with a lot of time-wasting nonsense of which he must get rid before he can receive the genuine instruction.

We waste no time in argument with persons who cannot see the need of keeping secret certain aspects of occult instruction. Such persons are not ready for the knowledge they clamor for, and will not receive it until they are intelligent enough to see

221

how vitally necessary secrecy really is. We frankly admit that we hold back not a little, in accordance with ancient usage that we feel to be binding upon us. But we do not give you false interpretations, nor waste your time with fruitless practices. When these preliminary steps of training have been taken by you, detailed explanation of the more advanced work will be available, under suitable reserves.

The nude water–bearer is Isis–Urania. She represents truth, and the practice of meditation reveals truth to us without disguise, hence she is nude. Her legs are bent so that each forms an angle of 90 degrees. 90 is the number of the letter Tzaddi, and an angle of 90 degrees is an ancient symbol of rectitude.

The weight of her body rests on her left knee, and is supported by earth, representing the facts of physical existence. Her balance is maintained by her right leg, and her right foot rests upon the surface of the pool. This implies that in meditation something occurs that gives to the usually unstable mind–stuff, symbolized by water, a solidity and stability comparable to that of the physical world. Here is a hint of the true meaning of the process termed by alchemists the "fixation of the volatile."

The two vases are the two personal modes of consciousness, like the two ministers in Key 5 and the man and woman in Key 6. The ellipses on the sides of the vases represent the zero sign, Spirit, or Akasha. Only two ellipses are shown but there are really four, signifying the expression of Spirit through the four elements.

From the vase in the woman's right hand falls a stream that sets up wave motion in the pool. Note that this wave motion is in the form of concentric rings, like the circles on Key 10. This wave motion in the pool represents the activity set up in subconsciousness by meditation.

From the other vase, a stream falls on land and it is divided into five parts. This represents the purification and perfection of the senses by means of right meditation. One important clue to the meaning of Key 17 is that the woman lifts the vases, and that the water comes from the pool and goes back to it.

The mountain in the background is the same as the one in Keys 6 and 8. It represents the perfection of the Great Work, which is man's conscious control of the inorganic forms of the Life–power's self–expression. That control begins with man's mastery of his own mind and body, so that they become open channels for the outflow of the higher aspects of the Life–power's true consciousness. When this preliminary work with the personal vehicle is completed, then becomes possible the culmination of that work in the actual mastery of the patterns of the inorganic world, by what appears to the uninitiated as a mysterious, miracle–working power of the adept. The adept himself, however, knows that this power is latent in all men, and he seeks eagerly for those who are ready to begin the journey leading to the mountain–peak of mastery.

The tree in the middle distance refers to the human nervous system. This is often symbolized in occult diagrams as a tree. The upper part of the tree is the brain, and the trunk represents the spinal cord and the sympathetic nerves and ganglia. The bird perched in the branches is an ibis, a fishing bird regarded by the Egyptians as being sacred to Thoth, identified by the Greeks with Hermes, and by the Romans with Mercury. Here in Key 17 the bird of Hermes reminds us that meditation is begun by, and supervised by, the self–conscious aspect of human personality, Mercury or Hermes, pictured in Tarot as Key 1, the Magician.

On the diagram of the cube of space, the line corresponding to Tzaddi and Key 17 is the line South–Above, which is the southern boundary of the upper face of the cube.

That upper face is represented in Tarot by the Magician, and since the line corresponding to Key 17 is the southern boundary, we see that Key 17 must represent the southern half of Key 1, where we see a table, with the implements of ceremonial magic.

Now, ceremonial magic itself is one form of meditation, because everything done in a magical ceremonial is intended to emphasize the central idea, or seed–thought, of the ritual. In this connection review Lesson Six.

At this point it may be well to indicate the direction of the currents of energy in the twelve boundary lines of the cube. You can indicate these in your diagram in Lesson Eighteen by adding arrows, pointing in the direction that the current flows.

In the line North–East (Key 4), the current moves downward from Above to Below. In the line South–East (Key 5), it moves from Below to Above. In the line East–Above, it moves from South to North, as can be seen by careful inspection of Key 6. In the line East–Below, (Key 7), it moves from North to South, like the river in the background of the picture. Thus it is possible to trace a continuous line round the boundaries of the East face of the cube, beginning with Key 4 from Above to Below, then through the line of East–Below from North to South, then from Below to Above up the line of South–East, and from the South–

East upper corner, through the line of East–Above, back to the North–East upper corner.

On the North face of the cube it is impossible to trace such a continuous line, for the current in the lines North–Above (Key 8) and North–Below (Key 9) moves in both lines from East to West. And the current in the line North–West (Key 11) moves, like the current in the line North–East (Key 4), from Above to Below.

It is also impossible to trace a continuous path round the Western face, because, although the line South–West carries a current up from Below to Above (Key 13), the lines West–Above and West–Below both carry currents from North to South (Keys 14 and 15).

But on the upper face of the cube, it is possible to trace a continuous line starting from any corner, for East–Above (Key 6) moves from South to North, North–Above (Key 8) carries a current from East to West West–Above (Key 14) runs from North to South, and South–Above (Key 17) carries the current from West to East.

No continuous line can be traced round the lower face, because the lines East–Below and West–Below both move from North to South. And no continuous line can be drawn round the Southern face because the lines South–East and South–West both move from Below to Above; and the line South–Below, like the line South–Above, carries a current from West to East.

Note that the line South–Above (Key 17) begins at the upper end of the South–West (Key 13) and runs back to the upper end of line South–East (Key 5). Thus this line does actually join the line of Nun, the fish, to the line of Vav, the hook. (See Lesson Thirty–Seven).

Note also that the current from the line West–Above (Key 14) and that from the line South–East (Key 13) meet at the point where the line South–Above begins. Thus it is apparent that the forces represented by Keys 13 and 14 are blended in Key 17. That is to say, the secret force of Scorpio is blended with the single aim represented by the arrow of Sagittarius, in every right act of meditation.

Furthermore, since the line corresponding to Key 17 ends at the upper point of the line corresponding to Key 5, and the current in the latter moves upward, it is evident that the force carried by Key 17 does not move downward against the current of the line South–East.

What happens is that at the end of a successful period of meditation, one receives through the activity pictured by the Hierophant, a revelation of some eternal principle bearing directly on one's problem.

After this has occurred, the current from the line South–Above passes into the line East–Above, symbolized by Key 6. That is, the revelation received at the end of a successful meditation becomes part of the conscious awareness of the person meditating. And this additional enlightenment is made at once a contributing element to the exercise of discrimination pictured by Key 6.

We shall not follow the course of the cube boundaries any further now. But the alert reader will have perceived the general principle, and should be able to carry it on as a means to making many interesting discoveries concerning the Tarot.

Continue your meditation practice this week. Begin it by giving five minutes to letting the pictured image of Key 17 make its impression on your subconsciousness. Remember that this Key is a picture of what adepts know about meditation, and that it gives to your subconsciousness definite suggestions which will make it easier for you to meditate successfully.

Finally, think well upon this passage from *The Book of Tokens*. It contains an important secret concerning Key 17.

> Thinkest thou, O seeker for wisdom,
> That thou bringest thyself into the Light
> By thine own search?
> Not so.
> I am the HOOK,
> Cast into the waters of darkness,
> To bring men from their depths
> Into the sphere of true perception.
> Entering that sphere,
> They must die to their old selves,
> Even as a fish cast upon the land must die!
> Yet do they die only to live again,
> And what before seemed life to them
> Now weareth the aspect of death.
> Men think they seek me,
> But it is I who seek them,
> No other seeker is there than myself,
> And when I find mine own.
> The pain of questing is at an end.
> The fish graspeth the hook,
> Thinking to find food,
> But the fisherman is the enjoyer of the meal.

LESSON THIRTY-NINE

THE MOON
(ORGANIZATION)

18 — THE MOON — ק

226

Key 18 symbolizes the fourth stage of spiritual unfoldment. After one has realized that the condition of bondage to appearances is but an illusion (Key 15); when by the flash of spiritual illumination false structures of wrong thought and action have been overthrown (Key 16); then comes a period of quiet, like the calm that follows a storm, and during it, new relations are revealed to us through meditation (Key 17). After this, begins the process of organization.

As here used, the term organization does not mean the association of human beings into groups or societies. It refers rather to the organization of the various parts of the human body into a higher type of organism than that which is spontaneously provided by the general averages of evolution.

The practical application of the principles of Ageless Wisdom is aimed at this change in the human organism. Creatures in the evolutionary scale below man are incapable of any great degree of self–modification. Animals and plants brought under the influence of man may be considerably modified in a relatively short period of time, but they show a tendency to revert to the primitive types when the cultural influence of man is for any reason removed.

The "Great Art," as the alchemists called their practice, is concerned with the production of a higher, finer, more sensitive and responsive type of human body. This is not effected by eugenic measures. It is not by selection and breeding, but by the direct action of man's will and imagination upon his own vehicle of flesh and blood, that the transformation is effected.

This transformation is the outcome of the working together of universal forces. It is not merely a consequence of personal efforts. Yet the culmination of the Great Work requires the introduction of the personal factor. No man accomplishes this work until he himself sees, understands, and applies the principles, laws and forces that are involved in that transformation of his own substance, which the alchemists called "The Operation of the Sun."

This accomplishment is made possible by the exercise of imagination, for imagination is what makes clear and definite our desires and aspirations. Mental images are the patterns, which we pass into subconsciousness, the builder of the body and the controller of all its functions.

If our patterns are clear and definite, and we keep them intact, subconsciousness will build a body to correspond to them. This does not mean that we can sit still and do nothing but hold mental images. Not by any such practice shall we transmute our bodies. What it does mean is that when our images are vivid, they not only provide us with patterns for bodily transformation, but also impel us into courses of action which help to bring about the necessary changes.

For example, a boy cherishes the image of becoming a concert pianist. This image dominates his action, so that he goes willingly through the hours of practice that would be drudgery to an unmusical person. The practice affects the muscular structure of his hands, arms and legs. It causes many subtle changes in the centers of sight and hearing. It affects many other groups of nerves and muscle cells. Eventually he becomes what he imaged, *because he has built for himself, by action corresponding to imagination, the specially conditioned body of a pianist.*

The same principle holds true in every other instance. A prize-fighter is dominated by his imagery, and so is a poet. Everything that human beings achieve is accomplished through some kind of bodily activity, and each type of activity is made possible by the development of a corresponding type of organic structure. This is as true of the prophet and seer as it is of anybody else. Whatever your object in life may be, you will achieve it when you have built a physical vehicle that can transform the Life–power into the particular kinds of action corresponding to your mental imagery.

The number 18 expresses the potency of the number 8, working through 1. Thus it represents the Law of Suggestion symbolized by Key 8 as being applied through the directive activity of attention typified by Key 1.

You will find it to your advantage to review Lesson Two of *Seven Steps in Practical Occultism* in connection with this study of Key 18. What that lesson has to say about subconsciousness should pass often through the conscious mind, for each review imprints upon subconsciousness itself a deeper impression of your conscious realization of these facts. In effect, when subconsciousness knows that we understand what it can do, it works better. The most advanced adepts are not too wise to remind themselves continually of this, and Tarot is a device invented for just that purpose.

228

In reference to the organization of a finer and more responsive physical vehicle, this self–direction from the level of the conscious mind is the application of a principle enunciated long ago by Lamarck, who wrote:

> The production of a new organ in an animal body results from the supervention of a new want continuing to make itself felt, and a new movement which this want gives birth to and encourages... Effort may be in a large measure unconscious and instinctive, but must in large measure be Conscious, being made with a mental purpose to produce some desirable result.

The Hebrew letter Qoph (ק) means "the back of the head." It alludes to the fact that some of the most important organs of the human body are located in the rear of the skull. This part of the head houses the posterior lobes of the cerebrum and cerebellum. The posterior lobe of the cerebrum contains the sight center, so that it is actually true that we see with the backs of our heads.

Just below the posterior lobe of the cerebrum is a knot of nervous tissue, called the *medulla oblongata*, that unites the brain to the spinal cord and its branches. Thus the medulla is the connecting link between the higher centers of sensation, thought and action located in the head and the subordinate centers located in the body. The medulla itself is indeed a knot, presenting many intricate problems to anatomists and physiologists. Many of these problems are unlikely to be solved by those who depend on ordinary methods of investigation.

Unsatisfactory as ordinary study of the nervous system must be, because tissues examined under the microscope are taken from dead bodies, it has been found that the medulla governs respiration, that it regulates the heart, and that it contains the principal center that controls the circulation of the blood throughout the body. Besides these, it has other functions of basic importance in the maintenance of the body. Thus this knot of nerve cells at the back of the head is really what keeps us alive, for its functions are carried on without interruption, even while we are asleep.

Sleep, therefore, is assigned in the Qabalah to the letter Qoph, because what consciousness remains active in personality during sleep has its most important centers in the back of the head. Sleep, moreover, is the period of rest and recuperation, during which the waste caused by the day's activity is eliminated, and new materials are woven into the bodily structure.

While we sleep, the plans and thoughts we have been concerned with during the day are ripened and brought to maturity. Thus it is proverbial that night brings counsel. Many a problem has been solved subconsciously during the night. Our mental processes continue at subconscious levels, even while the cells of the upper brain are resting.

It is during sleep that our aspirations and efforts are built into organic structure. What we have thought and done during the day goes on influencing the body while we sleep. This is why it is advantageous to review each day before falling asleep. We see where we have fallen short, and we vigorously determine to do better the next time we find ourselves in a similar situation. We intensify the effect of all our well-doing by this mental repetition of the original actions and thoughts. Then, before composing ourselves for slumber, we once more bring before us, as clearly as we can, the image of that which is our highest and truest desire. By this means we actually build our aspirations into our flesh and blood, impressing our dominant desire on every cell.

As you make yourself familiar with the details of Key 18 this week, while coloring it, try to work out this hint. The digits of the number 18 add to 9, and 9 is the Hermit. Review the two lessons on Key 9, with special reference to the instructions concerning the functions and secret power of the Virgo area of the human body. Then notice that Keys 9 and 18 are both night scenes, while both have the suggestion of a height and of a path leading to that height. This will prepare you to understand next week's lesson.

COLORING INSTRUCTIONS

Yellow: Moon and rays, path. Yods same as in Key 16.

Green: *Grass in foreground.* (Note that this does not reach the towers.)

Blue: Background, pool.

Gray: Towers, wolf, stones round pool.

Violet: Crawfish, mountains (dilute for mountains.)

Brown: Dog, plains between grass and the mountains.

White: Tower windows, highlights on pool, wolf's fang.

THE MOON
(Cont.)

Key 18's title, The Moon, is a direct reference to subconsciousness and its powers of duplication, reproduction, reflection, and the turning of energy back toward its source. In its deeper meaning Key 18 therefore symbolizes the Path of Return. Thus it has a sidelight of reference to the parable of the Prodigal Son.

An ancient esoteric maxim is plainly indicated by the symbols of this Key. "First the stone, then the plant, then the animal, then the man." At the lower end of the path, at the margin of the pool, are several stones. Just beyond them are the pointed leaves of a water–plant, looking like arrows, and suggesting aim and aspiration. The vegetation also continues in the field beyond. Climbing onto the path is a relatively low form of animal life, a crustacean, and a little farther along are a dog and a wolf. Then come the towers, human structures, but the path continues beyond them.

The pool below is the same as that of Keys 14 and 17. It is the great deep of cosmic mind–stuff, out of which emerges the dry land of physical manifestation. From it all form, inorganic as well as organic, proceeds. Thus it is a reservoir of that occult Water which the alchemists called the "seed of metals."

The crawfish is a crustacean, hard–shelled. Note that its shape is similar to that of a scorpion. This resemblance is one of the reasons for selecting this particular creature as a symbol. That which rises, and makes the whole journey on the Path of Return, is the force of the zodiacal sign Scorpio, as we have seen throughout these lessons. The crawfish also represents, on the negative side, selfishness, crabbedness, obstinacy; but on the positive side it is a type of purpose, determination, and pertinacity. On account of its shell this animal also typifies the early stages of unfoldment, wherein the student still thinks of himself as being separated from the rest of nature.

In some esoteric versions of Tarot the crawfish is replaced by an insect, the Egyptian scarab beetle, representing the god

231

Khephra, symbol of the sun at night, when it is hidden below the horizon. In many respects this is good symbolism, for *night* always represents the predominance of subconscious activities. Any symbol of the sun stands for what the alchemists mean by "our gold." The potable gold of the alchemists is just another way of designating this fluidic light–force at work in the field of subconsciousness, where it brings about the changes in the physical body that make that body the vehicle of adeptship.

The dog and wolf belong to the same fundamental genus, the canine family. But the wild, dangerous wolf, inimical to man, is what nature produces, apart from human interference and adaptation. The dog is the result of modifications effected in the wolf by human thought. Men tame wolves and modify the structure of their bodies by cross–breeding. Thus this detail of the symbolism is a direct allusion to control of the body–consciousness, and to development of specific patterns formulated by human intelligence. The wolf is a symbol of Nature, and the dog is a symbol of Art.

The path goes between these extremes. For it is the way of balance, the way or method that goes neither too far toward artificiality, nor toward the error of supposing that everything should be left to the ungoverned expression of natural impulses.

The path progresses over undulating ground, so that it is a succession of ascents and descents. Progress on the Path of Return is not an unbroken upward climb. As we traverse it, we attain one eminence after another, and after surmounting some lesser peak we seem to go downhill for a time. This is only the surface appearance. If we keep our faces toward the goal, every step forward is really part of the whole ascending journey.

We cannot be climbing all the time. In the Great Work there is periodicity. It is a work of the Moon, as well as a work of the Sun. In this operation there must be waning as well as waxing, reflux as well as flux, rest as well as activity. Assimilation, or taking in, must be balanced by expression, or giving out. Periods of intense effort must alternate with periods of relaxation. A bow always drawn never speeds the arrow.

Since the path rises over rolling ground, as one advances, there comes a time when the lowest point of descent is a higher level than the peak of a previous attainment.

This path symbol is of great importance to occult students. To all of us there come times when we cannot climb, and if we do not understand the law here represented, it may discourage us.

The one thing needful is to keep facing toward the goal. As long as we do this, we may be sure we are progressing, even in those periods when we find it impossible to study or practice.

The towers are the work of man. They have battlements, and form a gateway. The suggestion of the design is that each tower is connected with a wall, not shown in the picture. The occult interpretation we have received is that this is the wall of the ordinary limits of human sensation and perception. Yet this is not a final boundary. A vast region of experience extends beyond it. Many have entered that region, and their footsteps have marked a path whereby we may follow them. The way is open for all who will set out upon it.

The moon is so drawn that it has sixteen principal and sixteen secondary rays, though in the picture some of the secondary rays at the top of the design are not clearly shown. Thus there are thirty–two rays, and this number 32 is, first of all, the number of paths on the Qabalistic diagram of the Tree of Life, which shows the ten forces corresponding to the numbers from 1 to 10, and the twenty–two forces represented by the letters of the Hebrew alphabet and the Tarot Keys. Hence, the rays of the moon indicate the sum–total of cosmic forces at work in the field of human personality.

32 is also the number of the Hebrew noun לב, L B, *laib*, meaning "the heart (in all senses), especially as the seat of knowledge, understanding and thinking; also midst, center." Remember in this connection the quotation from Eliphas Levi in *Seven Steps in Practical Occultism*, given in Lesson One, which identifies the heart of man with the sympathetic nervous system.

The Hebrew word for Moon is לבנה, LBNH. Its first two letters spell *laib*, "heart." The second two spell *ben*, "son." The last two spell *nah*, "ornament, beautification." The first three letters spell *laban*, "white." The last three spell *bawnaw*, "to build, make, erect." This esoteric analysis of the word according to the methods of the Qabalah suggests: 1. That in the heart of the son (man) are to be found the sources of beauty; and 2. That in the aspect of the Life–power identified in yoga and alchemy as the "white work" of the moon, is concealed the real secret of building the mystic temple of regenerated human personality.

233

Eighteen Yods fall from the moon onto the path. In the colored Keys they are partly red and partly yellow, to intimate the combination of solar energy (yellow) with the vital forces in the blood (red). In some versions of Tarot these Yods are replaced by drops of blood, intimating the same underlying idea, which is that the powers of subconsciousness are developed as actual physical structure through changes in blood chemistry. The body is actually built from elements contained in the bloodstream, and the chemistry of the bloodstream is controlled by subconsciousness, the moon in Key 18.

The Way of Attainment is the Path of Return. The Beyond is really the Source. Thus there is a sense in which that which is before us, in the future, is also that which is behind us, in the past. This is the meaning of the saying, "The last shall be first, and the first shall be last," for when the cycle is completed, end and beginning are one.

The height to which the path leads is that whereon stands the Hermit of Key 9. Ancient teachers have left clear descriptions of this way. They say it is narrow, meaning that concentration is required to follow it. They intimate that it is a mode of life balanced between the conditions of nature and such modifications of those conditions as are possible to art. The beginning of the way is in the realm of the familiar, even commonplace. It leads us, by easy stages, from the known to the less–known, and from the less–known to the unknown. Every great Master of Life has followed this path to its goal. The path itself is the path of physiological reorganization. The goal is true Self–recognition, correct perception of the universal I AM, and mental identification with that One Identity.

Thus on the cube, the line corresponding to Qoph and Key 18 is the line South–Below, connecting the lower end of the line South–West to the lower end of the line South–East. The current in this line South–Below moves from West to East, that is, from *appearances* to *causes.*

Observe that this line receives no influence from the line South–West, because the current of energy moves upward in that line. But it does receive direct influence from the line West–Below, corresponding to Ayin, Key 15,and the sign Capricorn. This line of South–Below is that of the sign Pisces, the twelfth, and last, sign of the Zodiac. This sign is ruled by Jupiter (corresponding to West on the cube), and in it Venus (corresponding to East) is said to be exalted. In this connection, note that the line runs from West to East, and at the South–East corner communicates its influence to the line South–East, corresponding to Key 5. Compare this with what was said at the end of the third paragraph on this page. Mental identification with the One Identity is precisely what is symbolized by Key 5, and this identification results from the reorganization symbolized by Key 18. And as a further confirmation of the attribution of Key 18 to the sign Pisces, you will note that Pisces rules the *feet*, and is therefore suggested by the path, or trace left by the feet of those who have traveled over it.

This week begin the practice of reviewing your day's activities just before going to sleep. If you keep a diary, it provides an excellent method for reviewing your gains and failures. Your attainments are just the stepping–stones in your progress toward Self–realization. Your failures are warnings as to what you must avoid in the future.

Never muse too long on your failures. Remember that what we call "sin" is literally nothing but missing the mark. Do not worry. Worry is concentration on the negative appearances of life. If you can worry well and at length, then you possess the ability to concentrate. Change the polarity of your thoughts and emotions in your daily life. Impress your subconsciousness, before you fall asleep, with the most positive images of good that you can fashion. Persist in this practice, and you will sow seeds that subconsciousness will build into a new and better bodily structure.

LESSON FORTY−ONE

THE SUN
(REGENERATION)

The fifth stage of spiritual unfoldment, symbolized by Key 19, is the stage of the new birth from natural humanity to spiritual humanity. Every ceremonial presentation of the process of regeneration employs this symbolism of rebirth.

In the natural man, the powers of subconsciousness are stifled and perverted by suggestions implanted as a result of erroneous conscious thinking. By applying the correct conscious self–direction to his efforts to grow, a man becomes a truly new–born being, one "twice–born." In this new birth the physical body is transformed, and the practical method that effects this change is concisely summarized in the injunction: "Be ye transformed by the renewing of your mind."

Meditate on these words. The new birth is a very real process, a deepening inner realization of the true status of man in the cosmic order. It is a degree of adeptship, that of liberation from the limitations of physical matter and circumstance. It is also a grade of conscious identification with the One Life.

Yet it is not final. For though it is a stage wherein all material resources are under the control of the adept, who, having himself become childlike, experiences the fulfillment of the promise: "A little child shall lead them;" the person who has reached this grade still feels himself to be a separate, or at least distinct, entity. This is not full liberation, but it is a higher stage than any of those preceding it. It is, in particular, the stage at which all physical forces are dominated by the will of the adept because he is an unobstructed vehicle for the power of the One Will, which has ruled those forces always, ever since the beginning.

The number 19 stands for the expression of the power symbolized by 9 through that symbolized by 1. In Tarot this is the expression of the force represented by the Hermit through the activity typified by the Magician. In this connection remember that you learned from Lessons Twenty–one and Twenty–two that the Hermit is a Tarot symbol of the Universal Will, or the single free will–power of the *One Identity*. And as the Magician represents the plane of personal self–consciousness, it becomes evident that, in relation to Tarot, the number 19 must designate the expression of the One Will at the level of personal self–consciousness.

The Hebrew letter Resh (ר) means "head." With the noun "head" we associate the idea of beginning, since that which is in the beginning comes first, or takes the lead, and therefore has precedence, priority and superiority. So we have the head of a government in its ruler, the head of a class in its brightest pupil, and the heads of a speech in the principal points of argument or exposition.

Again, we speak of "head" in the sense of power, as when we say "a full head of steam," suggesting concentrated energy. The ideas of completion and accomplishment, moreover, are conveyed by such phrases as "to bring to a head," or "to come to a head."

The sun is the heavenly body assigned to the letter Resh. This connects the esoteric meaning of the letter with all the ideas that have been associated with the sun. In both Testaments, the Bible calls God the sun of life and lights and, in all other great scriptures, the sun is a principal emblem of Deity.

In the alchemical writings we are told that the Great Work is the Operation of the Sun. The sun is also the symbol for alchemical gold of which Eliphas Levi says:

> The gold of the philosophers is, in religion, the absolute and supreme reason; in philosophy it is truth; in visible nature it is the sun, which is the emblem of the sun of truth, as that is itself the shadow of the First Source whence all splendours spring; in the subterranean world it is the purest and most perfect gold. For this reason the search after the *magnum opus* is called the search after the Absolute, and the great work is itself called the work of the sun.

Note particularly the correspondence between the sun and gold, for it is a clue to the whole Hermetic mystery. Thus Sendivogius says that the Philosophers' Stone is nothing other than gold digested to the highest degree. Similarly, the anonymous German author of the *Golden Tract* says: "The reader now knows that the substance of our Stone is neither animal nor vegetable, and that it does not belong to the minerals or the base metals, but that it must be extracted from gold and silver, and that our gold and silver are not the vulgar, dead gold and silver, but the living gold and silver of the Sages."

This living gold, in its primary manifestation, is the radiant energy of the sun, which is truly the First Matter of the Great Work. Concerning the First Matter, the alchemists say that it has as many names as there are things on earth, that it swims with the fishes in the sea, and flies with the birds in the air. Compare their doctrine with the following quotation from Tyndall's twelfth lecture on Heat:

> Every tree, plant, and flower, grows and flourishes by the grace

and bounty of the sun.

As surely as the force that moves a clock's hands is derived from the arm that winds up the clock, so surely is all terrestrial power derived from the sun.

Leaving out of account the eruption of volcanoes, and the ebb and flow of the tides, every mechanical action on the earth's surface, every manifestation of power, organic and inorganic, vital and physical, is produced by the sun. His warmth keeps the sea liquid and the atmosphere a gas, and all the storms, which agitate both, are blown by the mechanical force of the sun. He lifts the rivers and glaciers up to the mountains; and thus the cataract and the avalanche shoot with an energy derived immediately from him. Thunder and lightning are also his transmuted strength. Every fire that burns and every flame that glows dispenses light and heat, which originally belonged to the sun. In these days, unhappily, the news of battle is familiar to us, but every shock and every charge is an application, or misapplication, of the mechanical force of the sun. He blows the trumpet, he urges the projectile, he bursts the bomb. And remember, this is not poetry, but rigid mechanical truth. He rears, as I have said, the whole vegetable world, and through it the animal; the lilies of the field are his workmanship, the verdure of the meadows, and the cattle upon a thousand hills. He forms the muscle; he urges the blood; he builds the brain. His fleetness is in the lion's foot; he springs in the panther, he soars in the eagle, he slides in the snake. He builds the forest and hews it down, the power that raised the tree, and that wields the axe, being one and the same. The clover sprouts and blossoms and the scythe of the mower swings by the operation of the same force. The sun digs the ore from our mines, he rolls the iron; he rivets the plates, he boils the water; he draws the train. He not only grows the cotton, but he spins the fibre and weaves the web. There is not a hammer raised, or a wheel turned, or a shuttle thrown, that is not raised and turned and thrown by the sun. His energy is turned freely into space, but our world is a halting place where this energy is conditioned. Here the Proteus works his spells; the selfsame essence takes a million hues and shapes, and finally dissolves into its primitive and almost formless form. The sun comes to us as heat; he quits us as heat; and between his entrance and departure the multiform powers of our globe appear. They are all special forms of solar power — the moulds into which his strength is temporarily poured in passing from its source through infinitude.

239

This quotation is a brilliant exposition of the *physical* manifestations of the One Radiant Energy. In Tarot, as in alchemy, this ALL POWER is often represented as water, for, as Eliphas Levi says: "It is substance and motion at one and the same time; it is a fluid and a perpetual vibration." And one of the alchemists, speaking of this spiritual radiance as the First Matter or Primal Substance, declares: "If you call it water, you will not be wrong."

Down through the ages, the wise men that compose the Inner School have preserved the knowledge of this living, fluidic radiance. Modern science has gone far since Tyndall's day, and now its high priests give out a doctrine different from the Ageless Wisdom in just one particular. The modern doctrine is a result of speculative reasoning, based on analysis of the elements composing man's environment. The Ageless Wisdom is an expression of direct experience, *possible* for all men, but *known* to relatively few. The spiritual, fluidic, golden water of the alchemist is a *reality*, and may be perceived as immediately and definitely as any other phenomenon in nature. Hence alchemists aver that they have seen the First Matter with their own eyes, and have touched it with their hands.

They say, too, that their First Matter is *seen by all*, though known by few. It is, then, something within the range of even our physical sight. Its effects are perceptible by ordinary sensation, but not every person knows the significance of this that is seen by all. Ageless Wisdom is a record of the experience of those who, looking in the right direction, have *seen into* something that the uninitiated only *look at*.

In the human body, the point of entrance that admits this living radiance into the field of personality is a group of nerve cells forming what anatomists call the cardiac ganglion. This ganglion is in the sympathetic nervous system, just above and behind the heart, whose beat it controls. Through this center the undifferentiated Life–power enters the body, as an electric current enters a building through the main switch. The nerve cells of the sun center charge the bloodstream, as it passes through the heart, with this current of radiant energy. Persons having the finer vision, which is one of the consequences of occult training, are able to see the fine vibrations of this force as they enter the body through this "main switch."

According to astrology, the Sun rules the sign Leo, which governs the heart, and this confirms the Inner School's attribution of the sun to the cardiac ganglion, instead of to the solar plexus. Modern writers who make the latter erroneous attribution do so because they are misled by the anatomical name of the great nerve center behind the stomach, which in our work is correctly attributed to Jupiter. In relation to Tarot, this makes Key 19 the dominant force manifested by the process depicted in Key 8. Thus, you will profit by rereading Lessons Nineteen and Twenty with the thought in mind that what they explain is actually the result of what is symbolized by Key 19.

Again, astrology tells us that the sun is exalted, or raised to its highest form of expression, in the sign Aries, represented in Tarot by Key 4. Here again you will find it worthwhile to review Lessons Eleven and Twelve, thinking of what is pictured by the Emperor as being the perfected manifestation of what is symbolized by Key 19.

In studying Key 18, we noted that its number indicates a correspondence between the body–building processes symbolized by that Key and the functions of the Virgo region, typified by Key 9. In our study of Key 19 we have also to do with the same functions. For it will be remembered that what the alchemists call their Stone is also termed their *Medicine*. (Review in this connection the explanation of the word "Stone," given in Lesson Eight, in Lesson Fourteen, and in Lesson Eighteen.)

Consider now the separate letters of the noun אבן, A B N, *Ehben*, "Stone." The first is א, Aleph, symbol of the LifeBreath, typified by the Fool. The second is ב, Beth, representing Mercury and self–consciousness, the Magician. The third is ן, Nun, corresponding to Scorpio and the Key named Death. Add the numbers of these Keys together (0, 1 and 13) and their total is 14, the number of Temperance, which, you have learned, symbolizes the Knowledge and Conversation of the Holy Guardian Angel. That is to say, when we establish communication with the Higher Self, we enter into a state of consciousness in which we recognize the truth that the Father (אב) and the Son (בן) are truly ONE IDENTITY. We enter into this consciousness through the influx of the ALL POWER (Key 0) into the field of personal self–consciousness (Key 1), whence it is directed to the subconscious levels so as to modify the serpent power or Scorpio force. (In this connection observe that the Magician is cultivating flowers in his garden, and that flowers are the reproductive organs of the vegetable kingdom.)

241

As a result of the exercises that are undertaken by the practical occultist, the force that analytical psychology terms *libido* is raised or sublimated, so that it awakens the brain centers which bring us the higher order of knowing in which the Father (אב),

AB, and the Son (בן), BN, instead of being regarded as being separate, are seen to be ONE IDENTITY. That conscious realization is therefore not only the Stone (אבן), ABN, but also the *Medicine*, for it truly heals all diseases of mind and body. Sometimes it is called *the Medicine of Metals*, for the alchemical metals are the seven interior stars, related to seven nerve centers in the body.

Remember, this is a physiological as well as a psychological transformation. The body chemistry is changed. The subtle structure of the cells is altered. The "metals" are *healed* or made *whole* by our success in the Great Work. Thus we become in very truth *newly born* or regenerated.

As you color Key *19*, *fix its details in mind*, so that it will be easier to follow the explanations in the next lesson. Keep up the practice of reviewing the day's activities, but this week endeavor to intensify your realization that the entire *physical* aspect of those activities is, as the long quotation from Tyndall shows, really a transformation of solar energy.

COLORING INSTRUCTIONS

Yellow: Sun and rays, sunflower petals.

Green: Grass (circle should be darker than the rest of the grass), leaves.

Blue: Background. (This should circle round the rays extending from the sun. Blue projections, similar to these on the face of the sun in the Key, should extend inward from the edge of the circle toward the sun. Make these projections very short.)

Brown: Sunflower centers.

Gray: Wall.

Orange: Yods.

Blonde: Hair.

THE SUN
(Cont.)

The title, *The Sun*, corresponds to the dominant symbol of the Key, a radiant sun with a human countenance. It also confirms the attribution of this Key to the letter Resh, and conveys all the meanings attached to the solar symbol in the preceding lesson.

The sun itself is the conventional alchemical representation of the day–star, but there are details in the design which are important as showing the relation of Key 19 to other Keys.

The sun has eight salient or pointed rays. Thus the lines passing through these rays form the same angles as the lines within the circles of the Fool's dress, the lines that form the spokes of the Wheel of Fortune, and the lines of the great star in Key 17. The suggestion is that one and the same power is represented by all these symbols, since their geometrical basis is identical.

When you studied Key 17, you were told that the secondary rays of the great star would be seen again in Key 19. Here they are extended to form eight curved, or wavy, rays of the sun. It is as if there had been a development of power, and the nature of that development is clearly indicated, because curved lines invariably represent feminine aspects of the Life–power. In other words, what is shown in Key 19 is the equal development of masculine (salient) and feminine (wavy) forms of the universal radiant energy.

Besides these larger rays there are shown forty–eight beams, in groups of three, each group placed between a salient and a wavy ray. These refer to the expression of the One Force in works of integration, preservation and disintegration. Their number, 48, not only reduces to 12, but is also 4 x 12, so that it suggests some connection with Key 12, as well as the operation of the law symbolized by that Key in the four phases of "matter," — fire, water, air and earth.

Again, the salient rays of the sun, as masculine, refer to the solar radiance itself, and to the alchemical sun, always designated by the pronoun "he." The wavy rays, as feminine, refer to the lunar current of the Life–power, and the moon is always designated as "she." The number 48 is the value of the Hebrew noun כוכב, K V K B, *Kokab*, the name of the planet Mercury. Hence the three types of rays extending from the solar disk hint at the combination of sun (salient), moon (wavy) and Mercury (the 48 beams). This, together with the fact that the sun has a human face, makes it evident that this symbol is a representation of the perfected Operation of the Sun, for the alchemists say: "The Great Work is performed by the Sun and Moon, with the aid of Mercury." That work is the work, which regenerates personality, and its perfection gives us the *Stone* (אבן), ABN, described over and over again as something which can never be made save by the grace of God. That is, to attain the goal, something *more* than personal effort is required and that something more is an influx of power from the superconscious level of the Life–power's self–expression.

Round the disk of the sun there are shown a series of short lines. Their number is not accidental. There are exactly 125, and 125, as the *cube* of the number 5 (5x5x5), represents the power of that number exercised in a threefold manner, or through the entire extent of the three–dimensional world. If we remember that the number 5 is represented in geometry by the pentagram, symbol of the dominion of Spirit over the elements, it will be evident that 125 conveys symbolically the idea of the extension of that dominion over and through every part of nature.

That dominion is the *Stone* and the *Universal Medicine*. But in the preceding lesson you learned that the letters of A B N, the Stone, correspond to Keys 0, 1 and 13, so that Key 14 sums up one aspect of the Stone. Then, since the digits of 14 add to 5, the number of the Hierophant, there is evidently a connection between Key 5 and the Stone. This is really true, for the Knowledge and Conversation of the Holy Guardian Angel is none other than continuous intuitive perception of reality, communicated through interior hearing. Hence we enjoy not knowledge only, but also *conversation*. Furthermore, the number 14 is the value of the word זהב, Zahab, referred to in Lesson Thirty–six.

There the point was made that Zahab is the alchemical gold, which is defined in the quotation from Eliphas Levi in Lesson Forty–one. This "gold" is what is symbolized by the Sun in Key 19 and, in Key 14, the same "gold" is pictured as an angel, on whose forehead gleams a solar disk.

In Key 19, the human features of the solar orb, as in all alchemical representations of the sun, are intended to show that it is a symbol of living, conscious intelligence. Ancient occult doctrine holds that all celestial bodies are vehicles of intelligence, and the deeper modern science goes in its analysis of the physical universe, the more evident does it become that this ancient notion is essentially true, though it may be true in a subtler, finer sense than was understood by some of our ancient brethren. The main point is that the sun, as a synthesis of all the active forces entering into the composition of human personality, is here shown as a *living force*, not as a merely physical energy.

It is a power like unto ourselves. We have something in common with it. It enters intimately into our lives. Tyndall's words, quoted in the preceding lesson, show that even on the physical plane our lives are part of a series of transformations of solar energy. That energy constitutes a circuit. It is not merely that energy coming *from* the sun flows through our bodies and takes form in their activities. It is that energy coming from the sun *and flowing back to it again* produces all the phenomena of human experience. Thus the solar energy shines in us, and our energy shines in the sun. There is a difference in the degree of radiance, but sun and man are lights on the same circuit of invisible spiritual energy. This is a central doctrine of Ageless Wisdom, and it has important practical consequences.

The letters Yod which are shown falling from the sun (six on each side, and one in the middle, between the children) are thirteen in number, so as to suggest first of all the ideas of Unity and Love, inasmuch as 13 is the value of the Hebrew nouns designating these two ideas. The letters that fall are Yods, to indicate the Law of Response associated with that letter, and also to show that in what is pictured here, the secret activity associated with the sign Virgo plays its part. A further suggestion of their number, 13, is that this number is that of the Tarot Key associated with the sign Scorpio. For it is a combination of the forces of Scorpio (13) and Virgo (Yods) that does bring about the state of regeneration wherein Unity and Love are made manifest throughout the personality.

The sunflowers are five in number. Four are open. These are symbols of four great stages in the development of form: 1. The mineral kingdom; 2. The vegetable kingdom; 3. The animal kingdom; and 4. The kingdom of the natural man. The unopened sunflower represents a stage of development as yet un–experienced by most persons. It is a symbol of the kingdom of spiritual humanity, composed of regenerated men and women. This kingdom goes as far beyond that of the natural man as that of the natural man goes beyond that of the animal.

The four sunflowers symbolizing the kingdoms already perfected are turned across the wall, so that they face the children, as if the latter were their suns, to which they turn for life and light. The idea suggested is that the kingdoms of nature so represented are actually turning to, and thus expressing their dependence on, the regenerated humanity typified by the children.

The fifth sunflower turns toward the sun above, for it and the children symbolize the same thing. It is representative of a state of being as yet in its earlier stages of development, in bud but not in full bloom. Thus at present it is more dependent on the working of universal forces than on any embodiment of those forces in human personality. The natural man and the three kingdoms below him are even now dependent on the new–born spiritual humanity, and receive their sustenance *through* that spiritualized flowering of the human race. Spiritual humanity itself, however, turns only to that which is above for support.

The wall behind the children is of stone. Thus it represents forms of truth, as opposed to the forms of error typified by the bricks of the tower in Key 16. It is, nevertheless, a wall, and it has five courses, to show that it is built of materials drawn from sense–experience. Those materials are aspects of truth, or reality. On this point Ageless Wisdom is explicit. It does not deny the truth of sense–experience. Even though our senses do not give us a full report, the report is true as far as it goes.

The difficulty is that most persons believe there are no aspects of truth other than those we learn through physical sensation. By limiting themselves to sensation, they build an artificial barrier that halts their further progress. Thus the wall says: "Thus far, and no farther, shalt thou go." Yet we shall see that Key 19 has intimations of another way.

The children are nude. Thus they repeat the symbolism of Key 17, where we see nature unveiling herself as truth. In Key 19, we see humanity so perfectly identified with that same truth that it has nothing whatever to conceal.

Here we anticipate an objection. Someone may say, "What about the secrecy with which Masters of Wisdom are supposed to surround themselves?" The answer is that they do nothing of the kind. The veils that hide them from us are of our own making, even as is the Veil of Isis. Our ignorance is the veil, rather than any effort of theirs to remain concealed. The Masters are the most childlike and transparent of human beings. Their lives are simple. Their words are simple. It is because they are so plain and direct that what they say is so seldom understood. Hence one of the old alchemical authors says:

> The Sages, then, do well to call their gold or earth water, for they have a perfect right to term it whatever they like. So they have frequently called their Stone their gold, their super–perfect gold, their regenerate gold, and by many other names besides. If any one does not perceive their meaning at the first glance, he must blame his own ignorance, not their jealousy.

A few lines back you read that Key 19 has intimations of another way than that which is barred by man's interpretations of his sense experience. This other way is hinted at by the fact that both children turn their backs to the wall. The nature of the other way is indicated by the fairy ring in which they are dancing.

These two concentric circles are symbols of the fourth dimension. The way of the spiritual man is not as the way of the natural man. The spiritual man centers himself in the inner circle of manifestation. By repeated practice, he has made habitual his inner identification with the ONE SPIRITUAL SELF.

Hence the children are shown as being of equal stature, and standing on the same level. In the natural man, subconsciousness, the feminine aspect of personality, is subordinate. She is subjected to the misunderstandings and misinterpretations of the masculine, or conscious mind. This is not so in the life of a spiritual man, whose subconsciousness is released from the bondage of erroneous suggestion. In spiritual humanity the powers of subconsciousness are rightly understood and rightly unfolded. Under correct application of the law of suggestion, subconscious habits have been established that repudiate utterly the notion that, because we cannot attain to certainty through sensation, we cannot attain to certainty at all.

For this reason the first of the Tarot Keys is named "The Fool." The certainty of freedom possessed by the spiritual man is knowledge gained by means, which go beyond sensation. Such knowledge seems folly to the uninitiated, and the world of sense–bound humanity derides it. For the Way of Certainty is the Way of Non–Sense, even as St. Paul said when he declared that his doctrine was "sheer folly" to the Greeks. Do not confuse this esoteric Non–Sense with the ordinary meaning of the word "nonsense." Some well–intentioned persons do, in this age of eager, but often ill–directed, quest for occult truth. Thus it seems, often, that the one sure way to gain a wide popular hearing for anything purporting to be occultism is to make it as fantastically preposterous as possible. This the Inner School permits, in order to test the discrimination of those who seek to approach its portals.

The little girl makes the gesture of repudiation toward the wall, this indicating that subconsciousness has been trained to accept the Other Way. The little boy holds the palm of his hand away from the wall, in a gesture of acceptance which complements what is expressed by the gesture of the girl. He is ready to receive the New Light on the Open Way.

These two figures represent the regenerated personality. Compare them with the kneeling figures at the feet of the Hierophant. Lay out Keys 5, 12, and 19, as shown in the Tarot tableau given in Lesson Two. Taken together in this manner the Keys have more power to evoke thought than they do when studied separately.

Let us now consider Key 19 in its relation to the direction South, or the southern face of the cube of space shown in the diagrams accompanying Lesson Eighteen.

We are to regard the Key as representing this face of the cube, so that the part of the design at the observer's right is the eastern half of the picture, and the part at the observer's left is the western half. We thus see that the little girl corresponds to the direction South–East, as do one of the sunflowers and the unopened bud. From this we learn that it is only in humanity that the function of subconsciousness as Intuition is really expressed. Subconsciousness is its agency of manifestation. In the kingdoms of nature below man, true Intuition cannot be manifest, because Intuition is conscious awareness of universal principles, and this conscious awareness is not among the functions of the various organisms in the three kingdoms of nature below that of the natural man.

In those three kingdoms, represented by the three sunflowers behind the boy, there is an ever–increasing development of consciousness, approximating, in the higher animals, something very like man's self–consciousness. Animals like dogs and cats have most decided personalities. So have birds accustomed to captivity, like canaries and parrots. It is far from being true that these higher animals are *completely* identified with a group–soul, and have no identity of their own. They have, in fact, almost as much distinct identity as many types of human beings, including some who are very glib with their patter about animal group–souls, learnt by rote from Theosophical primers. Thus it may be well to point out here that humanity has a group–soul just as truly as do the animals, and many are the men and women who are by no

248

means free from being dominated by it.

The little boy and the three sunflowers behind him represent the direction South–West, corresponding to the sign Scorpio and Key 13. And it really is through the operation of the force represented by Key 13 that the development of successive states of consciousness is made possible. For this force is the active principle of generation and reproduction that provides the Life–power with the millions of physical vehicles necessary to the evolution of human personality at the level of the natural man. And this same force, directed purposefully by the regenerated consciousness of man, typified by the little boy, is what completes the Great Work,

The upper part of Key 19 corresponds to the upper part of the southern face of the cube, and so we find that the Sun is a repetition of the Blazing Star of Key 17, here brought into full manifestation.

The lower part of Key 19 corresponds to the direction South–Below, and thus we learn that the fairy ring of Key 19 is another way of symbolizing what is taught by Key 18. The ring is the Ring–Pass–Not of the regenerated organism. The children clasp hands above its center. For the Other Way and the Way of Return are one, and that One Way leads *within*, or *from the surface to the center*. This we shall see very plainly expressed by the last two Keys of the Tarot series, to be studied in the next four lessons.

The student will do well to take the hint given in this part of the lesson, and study the other Keys corresponding to faces of the cube in the same way. Note that because the human mind can never get *behind* the plane of causes, the eastern face of the cube, corresponding to Key 3, must be viewed *from the west*, so that the right side of Key 3 is to be interpreted as South–East, and the left side as North–East. Similarly, the lower face of the cube must be viewed from above, so that the right side of the Key will correspond to South–Below, and the left side of the Key to North–Below, with the upper part corresponding to East–Below, and the lower part to West–Below.

North, again, is the place of the unknown, so that we cannot get behind that. Hence we look at Key 16 as if we were facing it from the south, which puts North–East on the right side of Key 16, and North–West on the left side.

The wise student will take these hints, but it should be understood that they are no more than hints. The complete exposition of the correlation of Tarot with the cube of space would require

249

a great many volumes. We most certainly advise you to give *some* time to it, recording your findings in your occult diary; but we warn you also, at this stage of your work, against becoming too much preoccupied with this phase of Tarot study.

LESSON FORTY–THREE

JUDGEMENT
(REALIZATION)

20 JUDGEMENT

Key 20 shows the sixth stage of spiritual unfoldment, in which the personal consciousness is on the verge of blending with the universal. At this stage the adept realizes that his personal existence is nothing but a manifestation of the relation between self–consciousness and subconsciousness. He sees, also, that self–consciousness and subconsciousness are not themselves personal, but are modes of universal consciousness. He knows that in reality his personality has no separate existence. At this stage his intellectual conviction is confirmed by a fourth dimensional experience that blots out the delusion of separateness.

The number 20 has already gained special significance for you as the number of the letter Kaph, to which Key 10, the Wheel of Fortune, is assigned. Thus 20 is for you a numeral symbol of mental grasp or comprehension.

This idea is basic in connection with Key 20, because in this Key we see the result of completing the cycle of manifestation represented by the Wheel. In the lesson on Key 10, it was pointed out that humanity at large is yet in the position of Hermanubis, and that the completion of the Great Work consists in the extension of the light of intelligence through that segment of the wheel that is marked by the letter Yod. In other words, when man comprehends his true nature, he sees that that nature is identical with the One Reality, the One Will of which the universe is a manifestation. Then he says, "I have no will but to do the will of him that sent me."

On the other hand, he *knows* that will. He knows it as a will to freedom, as a will to joy, as a will to health, as a will to abundance. He knows that it is a will to good, to the impartation of every good and perfect gift. He comprehends it as the Will that finds expression in all activity. Here and now, he sees that Will expresses no lack, no disease, no failure, and no poverty. He grasps the truth that whatever appearances of evil surround us, they seem as they do because we are not yet seeing the true relations.

For such a one, daily experience is a succession of miracles. When we begin to see the light, it is like the lightning–flash of Key 16. While it lasts, it breaks down structures of error, and shows all existence as it really is. Then the darkness of ignorance closes in again, and we have to wait for the next flash.

In the state represented by Key 20, however, there is a perpetual recognition of the power of Spirit. Thus 20, read from units to tens, expresses the operation of the No–Thing through memory, or the working of the Fool's vision through the law of the High Priestess. Here there is freedom from those lapses of memory that assail us earlier in the work. Moment by moment, without cessation, we see the truth and live it. With this recognition comes a new kind of consciousness. *We do not sleep any more.* Our bodies are put to rest, but *we* remain awake, able to function consciously in the fourth dimension, so that we actually do "serve God day and night."

This is one of the meanings of conscious immortality. I testify to my knowledge that it is an experience of normal men and women. To be unconscious eight hours out of the twenty–four is as unnecessary as to wear a gas–mask in ordinary air. We are immortal and, whether we know it or not, we can function consciously during the sleep of the body.

The greater number of persons, however, do not recall their nocturnal experiences, because they have not developed the physical instruments for recording it. Once this power of recalling the experience is developed, it is possible to plan for the night's work, and the recollection of it will be part of the day's activities. Until this is known experimentally, no human language can convey the alteration it makes in one's whole life.

The Hebrew letter Shin (ש) means "a tooth or fang." In its form this letter resembles three tongues of flame rising from a fiery base. Thus the element of fire is attributed to this, the third and last of the Hebrew *Mother* letters. The sound of the letter, "Sh!" is an admonition to silence understood by all men. So, but more imperative, is the sharper hiss of which this letter is also a sign in Hebrew. Thus the letter Shin corresponds by sound to the final admonition of the Masters: BE SILENT!

Serpents, everywhere recognized as symbols of wisdom, are silent, subtle creatures. Jesus told his disciples to be wise as serpents, thus emphasizing, for those who had ears to hear, the ancient doctrine of silence. Evidently, then, in beginning our study of the letter Shin, we are approaching a great wisdom, which has always been reserved, something about which silence must be kept.

Knowers of the Secret do not maintain silence because they are niggardly with their spiritual possessions. Nor is silence kept because any order of beings higher than man imposes a prohibition forbidding speech. Neither is silence observed because there is danger in the Secret. The one reason for silence is thus phrased by Lao–Tze:

"The Tao which is the subject of discussion is not the true Tao." This is identical with the statement of the alchemists, which is really negative, though it seems to be positive in its wording: "Our Matter has as many names as there are things in this world: that is why the foolish know it not."

The Great Secret simply *cannot* be told. Hence it is folly to try to tell it. The wise waste no time, invite no misconception, expend no energy in vain efforts to tell. When they speak, it is not to tell the Secret, but to point out the Way.

On the other hand, those who know the Secret are forever telling it, not only by their words, but also by their lives. Thus a correspondent writes: "How strange that though I had read the same statement hundreds of times, it is only now that I perceive it!" As when we learn a foreign language, so with the speech of the wise. At first the words are meaningless noises. Presently we apprehend some of the meanings. If we persist in our study, a day arrives when not only the dictionary definitions of the words, but also the subtle connotations and implications that no lexicographer may hope to capture, are conveyed to us *in the very same words* which meant nothing in the beginning.

So it is with these Tarot studies, where not only the written word, but also the more expressive language of picture symbols, is used to communicate the mysteries. I must again remind you that in these lessons you are given keys, which will open the doors of the prison–house of ignorance, and admit you to the freedom of the True World. The language of symbol is the common speech of the inhabitants of that True World. All languages of mankind are but poor translations from it.

If you ask, as some have done, "Why not put this into plain English?" I answer that wherever plain English will convey the meaning, it is my constant endeavor to use it. Yet no translation from the mystery language can ever be adequate. You must learn that *silent speech* of symbols for yourself. Then you will find that you are in communication with others who know it.

In old versions of Tarot, as in ours, Key 20 is invariably named *The Judgment*. On the surface this refers to that day which theologians regard as being afar off — the day when all souls shall be judged. This is a veil for the real meaning. Judgment is the consequence of weighing evidence. Hence Justice is always represented by the scales, and in ancient Egyptian representations of the judgment of the soul, the candidate's heart was put in the balance with the feather of truth.

Again, judgment implies estimation or measurement. One might say that the Great Secret answers the question: "How much do you weigh?" That is to say, we have to see that since all that is real of us is *identical* with the One Thing, our true weight must be the same as its true weight. The consciousness of totality comes in here. George Burnell expresses it beautifully: "Truth is that which is; there cannot be that which is not. Therefore that which is, or Truth, must be *all* there is." When the weight of the heart — the central consciousness in man — corresponds to the weight of the feather of truth, then the scales of judgment are balanced.

A judgment is a reasoned conclusion. Ageless Wisdom offers a reasonable doctrine. The sages forever say: "Come now, let us reason together." St. Paul, writing of the giving up of the false sense of personality, calls it a reasonable sacrifice. The Chaldean Oracles bid us join works to sacred reason. Thus in the symbols of Key 20 we shall find many references to the number 4, the Tarot number particularly associated with reason.

Yet, since a judgment is a reasoned *conclusion*, and reasoning leads to that conclusion, judgment is also the end of reasoning. In Key 20, reasoning has come to its term and a new order of knowing is manifested. Old things have passed away through the operation of the law pictured by Key 13, which is the agency of the principle of right discrimination pictured by Key 6. There is to be no more weighing of evidence, no more discussion of pros and cons, no more argument for and against. That is all done with, and in the picture we shall find abundant evidence of this.

Finally, a judgment is a decision. It has direct consequences in action. Note that word "decision," and its derivation from a Latin root meaning "to cut." In this you have the same hint that is given by the correspondence of the letter Shin to a Hebrew word meaning "separation." The Judgment cuts off, forever, our connection with the false knowledge of "this world." It puts an end to our limitation to three–dimensional consciousness. It terminates our sense of mortality.

Thus, in a Bible promise which is directly related to this doctrine of Judgment, we read: "They shall hunger *no more*, neither thirst *any more*,... and death shall be no more; neither shall there be mourning, nor crying, nor pain, *any more*."

To have done with all this misery. Nothing less. That is the promise, and to have done with it *forever*. Not a makeshift alleviation. A devouring flame of realization, which consumes the whole unhappy brood of lies.

This week try to practice SILENCE. Speak as little as you can, keep your emotions under control, and above all, try to make your thoughts quiet. Notice that this conserves energy for useful endeavors. Continue this practice, the rest of your life.

COLORING INSTRUCTIONS

Yellow: Bell of trumpet, rays from clouds.

Blue: Background, water, angel's dress.

Gray: Bodies of human figures, coffins (dark gray).

White: Clouds, banner (not cross), icebergs (blue highlights, very delicate), collar edging on angel's dress.

Gold: Trumpet.

Blonde: Hair of woman, child and angel.

Red: Angel's wings, cross on banner.

THE JUDGMENT
(Cont.)

The angel of Key 20 is obviously Gabriel, for he carries the trumpet, which summons the dead from their coffins. Gabriel is the archangel of the element of water, and he is also the archangel of the moon. In this connection, observe that 2, the number of the Key attributed to the moon, is the root–number of 20. Furthermore, in Key 2 all the water shown in Tarot has its source.

The idea here is that the presiding power in the scene is the power of reflection, the root–power of the Universal Memory. Gabriel means "Might of God," and the suggestion is, therefore, that human personality is raised from the "death" of three–dimensional consciousness by a power descending from above, rather than by its own efforts. The Spirit of Life in us never forgets itself, and when the Day of Judgment comes, we hear its trumpet call, proclaiming our real nature, and calling us from the deathlike sleep of belief in mortal existence.

In the composition of our version of this Key, care has been taken to enclose the angel in a geometrical design consisting of two equal circles, exactly filling a larger circle. The angel's head is in the upper small circle, his body in the lower one. This figure is an ancient symbol of the fourth dimension.

Clouds surround the angel because the true nature of the Self is veiled by appearances, and the substance of these appearances is really the same as the stream of consciousness typified by the robe of the High Priestess. It is the flow of the stream of consciousness, which gives rise to our ideas of time, and these ideas are what partly veil from us the true nature of the One Identity.

Twelve rays of light pierce the clouds. These have a technical Qabalistic meaning, for in Hebrew wisdom the number 12 refers particularly to the name הוא, H V A, *Hoa*, (pronounced *Hu*). This is the Hebrew third personal pronoun "He," attributed to Kether, the Crown of Primal Will. The intimation here is that the light piercing the veil is the light of the True Self, called "He" by Qabalists. Gabriel personifies one aspect of that light.

Descending from the trumpet are seven rays. The trumpet itself is made of gold, and in preceding lessons you have learned the occult significance of this metal. As an instrument for amplifying sound vibration, the trumpet refers to the fact that the awakening of the higher consciousness is actually accomplished by certain definite sounds. These are represented by the seven little rays, which correspond to the sound vibrations of the seven interior centers that we saw represented by the seven small stars of Key 17.

The icebergs in the background refer to a certain alchemical dictum that says that in order to perform the Great Work we must *fix the volatile*. The volatile is the stream of conscious energy, typified as water. Its flow gives rise to the illusions from which our delusions are derived. When we fix it, or make it solid by arresting the flow, we are emancipated from bondage.

Thus Key 12 shows the Hanged Man, or Suspended Mind, in connection with the element of water. The state of Samadhi, or perfect abstraction, there pictured, culminates in the Perpetual Intelligence symbolized by Key 20. The higher consciousness arrests the flow of the stream of mental energy and, because it does this by means of abstractions having their basis in mathematics, the arrested flow of consciousness is represented by ice, as it is in Keys 0 and 9.

The sea, moreover, is the *end* of a flowing of water. Thus it suggests the same notions of termination and conclusion that we found associated with the word "judgment."

The sea supports three stone coffins, intimating that the real support or basis for the appearances of physical form is really the vibration of mental energy. The sea is the great sea of the racial consciousness, operating at the subconscious level. This is the actual substance of all things in human environment. There is no difference whatever between the substance of an electron and the substance of a thought. In these days this ancient doctrine of Ageless Wisdom is receiving abundant confirmation from leading exoteric scientists.

The coffins are rectangular, to suggest the apparent solidity and impenetrability of three–dimensional forms. The human figures stand upright, so that their bodies are at right angles to the bottoms of the coffins. This intimates something that it is impossible actually to represent — the mathematical definition of the Fourth Dimension as that which is at right angles to all three dimensions of space as we perceive them.

The three figures represent self–conscious awareness (the man), subconsciousness (the woman), and their product, the regenerated personality (the child). They correspond also to the

Egyptian triad, Osiris the father, Isis the mother, and Horus the child.

Their postures hint to the initiated that each figure represents a Roman letter. The woman, by her extended arms, denotes L. The child lifts his hands over his head, so that his arms make a V. The man, in the traditional posture of Osiris risen, crosses his arms to form an X. Thus the three persons symbolize L.V.X., the Latin for *Light*.

The man is in an attitude of perfectly passive adoration. In fourth–dimensional consciousness, or the Perpetual Intelligence, the self–conscious mind realizes that it does nothing whatever of itself. It is merely a channel through which the higher life descends to lower levels. Its one virtue consists in what is intimated by the name of the mode of consciousness typified by the Magician, the Intelligence of *Transparency*. The more transparent self–consciousness becomes, the less interference it offers to the free passage of the One Thing. "Of myself I can do nothing," is the meaning of the man's crossed arms. The X crosses out, or cancels, the idea of personal origination for any action.

The woman actively receives the influx of power from above. Since her posture suggests the letter L, it is related to Lamed and to Key 11, which represents the Faithful Intelligence. Under the governance of right reason, subconsciousness expresses perfect faith. Unreasonable faith is impossible, however stoutly men may affirm that their creeds and dogmas deserve to be called *faiths*. Thus the woman represents the purification following right reasoning, the subconscious response to correct estimates of reality.

The child faces toward the interior of the picture. Thus he represents insight, the turning of the mind away from the false reports of external sensation. His posture corresponds to V, or Vav. He is thus a type of Intuition, and of the Triumphant and Eternal Intelligence. "And a little child shall lead them."

The three figures are nude, to suggest a state of perfect innocence, a state of freedom from shame, that false emotion engendered by our incorrect interpretation of the real nature of human life and its functions. Their nudity also suggests perfect intimacy. This, of course, is one of the conditions of the Perpetual Intelligence, in which the true relations between the conscious and subconscious minds and their offspring, personality, are clearly understood.

The flesh of the figures is gray, to show that they have overcome all the pairs of opposites, since gray is the tint resulting

259

from the blending of any two complementary colors, such as white and black, red and green, blue and orange, and so on.

Since the Tarot Keys which correspond to the seven interior centers correspond also to the pairs of opposites, here is also an intimation that in the Perpetual Intelligence there is a perfect blending of the seven pairs of opposites: Life and Death (Key 1); Peace and Strife (Key 2); Wisdom and Folly (Key 3); Wealth and Poverty (Key 10); Beauty and Ugliness (Key 16); Fertility and Sterility (Key 19}; and Dominion and Slavery (Key 21}. In other words, the gray flesh of the figures shows that the forces of the centers have been perfectly coordinated, even as the seven rays issuing from the trumpet hint at the same thing.

The banner on the trumpet is a square, measuring 5x5 units, so that it is really a magic square of twenty–five cells, or magic square of Mars. Thus it refers to the activity associated with Mars in Tarot. Fire, the quality of Mars, predominates in Key 20, and Key 20 is placed in the tableau beneath Key 13, which represents the sign Scorpio, ruled by Mars.

Since the banner is square and bears an equal–armed cross, both the banner and the cross are symbols of the number 4. The same number is indicated by the four figures in the picture. There are also four principal elements in the scene: the icebergs, the sea, the group of human figures, and the angel.

For Tarot students, 19 represents Key 4, the Emperor. The Emperor stands for Aries, a fiery sign ruled by Mars. The Emperor is also the Tarot symbol of the sovereign reason, which leads to decision or right judgment. The number of Key 20 is 4x5, and this is suggested also by the fact that the square banner is bounded by four lines each five units in length, so that the perimeter of the square is 20. The Perpetual Intelligence may also be thought of as being the product of the interaction of Reason (Key 4) and Intuition (Key 5). We must reason rightly before we receive the inner teaching of Intuition. Lazy minds will not hear the angel's trumpet call.

In the cube of space, the line corresponding to the letter Shin is the coordinate line joining the north face to the south. This line moves from the *center*, as do all three coordinates. The reason for this is that the cube is brought into manifestation *from the central point.*

The first coordinate is the line of the Mother letter Aleph, extending upward from the center to the face Above, corresponding to the letter Beth, and downward from the center to the face Below, corresponding to the letter Gimel.

The second coordinate is the line of the letter Mem, extending eastward from the center to the face East, corresponding to Daleth, and westward from the center to the face West, corresponding to Kaph.

Note that the first co–ordinate, because it corresponds to Aleph and the Fool, is that of the Life–Breath. The mode of consciousness it represents is *spiritual consciousness*, which we usually term "superconsciousness." But, as has been said elsewhere in these lessons, the terms "above" and "within" are often interchangeable in occultism. Our habits of thought are vestiges of ancestral thinking, when "heaven" was identified with the sky, which appears to be *above* the surface of the earth. But Masters of life know that the true location of "heaven" is not up, but in. Hence Jesus declared: "The kingdom of heaven is *within* you."

Superconsciousness, therefore, is *interior consciousness*. Thus in Key 18, the Path of Return *appears* to ascend, but really it leads *within*. Similarly, in Key 20, the little child faces *into* the picture, as do the listening ministers in Key 5.

Hence each of the cube coordinates is a symbol for an aspect of superconsciousness, or *awareness of the within*. In Key 12 that awareness is shown as a reversal of the mental attitude of the average man, who is concerned almost wholly with outer appearances, and his mental and emotional reactions to them. Key 12, through the letter Mem, is related to the element of water, and thus it connects the eastern face of the cube, attributed to Venus, fabled to have been born from the foam of the ocean, to the western face, attributed to Jupiter, the sky–father who is ruler of rains and storms.

The third coordinate is associated with the element of fire, and links together the northern face of the cube, attributed to the fiery planet Mars, and the southern face, attributed to the Sun, source of all manifestations of fire in our world–system.

The first coordinate, that of Aleph, is associated with *life*. The second coordinate is assigned to Mem, and to *substance*, which is symbolized universally as water. The third co–ordinate is that which has to do principally with *activity*, symbolized as fire by the Hermetic philosophers.

Thus Key 0 is mainly concerned with the superconscious awareness of *life*, Key 12 with superconscious awareness of the nature of *substance*, and Key 20 with superconscious awareness of the true nature of *activity*. If you will develop these hints, you will find out for yourself many aspects of truth that will be all the more valuable to you because they will be your own discoveries.

Note also that since in each of these coordinate lines the direc-

261

tion of movement is double, away from the center in two opposite directions, it is impossible to follow any of these lines *back to the center*. How, then, shall one get to that center? By following one or other of the four interior diagonals. These are not shown in the diagrams accompanying Lesson Eighteen, because they would have been confusing, but you can work them out without any difficulty, if you attend closely to what follows.

These four interior diagonals correspond to four of the five *final* forms of certain letters in the Hebrew alphabet. When the letters Kaph, Mem, Nun, Peh or Tzaddi come at the *end* of a Hebrew word, they are always written in a special way. Kaph at the end of a word is always ך, not כ. Mem at the end of a word is ם, not מ. Final Nun is always ן, final Peh always ף, and final Tzaddi always is written ץ.

The four diagonals all extend *upward* from the bottom of the cube, and they all pass through the center. The path of final Kaph (ך) begins at the south–east lower corner and runs diagonally through the center to the north–west *upper* corner, connecting the *lower* end of the south–east line with the upper end of the north–west line. The path of final Nun (ן) begins at the north–east lower corner, and runs upward through the center to the south–west upper corner., connecting the lower end of the north–east line to the upper end of the south–west line. The path of final Peh (ף) is the diagonal connecting the lower end of the south–west line with the upper end of the north–east line. The path of final Tzaddi (ץ) joins the lower end of the north–west line to the upper end of the southeast line. The place of final Mem (ם) is at the center of the cube, the point of perfect equilibrium and stillness.

From this it will be evident that it is by means of the psychological and other activities represented by Keys 10, 13, 16 and 17 that the steps are taken that lead consciousness inward to the *center*. Because the four diagonals all move upward toward the center from the plane represented by the lower surface, and in Tarot by Key 2, it is also evident that the life–force of the person undergoing occult training moves along these paths as a result of responses originating at the subconscious level. That is to say, the upward movement along the diagonals is a consequence of, or response to, a prior *downward* movement originating at the conscious level represented by the cube's upper face.

For example, the *shortest* way to get to the beginning of the diagonal corresponding to final Kaph is to descend through the line North–East, corresponding to Key 4, thence along the line

East–Below, corresponding to Key 7, and then upward through the diagonal corresponding to final Kaph and Key 10.

The shortest way to reach the starting–point of the diagonal corresponding to final Nun is simply to descend the line corresponding to the Emperor.

The shortest way to reach the beginning of the diagonal corresponding to final Peh is to descend the north–east line, thence to go westward through the line North–Below, and thence southward through the line West–Below.

The shortest way to reach the beginning of the diagonal corresponding to final Tzaddi is to descend the line North–East, and go west to the end of the line North–Below, which is also the beginning of the diagonal of final Tzaddi.

Note that the first of these diagonals is that of Kaph, hence it cannot be traversed until the western face of the cube, corresponding to Kaph, has been bounded. That is, *none of the interior diagonals can be entered until one has passed through the line West–Below, corresponding to Key 15.* It is to be understood, of course, that this is purely diagrammatic. What is meant is that one is not ready for the journey toward the Center until one has faced the definite problem, which happens to be one's own Dweller on the Threshold.

Having arrived at the center by way of any one of the four interior diagonals, one may then pass in any of ten different ways to the exterior. Four lines lead to the upper corners through the diagonals, and six lines lead to the faces through the lines of the mother letters. Thus we learn that Keys 0, 12, 20, 10, 13, 16 and 17 represent the ways leading from the center to the external faces and corners of the cube.

All this is probably difficult at first reading, but it is included in the lessons at this point because nothing in this whole system of Tarot symbolism, with the possible exception of the Cabalistic Tree of Life, is of greater value. Thus we advise you most emphatically to follow all these descriptions of the cube symbolism and directions *with the diagrams, and with the various Tarot Keys.*

We approach the end of this course. Now is the time to bring your occult diary up to date. Go back through the lessons, and make sure that you are actually carrying out the practical instruction. The cumulative effect of the comparatively simple tasks that have been set for you is most valuable. Do not be deceived by the seeming simplicity of some of this work. Nature operates by simple means, and the Great Work is an imitation of those simple methods whereby she accomplishes marvelous results.

LESSON FORTY–FIVE

THE WORLD
(COSMIC CONSCIOUSNESS)

21 THE WORLD

The last card of the major Tarot Keys, *The World*, is a symbol of cosmic consciousness, or Nirvana. The central fact of this experience is that he to whom it comes has first–hand knowledge of his identity with the One power which is the Pivot and Source of the whole cosmos. He knows also that through him the governing and directing power of the universe flows out into manifestation.

Words fail to give any adequate idea of this seventh stage of spiritual unfoldment. It must be left to your intuition to combine the suggestions of the picture with the meaning of the letter Tav (ת), which is assigned to this Key. Here is a picture of what you really are, and of what the cosmos really is. The universe is the Dance of Life. The inmost, central Self of you — THAT is the Eternal Dancer.

21 is the sum of the numbers from 0 to 6, so that as a Key number in Tarot it shows the completion or extension of the power of the principles represented by the seven Keys from Key 0 to Key 6. Thus there is a close affinity between Key 21 and Key 7, for as 21 is the consequence of adding the digits from 0 to 6, so 7 *follows* 6 in the numeral scale. Furthermore, we shall find that Saturn is attributed to Key 21, and Saturn is the *seventh* of the planets known to the ancients. From Saturn's Hebrew name, *Shabbathai*, we get the same meaning as from Sabbath, the day of rest or inertia, and the seventh day of the week. In the Tarot tableau, moreover, Key 21 (3x7) is placed immediately below Key 14(2x7), and Key 14 is placed immediately below Key 7. Thus the principle at work in Key 21 is represented by Key 7, and the secret of Key 7, is beautifully explained in the following words:

Stand aside in the coming battle and, though thou fightest, be not thou the warrior.

Look for the warrior, and let him fight in thee. Take his orders for the battle and obey them.

Obey them not as though he were a general, but as though he were thyself, and his spoken words were the utterance of thy secret desires; for he is thyself, yet infinitely wiser and stronger than thyself. Look for him, else in the fever and hurry of the fight thou mayest pass him; and he will not know thee unless thou knowest him. If thy cry reach his listening ear, then he will fight in thee and fill the dull void within. And if this is so, then canst thou go through the fight cool and unwearied, standing aside

and letting him battle for thee. Then it will be impossible for thee to strike one blow amiss. But if thou look not for him, if thou pass him by, then there is no safeguard for thee. Thy brain will reel, thy heart grow uncertain, and in the dust of the battle field thy sight and senses will fail, and thou wilt not know thy friends from thine enemies. He is thyself, yet thou art but finite and liable to error. He is eternal and is sure. He is eternal truth. When once he has entered thee and become thy warrior, he will never utterly desert thee, and at the day of the great peace he will become one with thee.
—Light on the Path, II, 1–5.

"He is thyself." The quest is for the Self. The goal is the Self. The knowledge is Self–knowledge. The power of the infinite and eternal Self is the only power. The Self is the ONE, working through the mysterious, glamorous power of reflection and duality. All this is plainly shown in the very number of this Key 21.

The Hebrew letter Tav means *signature* or *mark*, but the mark is the cross. The Egyptian TAU, corresponding to this letter, is said to have been a tally for measuring the depth of the Nile, also a square for measuring right angles. Among the Hebrews the letter Tav, written in the old alphabet as a simple cross of equal arms like that on the breast of the High Priestess, or that on the banner of the angel in Key 20, was a sign of salvation (See Ezekiel 9:4). Thus it is a symbol of salvation from death, and a signature of eternal life. As representing a signature, this letter implies security, pledge, guarantee, and so on. A signature makes a business instrument valid. Thus Tav indicates the final seal and completion of the Great Work.

The great secret of the letter Tav is the point where the two lines cross. This point represents the inner *center* at which the One Identity has its abode. Thus *The Book of Formation* says: "The only Lord God, the faithful King, rules over all from His holy habitation forever and ever." And the same book indicates the place of that holy habitation thus: "The seven double consonants are analogous to the six dimensions: Height and Depth, East and West, North and South, and the Holy Temple that stands in the center, which sustains them all." That innermost point is in itself nothing, and thus the Clementine Homilies report St. Peter as saying that the Place of God is That–which–is–not. Yet this same text goes on to say:

This, therefore, that, starting from God, is boundless in every direction must needs be the heart holding Him Who is verily above all things in fashion, Who, wheresoever He be, is as it were in the middle of a boundless space being the terminal of the All. Taking their origin therefore from Him, the six extensions have the nature of unlimited things. Of which the one taking its beginning from God is displayed upwards towards the height, another downwards towards the depth, another to the right, another to the left, another in front, another behind. For at Him the six boundless lines do terminate and from Him they take their boundless extension.

Read this quotation several times, comparing it with what is said in Lesson Forty-four and with figure 3 in the diagram accompanying Lesson Eighteen. Note that the abode of God is called the *heart*. It is also termed That-which-is-not, because it has no physical form or fashion, and might perfectly well be indicated by the zero sign, which we attribute to the Fool. Yet it is by no means a nonentity, for this inner POINT is a positive metaphysical and intellectual reality. Hence, if you can grasp the idea that this Place of God, or Holy Temple that stands in the center, is necessarily *everywhere*, you will see that it must be the center of your own being.

Hence to Tav is also assigned the Administrative Intelligence, of which it is written: "It is so called because it directs all the operations of the seven planets, associates their activities, and guides them all in their proper courses.'"

Remember that the occult planets are the same as the interior stars mentioned in connection with Key 17. Remember also that each of these planets corresponds to a Hebrew double letter, and thus to one of the six directions, as follows: Height, Mercury, Beth, Key 1; Depth, Moon, Gimel, Key 2; East, Venus, Daleth, Key 3; West, Jupiter, Kaph, Key 10; North, Mars, Peh, Key 16; South, Sun, Resh, Key 19; CENTER (The Holy Temple), Saturn, Tav, Key 21.

Thus Tav represents the point of control, at the CENTER, or at the heart. Not the physical organ, understand, but heart in the sense of *midst, inmost, core*. To get at the heart of your personal existence is to enter the Palace of the King. There the One Self is enthroned. There the Lord of the Universe has His abode. There is the central point of authority and rulership, extending its boundless influence throughout the cosmos. There, when the Great Work is accomplished, and the Father and the Son are One,

the New Kingdom is established.
Concerning this an ancient alchemical treatise says.

> The Son ever remains in the Father,
> And the Father in the Son.
> Thus in divers things
> They produce untold, precious fruit.
> They perish nevermore,
> And laugh at death.
> By the Grace of God they abide forever,
> The Father and the Son, triumphing gloriously.
> In the splendour of their New Kingdom,
> Upon one throne they sit,
> And the face of the Ancient Master
> Is straightway seen between them.
> —*The Book of Lambspring.*

That Center within. Seek it diligently, and you will surely find it, and find there the Stone of the Wise, so perfectly described in this quotation you have just read.

Key 21 summarizes the whole Tarot, and so summarizes all that can be put into any kind of symbolism concerning the culmination of the Great Work. Stamp the symbols deep upon your subconsciousness as you color them this week.

COLORING INSTRUCTIONS

Green: Wreath.

Blue: Background (leave blank ellipses round   spirals in hands).

Brown: Animals (as in Key 10).

White: Clouds, as in Key 10. Rays should be painted with white, extending from the ellipses round the spirals into the blue of the background.

Blonde: Hair on man and dancer; beak of eagle.

Violet: Veil round dancer.

Red: Binding at top and bottom of the wreath; the cap–like wreath on the head of the dancing figure.

THE WORLD
(Cont.)

The title of Key 21, *The World*, suggests "World—consciousness." He who attains to this state finds himself in tune with the whole universe; and discovers that the center of conscious energy at the heart of his personal life is one with the power that rules creation. In this consciousness, the whole universe becomes the body of the I AM, and one knows that the directive *Center* of the entire field of cosmic activity is identical with the innermost Self.

The four corners of this Key are occupied by the same mystical figures that appear on Key 10. Here there is a difference in one detail. The face of the bull in Key 10 is turned away from the lion, and thus also away from the central figure of the design. This is intentional, and follows an ancient tradition observed in most early versions of Tarot.

The bull represents the element of earth, or that which gives form. In Key 10, this is turned toward the lion and also toward the center of the Key, where the symbol of Spirit is shown at the heart of the wheel, because the mental activity pictured in Key 10 is one that turns the mind away from form to the consideration of energy, away from body to the consideration of Spirit. The comprehension of the Law of Cycles (Key 10) is an act of mental abstraction, in which attention is turned away from the forms of things to their fiery essence (the lion).

In Key 21, on the contrary, the emphasis is upon concrete manifestation. For this Key is attributed to the planet Saturn, representing the cosmic forces that limit energy in producing form. In this Key, therefore, the bull faces away from the lion, and away from the center of the design, in order to indicate that the forces pictured by The World move toward concrete manifestation.

269

The goal of the Great Work is not abstraction. It is demonstration, expression, orderly procession of energy into suitable forms — the adornment of the Life–power with suitable garments.

For the other meanings of the four figures at the corners of Key 21 see the explanations in Lesson Twenty–four. Remember that the general significance is that, as these creatures represent the Great Name, I H V H, their positions at the corners of the Key suggest that all manifestation is included within the boundaries of that Name and the Reality for which it stands.

The wreath is an ellipsoid figure. Its longer axis is exactly eight units, and its shorter one exactly five units. Thus a rectangle that would exactly contain it would be eight units high and five units wide, The rectangle of 5x8 is mentioned in the first of the Rosicrucian manifestoes, *The Fama Fraternitatis*, which speaks of "a vault of seven sides and seven corners, every side five foot broad, and the height of eight foot." Note that the area of such a rectangle is 40 square units, and that 40 is the number of the letter Mem, the letter corresponding to Key 12, the Hanged Man. The total length of the four boundary lines of such a rectangle is 26 units, the number of the name I H V H. Furthermore, 5 is to 8 in very close approximation to the Golden Section, or Extreme and Mean Proportion, and these two numbers were used again and again by the ancients to express that proportion, which is related also to the *fifth* and the *octave* in music. Extreme and Mean Proportion may be thus defined: "That proportion in which the lesser part is to the greater part as the greater part is to the whole." It is paraphrased in the occult maxim: "Nature (the lesser part) is to Man (the greater part) as Man is to God.

To students of dynamic symmetry, the 5x8 rectangle is known as the "Rectangle of the Whirling Square." It is the basis of the logarithmic spiral, concerning which Claude Bragdon says:

> Now the generic or archetypal form of everything in the universe is naturally not other than the form of the universe itself. Our stellar universe is now thought by astronomers to be a spiral nebula; and the spiral nebulae we see in the heavens, stellar systems like our own. The geometric equivalent of the nebula form is the logarithmic spiral. This is therefore the unit form of the universe, the form of all forms.

Thus the wreath represents the NAME (IHVH) as the FUNDAMENTAL PRINCIPLE OF FORM, of which the entire cosmos is the representation or manifestation.

The wreath is composed of twenty–two triads of leaves. Every triad corresponds to a Hebrew letter, to one of the twenty–two aspects of conscious energy represented by those letters, and to one of the twenty–two Tarot Keys. Every mode of the Life–power has three kinds of expression: 1. Integrative; 2. Disintegrative;

3. Equilibrating. The third balances the other two.

Note that a wreath is a work of man. Nature provides the leaves. Man weaves them into a chaplet for the victor. Thus the wreath is a symbol of human adaptations of the forces of nature. It also suggests that cosmic consciousness is not spontaneously provided by natural evolution. It is the completion of the Great Work, and man is the workman.

At top and bottom, the wreath is fastened with bands similar to the horizontal figure 8 over the head of the Magician. All that is visible of this band is that portion which makes a form of the letter X, which is the shape of one of the ancient Hebrew characters for the letter Tav. This intimates that the power represented by Tav is what man uses to bind the forces of nature into a wreath of victory. It is also a hint that the X form is more accurately shown as the horizontal 8, figure of mathematical infinity, and symbol of the truth that opposite effects are produced by *identical* causes.

The wreath rests on the bull and the lion, because man's power of giving form (the bull) to the formless, fiery essential energy (the lion) is what enables him to weave together the twenty–two modes of force derived from that one energy.

Finally, the outline of the wreath is a zero symbol. The ellipse of manifestation, woven by man from the forces that play through him, is *No–Thing*. It has just as much power over him as he gives it, and not one whit more. It does not really bind him, when he understands what it is. The "world" of a Master of life is a wreath of victory.

The dancer in the wreath appears to be feminine, but has been so drawn that the legs are more masculine than womanly in appearance. The World–Dancer is the Celestial Androgyne. Her purple veil (in our version, as in ancient Tarot Keys) is in the form of a letter Kaph. Because Kaph is represented in Tarot by Key 10, the meaning here is this: The mechanistic appearance assumed by natural phenomena (Kaph, the Wheel of Fortune) veils their true character. The cosmos seems to be a system of wheels within wheels. It presents itself to our intellectual consciousness as a vast machine. Cause and effect seem to be rigidly and unalterably connected.

This is only relatively true. The Life–power is the author, and therefore the master, of the Law of Cause and Consequence. All "laws" are part and parcel of the drama of manifestation. *No law binds the Self.*

The World–Dancer is perfectly free, and that state of freedom is NOW. Hence the Dancer stands on nothing. She is self–supported. She herself is in perfect equilibrium.

A spiral in her right hand turns toward the right. One in her left hand turns toward the left. These spirals represent integration and disintegration. They are complements, and they turn simultaneously.

In the picture, each spiral has a definite beginning and a definite end, but this is simply a limitation due to the impossibility of picturing the infinite. Understand that the process the spirals symbolize has neither beginning nor end. Each spiral has exactly eleven loops, so that the two together represent the twenty–two modes of conscious energy symbolized by the Hebrew letters and Tarot Keys.

He who enters into cosmic consciousness *experiences directly* what is symbolized by this Key. He knows that every particle of the manifested universe is a living center of the One Reality, *within* that One Reality. He perceives directly that whatever is being disintegrated is exactly balanced by that which is simultaneously being integrated. He knows that the universe is a universe of conscious motion, consisting of endless sequences of production, destruction and reproduction. Evolution is balanced by devolution, association by dissociation, integration by disintegration.

Says *The Book of Concealed Mystery*, an old Qabalistic work: "Before there was equilibrium, countenance beheld not countenance. This equilibrium hangeth in that region which is NOT." (Compare this with what is said of the Place called "That–which–is–not" in the Clementine Homilies, quoted in Lesson Forty–Five)

This region that is NOT is the central point in the cube of space, where the three co–ordinates and the four interior diagonals cross. It is the point of perfect balance, through which pass the thirteen axes of symmetry of the cube. At this point our occult attribution of the letters places the generating center of the three co–ordinates. That is to say, the three mother letters, Aleph, Mem and Shin, are all *located* at this center, and the coordinate lines corresponding to these letters radiate from this center. At this center, too, is placed the letter Tav, the Temple of Holiness in *the midst*. Final Mem is also located here. From these letters we may form the two words, *Emeth*, A M Th, and *Shem*, Sh M. *Emeth* means, fundamentally, *stability*, hence truth. *Shem* signifies sign, *token, memorial, monument, name*. It is used often in the Qabalistic writings to designate the special Divine Name, *Jehovah*, or I H V H. Thus the letters assigned to the central point of the cube signify the *Truth of That which was, is, and will be*.

That same truth is the central reality at the core of human personality. Therefore is the name of God declared by Moses to be I AM. For the same reason the Hindu philosophers term this Reality the Supreme Self.

The *point* where it is centered, however, is without form or dimensions. Hence it is the region that is NOT. Here is the same suggestion that the Qabalah gives us when it calls *En*, AIN, the No–Thing, the "First Veil of the Absolute." It is what Tarot means by numbering the Fool, symbol of the Spirit that manifests the whole creation, with the zero sign. *No conditions of time, space or quality limit the perfect freedom of the Central Reality. At this center is the focus of all possibilities, conceivable and inconceivable, known and unknown.*

Walt Whitman emphasizes the idea of equilibrium also, for he tells us that cosmic consciousness is "an intuition of the absolute balance, in time and space, of the whole of this multifariousness, this revel of fools, and incredible make–believe and general unsettledness we call *the world*; a soul–sight of that divine clue and unseen thread which holds the whole congeries of things, all history and time, and all events, however trivial, however momentous, like a leashed dog in the hand of a hunter."

Leashed, but ready to be let loose to fulfill the hunter's bidding. When the Self is known, it is known as the Master of the Show of Illusion named the World. The name of that Master in Hebrew is *Eheyeh*, A H I H, or I AM, and this is the supreme Divine Name attributed to Kether, the Crown of Primal Will. It is connected with this final Tarot Key because its number, like that of the Key, is 21.

What we most wish to leave with you in closing this lesson and this course is the realization that states of consciousness are states of power. The goal of the Great Work is to know the Self; but to know, as we mean it here, is not merely to witness, not merely to be aware of something external, as when we say we "know" the various phenomena of our environment. The knowledge that completes the Great Work is *identification* with the Central Reality of the universe, and such knowledge is really the acme of practical power.

Thus, in alchemical books, this knowledge is symbolized by the Philosophers' Stone — that is to say, the mineral kingdom as the truly wise perceive it. For the mineral kingdom is the basis of all form manifestation throughout the universe, and to see that kingdom as it really is to understand all else. Hence the alchemists assure us that whoever knows the First Matter knows all

273

that is necessary, because, as Philalethes puts it in his *Fount of Chemical Truth*, "Our appliances are part of our substance."

In the consciousness of one who has reached this goal, Father and Son have become one, and rule from the throne at the center of the ALL. This is the secret meaning of *Ehben*, A B N, the STONE, as we have told you before. Therefore it is written that they who possess this STONE have the means for preserving their youth, expelling disease, preventing suffering, and providing themselves with all they require. All this is exactly and actually true, without any metaphor whatever. Success in the Great Work so unites the personal self with the One Identity that every detail of the personal existence is a conscious expression of the ALL POWER.

A life so lived is a life of perfect freedom, perfect health, perfect joy. It is a life in which there is no trace of want or insufficiency. It is a life in which every circumstance of daily experience affords an opportunity for the demonstration of what is termed, in connection with the letter Tav, the Administrative Intelligence.

Such a life is, in highest measure, a perfect fulfillment of one's real heart's desire. It is the actual and practical realization of heaven on earth, here and now. He who lives it ceases to be a bond–slave of appearances, a mere subject of the cosmic government. He enters into joyous participation in that government, as one whose life is a continual administration of the perfect law of liberty.

Make this your goal. Devote yourself with all your heart to it, and, like thousands who have gone this way before you, you shall be among those who tread the joyous measures of the Dance of Life.

* * *

Next week you will receive the Supplement to this course. It is a series of meditations to be used in conjunction with the Keys of Tarot. Be sure to follow the instruction given in this Supplement, with full attention to all its details.

LESSON FORTY–SEVEN

SUPPLEMENT: A MONTH
OF TAROT PRACTICE

You now possess the fundamental knowledge required for your further progress. You have had your introduction to Tarot. You know enough about each Key to enable you to grasp more advanced instruction. Yet to make Tarot serve you as it should, you need to become even better acquainted with it. In the hands of experts, it is a powerful instrument for self–transformation and self–mastery. Yet the greatest adepts in its use once knew less about it than you do now.

Do not make the mistake of trying at this time to review *Tarot Fundamentals*. You don't repeat the formula of introduction every time you meet a new acquaintance. No, you watch his behavior every time you see him in a different set of circumstances. You get to know him better by hearing what he says and seeing what he does. So it is with Tarot. The best way to deepen and broaden your knowledge of it is to see it from as many different points of view as possible.

Remember that you can arrange these twenty–two Keys (using them all in each arrangement) NO LESS THAN ONE SEXTILLION WAYS. The exact number is 1,124,000,727,777,607,680,000. Besides this there are innumerable other groupings, in which only part of the series is used, so that the total number of possible arrangements is practically infinite.

Every combination has its own special meaning. Every combination calls forth its own particular subconscious response. Every combination brings to the surface of your mind some fresh perception of relationships between ideas and things. Thus every combination helps you to organize your mind, and enables you to knit more closely the fabric of your thought.

In the following pages, you will find twenty–four combinations. Use one each day, six days a week, beginning the Monday after you receive this instruction. Do no work on Sundays except the recitation of the Pattern.

Begin by picking out the Keys selected for the day. Put them before you. Study them carefully in relation to one another. Then read the meditation aloud. The meditations have potent suggestive power. Every meditation is completed by the key sentence for the day, printed in capitals. Write this on a slip of paper, and carry it with you during the day. Repeat it at least three times as the day passes.

Before going to bed, look at the combination of Keys at least three times. See if it suggests to you any ideas other than those in the meditation. Make a note of them in your occult diary. Then read the meditation once more, recite the Pattern, and go to sleep.

By carrying out this instruction carefully you will accomplish several desirable results. You will charge your subconsciousness daily with seeds of creative thought. You will also review the entire series of Tarot Keys, from a fresh point of view. You will begin to understand from actual experience how wonderfully Tarot can aid you in living the liberated life.

After you have completed the four weeks' practice, you will be ready to apply for the first Proficiency Test, by which you will be able to check your grasp of *Tarot Fundamentals*.

The tools are now in your hands. From *Tarot Fundamentals* you have learned what they are. You now begin to do the work, which will enable you to be what you want to be, do what you want to do, and have everything requisite to that being and doing. From now on, you are beginning to *live* your daily life in accordance with the principles and laws represented by the Tarot Keys. Your feet are firmly planted on the Way of Liberation.

MEDITATIONS

First day: Keys 0 & I.

Life limitless flows through me to complete its perfect work. The power, which guides all things, finds in me an open channel of expression. Receiving that power freely, I freely give it to all things and creatures in the field of existence that surrounds me.

276

THROUGH ME LIFE ETERNAL TRANSFORMS ALL THINGS INTO ITS LIKENESS.

Second day: Keys 2 & 3.

The law of truth is written in my heart; all my members are ruled by it. Through my subconsciousness I am united to the source of all wisdom, and its light banishes every shadow of ignorance and fear. I share the perfect memory of the Universal Mind, and have free access to its treasures of knowledge and wisdom.

THE PEACE OF THE ETERNAL AND THE LIGHT OF ITS PRESENCE ARE WITH ME NOW.

Third day: Keys 4 & 5.

The Mind that frames the worlds is ruler of my thoughts; I listen for its instruction. Through me, the One Life sets its house in order and makes known the hidden meaning of its ways and works. It arms me against all appearances of hostility and, by its revelation of truth, I meet and solve the problems of this day.

DIVINE REASON GUIDES MY THOUGHT AND DIRECTS MY ACTION THROUGH THE INSTRUCTION OF THE VOICE OF INTUITION.

Fourth day: Keys 6 & 7.

The healing radiance of the One Life descends upon me; it fills the field of my personal existence with the heavenly influences of strength and peace. All the forces of my being are rightly disposed, for I yield myself utterly to the sure guidance of the One Will, which governs all things. I see things in their true relationships and proportions, and my words, expressing this clear vision, are words of power.

THIS DAY I THINK AND ACT WITH TRUE DISCRIMINATION, FOR MY PERSONALITY IS A VEHICLE FOR THE LORD OF LIFE.

Fifth day: Keys 8 & 9.

My strength is established, and I rejoice, for I am one with the single source of all power. Nothing is, or can be, my antagonist, for I am a perfectly responsive instrument through which the Primal Will finds free expression. All the subtle vibrations of cosmic energy work together for my liberation, and even now the Hand of the Eternal leads me step by step along the way to freedom.

ALL THE FORCES OF THE UNIVERSE ARE OBEDIENT SERVANTS OF THE ONE IDENTITY, MY OWN TRUE SELF.

Sixth day: Keys 10 & 11.

One power spins electrons round the nucleus of an atom, whirls planets round suns, expresses itself in all cycles of universal activity, yet remains ever itself and perpetually maintains its equilibrium. The sum total of the revolutions of the great universe, including all activities, is inseparable from the successive transformations of energy that constitute my life history. Every detail of my daily experience is some part of a cosmic cycle of transformation and adjustment.

THE WHIRLING FORCE, WHICH MOVES THE WORLDS, IS THE MOTIVE POWER IN ALL MY PERSONAL ACTIVITIES.

Seventh day: Use only the Pattern today.

Eighth day: Keys 12 & 13.

I do nothing of myself. These thoughts and words and deeds are but the ripening of the seeds of past activities. Every phase of my personal existence depends utterly on the motion of the One Life; therefore I am free from fate, free from accident, free even from death, since what I truly am can suffer neither decay nor change. By knowledge of truth I reverse all former pain–bearing errors; and as the darkness of ignorance passes away, the light of a new understanding is dawning in my heart.

I SUSPEND THE ERROR OF PERSONAL ACTION, AND THUS DISSOLVE THE LIE OF SEPARATION.

Ninth day: Keys 14 & 15.

Recognizing every detail of my life experience to be the operation of the One Life, I perceive that every appearance of adversity must be in truth but a mask worn by that same Life, to test my power to know it, even through the most forbidding veils. Like a wise teacher, the One Life sets me problems, that in the solutions I may receive renewed proofs that nothing whatever may be excluded from the perfect order of the Great Plan.

THAT WHICH WAS AND IS AND WILL BE IS THE ONLY REALITY. THIS DAY I SEE THE FACE OF THE BELOVED BEHIND EVERY MASK OF ADVERSITY.

Tenth day: Keys 16 & 17.

I am awakened from the nightmare of delusion, and now the truth that God, Man and Universe are but three names for the One Identity, is clear to me. Fear makes some men build them prisons that they call places of safety, but he who has seen the vision of the Beloved has no room in his heart for fear.

I NEED NO BARRIERS OF PROTECTION, FOR THE LIFE OF ALL CREATURES IS MY TRUEST FRIEND.

Eleventh day: Keys 18 & 19.

My feet are set upon the path of liberation, which shall lead me far from the limits of the world of sense illusion. I follow the Way of Return, as a child turns its face homeward at the end of the day. I do not see the end of the road, for it goes beyond the boundaries of my present vision; but I know the sun shines there, and that joy is there, for I have heard the messages of encouragement sent back by those who have gone on ahead.

MY EYES ARE TURNED TOWARD THE HEIGHTS. I PRESS ON TOWARD THE NEW LIFE OF A NEW DAY.

Twelfth day: Keys 20 & 21

The life of the heavens is manifested in me, here on earth. The fire of right knowledge burns away the bonds of illusion, and the light of right understanding transforms the face of the world. Through me, the Perpetual Intelligence that governs all things administers its perfect law.

MINE IS THE LIFE ETERNAL, TREADING THE JOYOUS MEASURE OF THE DANCE OF MANIFESTATION.

Thirteenth day: Keys 0, 1, 2.

This "self–consciousness" of mine is the means whereby the cultural power of the One Life may be directed to the field of subconscious activity. Its primary function is that of alert attention. As I watch closely the sequence of this day's events, their meaning will be transmitted to ray subconsciousness, there to germinate in forms of right knowledge and right desire.

TODAY I AM ON THE ALERT.

Fourteenth day: Use only the Pattern today.

Fifteenth day: Keys 3, 4, 5.

My personal world is *as I see it*. If the images rising from my subconsciousness are consequences of my faulty perceptions of other days, the new knowledge I have gained will help me to detect and destroy them. By being thus ever on the watch, I shall set my world in order. Thus, too, shall I make ready to hear the Voice of Intuition, which will enable me to solve my problems when I am confronted with appearances of disorder that my reasoning will not set straight.

I SEE THINGS AS THEY ARE.

Sixteenth day: Keys 6, 7, 8.

Consciousness and subconsciousness work together in my life as harmoniously balanced counterparts. I yield my whole personality to the directive and protective influx of the One Life. All the mighty forces of vibration below the level of my self—consciousness are purified and adjusted by the Master Power of which I am a receptive vehicle.

HARMONY, PEACE AND STRENGTH ARE MINE.

Seventeenth day: Keys 9, 10, 11.

The Will of the Eternal guides me to perfect union with the One Identity. Every detail of my daily experience is in truth a revelation of that Will through the cycles of its expression. What I do now is inseparable from the cosmic sequences of manifestation that establish the reign of justice throughout creation.

THE ONE POWER, MANIFESTING THE PERFECT ORDER OF THE UNIVERSE, KEEPS ME POISED THROUGH ALL CHANGES.

Eighteenth Day: Keys 12, 13, 14.

Every detail of my personal activity is really some part of the operation of the cosmic life. Today I reap the fruits of the thoughts and words and deeds of other days, and pass on to better things. I am guided, moment by moment, by the overshadowing presence of the One Identity.

MY PERSONALITY DOES NOTHING OF ITSELF, PASSING FROM STAGE TO STAGE OF ITS GROWTH BY THE POWER OF THE ONE LIFE, TOWARD THE GOAL OF FREEDOM.

Nineteenth day: Keys 15, 16, 17.

Every appearance of adversity and antagonism is but an evidence of my faulty vision. Let me be freed today from the delusion of separateness, and let my eyes be opened to the radiant splendor of the Truth of Being.

I REJOICE IN MY PROBLEMS, FOR THEY STIMULATE MY CONSCIOUSNESS TO OVERCOME ERROR, THAT I MAY SEE THE BEAUTY OF THE DIVINE PERFECTION.

Twentieth day: Keys 18, 19, 20.

Every cell of my body is animated by the cosmic urge to freedom. I turn my back upon the limitations of the past, and face courageously toward the new way which opens before me.

MY VERY FLESH IS THE SEED–GROUND FOR A NEW LIFE, FREE FROM THE BONDAGE OF TIME AMD SPACE.

Twenty–first day: Use only the Pattern today.

Twenty–second day: Keys I, 2, 3,

I am not deceived by the manifold illusions of sensation. For I continually remember that all these appearances are but reflections of a single Reality. By its power of deductive reasoning my subconsciousness develops the seed of right observation into a rich harvest of wisdom.

ALERT AND CONCENTRATED, I SEE CLEARLY, MAKE CLEAR AND

DEFINITE MEMORY RECORDS OF EXPERIENCE, AND THUS COL-
LECT MATERIAL FOR THE GROWTH OF RIGHT UNDERSTANDING.

Twenty–third day: Keys 4, 5, 6.

The empire of the Universal Order includes the little province of
my personal existence. All experience teaches me the perfection
of the Great Plan. Consciously and subconsciously I respond to
the perfect Wisdom, which rules all creation.

THROUGH ME THE ONE LIFE ESTABLISHES ORDER, REVEALS THE
SIGNIFICANCE OF EVERY PHASE OF MANIFESTATION, AND RIGHT-
LY DISPOSES ALL THINGS.

Twenty–fourth day: Keys 7, 8, 9.

The One Life lives through me. Its vital fire pervades my being.
Its unfailing Will sustains me continually.

THE MASTER PRINCIPLE OF THE UNIVERSE, DWELLING IN MY
HEART, PURIFIES AND PERFECTS ME, AND LEADS ME TO THE
HEIGHTS OF UNION WITH ITSELF.

Twenty–fifth day: Keys 10, 11, 12.

The revolutions of circumstance in the outer world are manifestations of the One Power seated in my heart. That Power maintains its perfect equilibrium through all these sequences of cause
and effect. My personal activities have no existence apart from
the Power.

THE WHEEL OF LIFE REVOLVES ROUND THE CENTER OF PURE
SPIRIT, PRESENT EVERYWHERE, AND THEREFORE CENTERED IN
MY HEART. THIS UNMOVED MOVER OF ALL CREATION IS MY UN-
FAILING SUPPORT.

Twenty–sixth day: Keys 13, 14, 15.

Out of the darkness of the unknown comes the power, which
sets me free. The Way of Liberation stands open before me. I face
this day's tests with joyful heart.

AS I DIE TO THE OLD PERSONALITY, FULL OF DELUSION, AND FACE THE UNKNOWN FUTURE BRAVELY, CONFIDENT OF SUPPLY FOR EVERY NEED, MY FEARS DISSOLVE IN THE CLEAR SUNLIGHT OF RIGHT UNDERSTANDING.

Twenty–seventh day: Keys 16, 17, 18.

Let others imprison themselves in their towers of false knowledge. I will be free! Let others dread the workings of our Mother Nature. I will love all her ways! Let others be servants of the body, which they hate, because they are its slaves. I will make it my servant, and love it for its faithfulness in responding to my commands!

RENOUNCING EVERY ERROR, I SEEK TO GROW IN KNOWLEDGE OF TRUTH, AND WORK TO MAKE MY FLESH AND BLOOD A GLORIOUS EMBODIMENT OF LIFE ETERNAL.

Twenty–eighth day: Use only the Pattern today

Breinigsville, PA USA
11 November 2009
227369BV00002B/108/P